CW00547312

Lighter-than-Air

The Pioneer

Upon this marble bust that is not I
Lay the round, formal wreath that is not fame:
But in the forum of my silenced cry
Root ye the living tree whose sap is flame.
I, that was fierce and valiant, am no more –
Save as a dream that wanders wide and late.
Save as a wind that rattles the stout door,
Troubling the ashes in the sheltered grate.

The stone will perish; I shall be twice dust.
Only my standard on a taken hill
Can cheat the mildew and the red-brown rust
And make immortal my adventurous will.
Even now the silk is tugging at the staff;
Take up the song – forget the epitaph.

Edna St Vincent Millay

Lighter-than-Air

The Life and Times of Wing Commander N.F. Usborne, RN, Pioneer of Naval Aviation

Guy Warner

Pen & Sword
AVIATION

First published in Great Britain in 2016 by
Pen & Sword Aviation
an imprint of
Pen & Sword Books Ltd
47 Church Street
Barnsley
South Yorkshire
S70 2AS

ISBN 978 1 47382 902 2

Typeset in Ehrhardt by
Mac Style Ltd, Bridlington, East Yorkshire
Printed and bound in the UK by CPI Group (UK) Ltd,
Croydon, CRO 4YY

Pen & Sword Books Ltd incorporates the imprints of Pen & Sword
Archaeology, Atlas, Aviation, Battleground, Discovery, Family
History, History, Maritime, Military, Naval, Politics, Railways, Select,
Transport, True Crime, and Fiction, Frontline Books, Leo Cooper,
Praetorian Press, Seaforth Publishing and Wharncliffe.

For a complete list of Pen & Sword titles please contact
PEN & SWORD BOOKS LIMITED
47 Church Street, Barnsley, South Yorkshire, S70 2AS, England
E-mail: enquiries@pen-and-sword.co.uk
Website: www.pen-and-sword.co.uk

Contents

Foreword   vi
Introduction   viii

Chapter 1   From the 1850s to the 1890s   1

Chapter 2   From the 1890s to the start of Neville's Aviation Career   28

Chapter 3   The 'Golden Age' before August 1914   74

Chapter 4   From August 1914 to February 1916   185

Chapter 5   Usborne's Achievements and his Legacy   223

Appendix I: Lighter-than-Air Flight Before the Advent of the Dirigible   258
Appendix II: Airship Terms   266
Appendix III: 'Air Battles of the Future'   270
Appendix IV: The *Clément-Bayard* Airship   273
Appendix V: The Lebaudy Airship of 1910   274
Appendix VI: The British Army – Early Heavier-than-Air Craft   276
Appendix VII: The Origins of Fixed-wing Aviation in the Royal Navy   277

Notes   280
References   293
Index   300

Foreword

Commander Neville Usborne was a career naval officer who entered the Royal Navy at a time of significant technological change. He was one of the first to appreciate the value of air reconnaissance for the fleet and, as a torpedo specialist with a practical knowledge of electrical and weapons systems, he was better placed than many seaman officers to become closely involved with the development of airships which were expected at first to have much greater utility than fixed-wing aeroplanes. He was appointed to the small team that stood by the first rigid airship, R1, unofficially known as the '*Mayfly*', during her construction by Vickers at Barrow-in-Furness, and was selected to command her on her completion. Whilst at Barrow he designed and patented a clever system to capture the water vapour produced during the combustion process in the craft's engines for use as ballast. In the event she was never completed and the Admiralty temporarily abandoned airships in favour of fixed-wing aircraft development, but this did not harm Usborne's career.

He was one of the outstanding personalities among the early aviation specialists, and a measure of the respect he earned can be drawn from his selection to become an associate fellow of the Royal Aeronautical Society in February 1912, at the same time as Frederick Handley Page and Horace Short. He qualified to fly both heavier-than-air aircraft – awarded pilot's certificate number 449 – as well as airships, and his drive and enthusiasm allowed him to continue at the forefront of development. Promoted to commander in January 1914, he was one of only six officers of that rank serving in the Royal Naval Air Service (RNAS) on its official formation on 1 July 1914 and was appointed to command the new Royal Naval Air Station at Kingsnorth in Kent, which was to be used as an operational, experimental and construction base for airships. From this new air station, Usborne flew some of the very first war patrols by RNAS airships in 1914, searching the eastern approaches to the English Channel in HM Airships 3 and 4 for signs of an enemy attack on shipping carrying the British Expeditionary Force (BEF) to France. He never lost sight of the need to make the best use of the material the RNAS had available, but recognised the urgent requirement for technical innovation to overcome the immediate problems that faced the Navy's air arm.

Usborne was closely involved in the design evolution of the SS class non-rigid airships that proved to be very successful in coastal patrol work, an achievement recognised by his appointment as the Admiralty's Inspecting Commander of Airships (Building) in August 1915. The RNAS had responsibility at the time for the air defence of the UK, since the whole of the Royal Flying Corps had been sent to France. However, fixed-wing aircraft proved unable to take off and climb fast enough to intercept Zeppelins over south-eastern England after they were detected, and nor could they maintain patrols at altitude for long against the possibility of an attack. The RNAS' primary tactic was to attack the Zeppelins at source in their factories and sheds in Germany and Belgium, but something had to be done to intercept airships that penetrated UK airspace, and Usborne designed a remarkable solution, the airship-plane. This was a hybrid aircraft that comprised of a standard BE2C scout aircraft suspended beneath an SS-type airship in place of its control car. It could patrol for several hours at 4,000 feet and Usborne believed that the BE2C could be released with a realistic chance of attacking and destroying an enemy airship once it had been sighted. Unmanned release trials worked successfully with a prototype hybrid, and, on 21 February 1916, Usborne flew the first manned example, AP-1, with Squadron Commander W.P. de Courcy Ireland as co-pilot. As you will discover in the following pages, both men were killed when something went badly wrong, with the result that the RNAS lost an innovative and driving force who had played a not inconsiderable part in its early development.

In this fascinating book, Guy Warner goes much further than simply recounting the biographical details of one individual, albeit a very remarkable one. He traces the development of lighter-than-air flight in the British armed forces from its very beginnings in the mid-nineteenth century in order to place Usborne's career and achievements in their due context. Historians have often, hitherto, paid too little attention to the development of airships by the Royal Navy, and the important part they played in the First World War has been overshadowed by the exploits of heavier-than-air aircraft. Commander Usborne himself has not been given the degree of recognition he deserves, as one of the outstanding personalities in the first decade of naval aviation. This book redresses that imbalance, and is a worthy tribute to the memory of a brave and resourceful officer and his contemporaries.

David Hobbs
January 2016

Introduction

Our views on the viability of the airship are conditioned by images of the wreckage of the R101 on the hillside at Beauvais on 5 October 1930, and the *Hindenburg* in flames at Lakehurst, New Jersey, in 1937. However, in the first decade of the twentieth century, the airship was just as exciting and promising a piece of advanced technology as the frail and unreliable, short-ranged, heavier-than-air craft. Airships offered stability, endurance, range, payload and reasonable speed when compared to contemporary surface transport. Airships appealed to the Royal Navy as they offered a means of extending the eyes of the fleet above the oceans.

A number of young and ambitious naval officers seized the opportunity to become involved with this new branch. Many served with distinction in the First World War and achieved high rank in the Royal Navy or the Royal Air Force. One of these pioneers was recognised by his contemporaries as having an inventive mind, allied to a powerful and thrusting personality. According to the airship historian, the late Ces Mowthorpe, he was, 'a brilliant and famous (in his time) airshipman.' Owing to his untimely death at the age of only thirty-three, in 1916, he is all but forgotten. His name was Neville Usborne and this is his story, set within the context of the technological and strategic developments of his time in the British Isles and Europe, and also of the technical and social climate in which he grew up. In the course of this study, I hope to draw together and shed light on several important subject areas in which he was intimately involved:

(a) How the RN had to adapt to and embrace new technology in the late nineteenth and early twentieth centuries, within a service ethos and training environment that still harked back to Nelson's times.

(b) How and why a bright, ambitious, technically minded young officer of the late-Victorian/Edwardian period could come to choose lighter-than-air aviation as a promising and fulfilling career path.

(c) The general loss of confidence in Edwardian Britain as it faced the possibility that this new technology (which as well as aviation, included submarines, radio-telegraphy, torpedoes, Dreadnought Class battleships, optical fire control and the introduction of oil fuel to replace coal) would erode the comfortable and complacent feeling of security from continental disturbances which had existed since the time of George IV.

(d) The very real and important debate in the early twentieth century between the comparative merits of lighter-than-air (balloons and airships) and heavier-than-air aviation (aeroplanes). How the role and organisation of a military air service was defined from the Royal Engineers Balloon School, to the RE Air Battalion, the RN Airships Branch, the RFC, and eventually the RAF.

(e) The political, public, press and military perceptions of the above.

(f) The differing strands of lighter-than-air flight – rigid airships as favoured in Germany, semi-rigid as the French preferred, non-rigid, which came to be the British speciality, balloons, kites and kite balloons. Which would prove to be of the greatest utility in the war, the advent of which was greatly feared in the first decade or so of the twentieth century?

(g) The particular involvement of Neville Usborne in the construction of the first British rigid airship, pre-war pioneering with small non-rigid airships – which would directly result in the design and construction of the two most successful and widely used classes of non-rigid airship – and the ultimately unsuccessful effort to develop a hybrid aircraft as a means of anti-Zeppelin countermeasures.

(h) Putting Usborne's story, and all of the above, within the overall framework and context of an examination of the military experience of lighter-than-air flight in Britain between 1878 and 1930, with attention also being paid to parallel developments in Europe and the USA during this period. Annexes sketch out the place of all of this within the history of lighter-than-air aviation from 1783, through the search for motive power and dirigibility in the nineteenth century, and also show briefly how airships found a niche in the Second World War and the Cold War.

The several classes of non-rigid airships operated by the Royal Naval Air Service during the First World War may, with some justification, be regarded as some of the most successful types of dirigible ever built. This did not come about by accident, and was based on over thirty years' experience accumulated by the British Army and the Royal Navy, and which progress Neville Usborne, among several others described in the text, played a significant role. No previous work has put all this together and no account has ever been given of the life story of this Anglo-Irish airman.

My very grateful thanks are due to the following for their very valuable help: Sara Bevan, Anne Boddaert, Den Burchmore, Nigel Caley, Michael Clarke, Ernie Cromie, Allen Crosbie, Peter Devitt, Richard Forrest, Sam Gresham, Dr Jane Harrold, Commander David Hobbs, Sue Kilbracken, Christopher Kilbracken, Diana King, Stuart Leslie, Tom McCarthy, Sara Mackeown, Phil Maguire, George Malcolmson, John Montgomery, Philip Moody, Betty Moss, Ces Mowthorpe, Tim Pierce, Dr Ian Speller, Nick Stroud, Julian Usborne, Doreen Warner, Beverley Williams, Christine Woodward and Sam Wynn. BRNC Dartmouth, Crawford Art Gallery, Imperial War Museum, History Department NUI Maynooth, National Aerospace Library, National Library of New Zealand, National Physical Laboratory, Port of Cork, RAeS, Royal Aero Club, RAF Cranwell, RAF Museum, Royal Engineers Museum, RN Submarine Museum, RUSI.

Finally, sincere thanks to my editor Ken Patterson and to all the staff at Pen and Sword, especially Charles Hewitt, Lori Jones, Laura Hirst, Laura Lawton and Matthew Blurton.

Except where stated, photographs are from the author's collection.

Chapter One

From the 1850s to the 1890s

Family Background

Neville Florian Usborne was born on 27 February 1883, in Queenstown (now Cobh), in Co Cork, on the south-eastern coast of Ireland, the son of Captain George Usborne, RN, and his wife, Josephine Scott, whom he married in Queenstown in 1875 and who was the daughter of a wealthy local shipping merchant, Philip Scott (1808–1879) [Philip Scott's father had founded James Scott and Co. of Cove in 1835. The family would be synonymous with shipping in Cork for more than 100 years. Philip, in his role as one of two town commissioners, presented the Address of Welcome to Queen Victoria and Prince Albert in 1849, and also requested the change of name from Cove to Queenstown. His son, James William, was a Cork Harbour Commissioner for forty years].

This view of the waterfront at Queenstown (now Cobh) is dominated by St Colman's Cathedral, construction of which began in 1868. (*Via Allen Crosbie*)

George was born in 1845 and entered the Royal Navy in 1860. He became a sub-lieutenant in 1865 and full lieutenant in 1867. He was appointed to the battleship HMS *Zealous*, a broadside armed, wooden hulled, ironclad, screw vessel serving as a flagship in the Pacific. In 1871 he was made flag-lieutenant in HMS *Revenge* (launched in 1859, a wooden hull, two-deck, second-rate of ninety-one guns, renamed *Empress* in 1890) at Queenstown, where it was the flagship of Rear Admiral Edmund Heathcote, the Port Admiral. George received a 'haul-down' promotion to commander in 1874. After studying at the Royal Naval College, Greenwich, he became Inspecting Officer of Coastguard at Moville, Co Donegal, in 1877 and later at Folkestone in Kent. It was there that he received the thanks of the German Emperor, together with a Berlin vase bearing the Emperor's portrait, for his assistance during the loss of a German ironclad warship.

Developments in Lighter-than-air aviation

As George approached his mid-30s there had already been several important developments in aviation during his lifetime. In July 1849, the Austrian steamship *Vulcano* had launched several hot-air balloons in an unsuccessful attempt to drop high explosive on the city of Venice, during the siege of the city.[1] On 24 September 1852, the first manned flight in a mechanically-driven aircraft took place – 17 miles (27 km) at 6mph (9.6kph) – by the French engineer, Henri Giffard (1825–1882), who was also the inventor of the steam injector, in a 3hp (2.22kW) steam-powered dirigible – the engine, coke, boiler and water weighed 900lbs (408kg) – driving an airscrew with a diameter of 11 feet (3.35 metres). It was 144 feet (43.89 metres) in length, with a maximum diameter of 39 feet (11.84 metres) and had a capacity of 88,000 cubic feet (2500 cubic metres). The

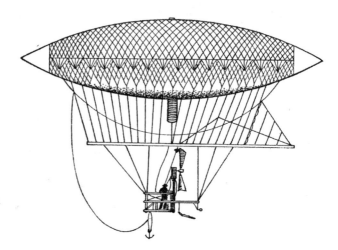

Giffard's Airship, which made its historic flight in 1852.

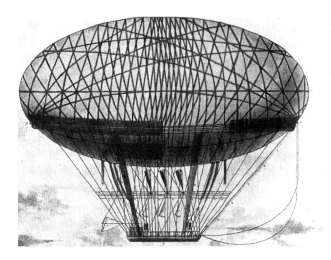

Meusnier's design of 1784 for a dirigible was sound, he simply lacked a suitable source of motive power.

envelope, which was filled with coal-gas, was elongated, symmetrical, and with pointed ends. The car containing the engine and aeronaut was suspended some 20 feet (6 metres) below the gasbag, the stokehole of the boiler was screened with wire gauze, and the engine was inverted so that the exhaust products were directed away from the inflammable material above. He had been inspired and assisted with his design by the ideas and sketches of Lieutenant Jean-Baptiste Marie Meusnier of 1783 and Sir George Cayley in 1817.

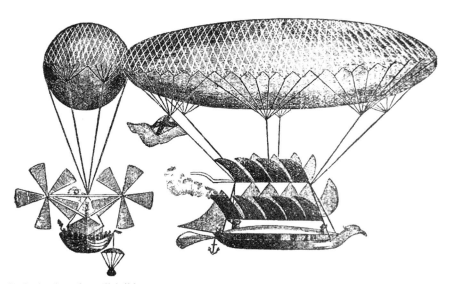

Cayley's plans for a dirigible.

Meusnier's design for a non-rigid airship anticipated many of the most important principles and featured ballonets (airbags mounted inside the gasbag to help keep it in shape and to maintain the internal pressure), rigging to suspend the car and an elongated shape – but he knew of no suitable power source. Cayley's design was similar and planned to use a steam engine to drive propellers or moveable wings. Giffard described his experience thus:

Henri Giffard.

> 'I took off from the Hippodrome at a quarter past five. The wind was blowing fairly strongly. Not for a single moment did I dream of struggling directly against the wind, the power of the engine would not have permitted it; that had been thought of in advance and proved by calculations; but I carried out various manoeuvres of circular and lateral movement, successfully. The influence of the rudder could be felt immediately and I hardly had to pull lightly on one of the two steering lines before I saw the horizon move around me.'[2]

After rising to 6000 feet (1828 metres), and as night was approaching, he extinguished the firebox, vented off the steam and landed successfully at Elancourt, near Trappes.

Just a few years later, the earliest known aerial photographs were taken over Paris in 1858 by Nadar, whose real name was Felix Tournachon (1820–1910). The Franco-Italian War of 1859 heralded the return of military ballooning by French forces after a gap of more than half a century[3], with a short series of reconnaissance flights in hot-air balloons by the French aeronaut Eugène Godard (1827–1890) during the Battle of Solferino. The event was reported upon by many European newspapers, including the *Irish Times*:

> 'Having first mounted on the campanile to take the bearings and make himself somewhat acquainted with the country, he entered his little skiff and went up in the air with a regularity which, according to those who saw the ascent, showed that he was master of his eccentric conveyance.'[4]

The First American Army Balloon Corps was formed on 1 October 1861, with five balloons and sixty men. Between 1861 and 1863 at least ten balloons were used for observation in the American Civil War, including the *Atlantic*,

A very obviously staged photograph of
Nadar.

The French aeronaut Eugene Godard.

Saratoga, *Enterprise*, *Intrepid*, *Washington*, *Union*, *Excelsior*, *United States*, *Eagle*
and *Constitution*. Balloons were present at the battles of Manassas, Bull Run,
Fair Oaks, Chancellorsville, Seven Pines and Fredericksburg, where they were
particularly of use in directing artillery fire. The first telegraph message to be

Lowe ascends at Fair
Oaks on 31 May 1862.

transmitted from a balloon was sent by the American aeronaut Thaddeus Lowe (1832–1913)[5] from the balloon *Enterprise* on 18 June 1861. A prominent Union officer, Major General William Farrar "Baldy" Smith, later noted, 'the signals from the balloon have enabled my gunners to hit, with a fine degree of accuracy, an unseen and dispersed target area.'[6] Then, on 3 August, John La Mountain (1830–1878) ascended in a captive balloon from the deck of the gunboat *Fanny*, to observe Confederate positions on the shores of Hampton Roads.[7]

At the Battle of Richmond, in June 1862, it was reported in the *Irish Times*[8] that the Federal forces sent up a balloon which supplied General McClellan with information by telegraph. It was discovered that even from a height of 200 feet (61 metres), an observer with a good telescope could spy on enemy activity as much as five miles (eight kilometres) away. Attempts were also made with regard to aerial photography. A converted coal barge, the *George Washington Parke Custis*, was used to convey and also tow balloons along the Potomac River, and may be termed the first operational aircraft carrier, or more accurately, 'the first surface vessel to be specifically configured for the operation of an aerial device.'[9] The greatest drawback was the requirement of heavy equipment needed to generate gas on-site, which was time consuming and cumbersome. The famous rigid airship constructor, Count Ferdinand von Zeppelin (1838–1917), there as a Prussian military observer, made his first ascent in August 1863 at St Paul, Minnesota. The Confederacy had also attempted to release a reconnaissance balloon from the steamship *Teaser* on the James River in 1862. Legend has it that it was manufactured from silk dresses patriotically donated by southern belles, but the true story is much more prosaic and it was actually made from raw silk at Savannah, Georgia.[10]

In 1870–71, during the Siege of Paris, balloons made sixty-six flights, carrying 164 passengers, 381 carrier pigeons, five dogs, three million letters and other cargo over the encircling Prussian Army between September 1870

A model of the *George Washington Parke Custis*. (*Mariners Museum, Newport News*)

and January 1871.[11] The letters were written on rice paper to save weight and included communications from the author's great-grandfather's Paris office. The *Irish Times* Military Correspondent sent 'Balloon News' from Paris by means of telegraph from Rouen, describing combat under the walls of the city which had happened only a few days before. Five of the balloons were captured by the Prussians and two were lost at sea. Three captive balloon stations were also established in the city, from which ascents for the purpose of reconnaissance were made. The French statesman and future Prime Minister, Léon Gambetta, escaped from Paris in a balloon on 7 October 1871.

The Prussian Army also formed two *Luftschiffer* detachments with the advice and direction of the English balloonist, Henry Coxwell, but these were soon disbanded. Some years earlier, Coxwell had demonstrated to German officers in Berlin the practicability of dropping bombs from a balloon.[12] Indeed, he maintained his interest in military ballooning right to the end of his long life, as not long before he died, on 5 January 1900, at the age of eighty, one of his last letters to the press was on the subject of the use of balloons in the Boer War.[13]

Perhaps inspired by the Parisian airmail, in March 1874, the German Postmaster General, Heinrich von Stephan, and founder of the World Postal Union, wrote a prophetic article on '*World Postal Service and Airship Travel*' in which he stated:

The Balloon *Neptune* during the Siege of Paris.

'Providence has surrounded the entire world with navigable air. This vast ocean still lies empty and wasted today, and is not yet used for human transportation.'[14]

Count von Zeppelin read this and afterwards was inspired to make some notes in his diary:

'Thoughts about an airship. The craft would have to compare in dimensions with a large ship. The gas volume so calculated that the weight of the craft would be supported except for a slight excess. The ascent will then take place through forward motion of the machine, which will force the craft, so to speak, against the upward inclined planes. The gas compartments will be divided into cells which can be filled and emptied individually.'[15]

Thoughts were also turning to a more organised military use of the air in France, with the formation of *L'Établissement Central de Aérostation Militaire*, at Meudon, to the south-west of Paris. Its first director was Captain Charles Renard, who would, within a few years, make airship history. Another French officer with an interest in aeronautics, Captain F. Ferber, summed up the challenge well: 'To design a flying machine is nothing; to build one is nothing much; to try it in the air is everything.'[16]

First Steps in England

During these years the British Army, or at least a few technically minded officers, had become more aware of the benefits of 'airmindedness'. In the 1850s, Henry Coxwell tried to interest the authorities in using balloons in the Crimea and elsewhere. Apart from some discussion and swift rejection of the topic of military ballooning by a War Office committee in 1854, it was not considered seriously until 1862. Lieutenant George Grover, RE,[17] wrote two well-argued papers on the military use of balloons, which were published in the professional journal of the Royal Engineers. He firstly posed the question:

'Are balloons capable of rendering sufficient service to an army, engaged in active operations, to make it worthwhile to authorise their employment as one of the resources of modern warfare?'[18]

He analysed the possible uses of balloons and rapidly dismissed the notions of either dropping explosive devices on enemy-held positions, or of transporting supplies into a besieged fortress or town, because no means of steering or motive power had been devised. He regarded the potential for, 'assisting reconnoitring officers' as having much greater potential, even from an elevation of a few hundred feet. He contended that they had not been employed by the British Army because of an overestimate of the problems involved and a lack of appreciation of the advantages. He listed the perceived problems as – vulnerability to ground fire, difficulty of transportation to a suitable operational site, adequate provision of gas in the field, the training of sufficient aeronauts and the general belief that ballooning was dangerous. He dealt with all of these in turn and answered all the points at issue very lucidly and clearly, coming to the following conclusion:

George Edward Grover of the Royal Engineers was an early advocate of Air Power.

'The subject is certainly worthy of the consideration of the Scientific Corps of the English [sic] Army, more particularly in the present day, when the resources of science are so especially directed towards the attainment of success in all military operations.'[19]

Captain Frederick Beaumont, RE,[20] who had observed the use of balloons by the Federal forces in the American Civil War, also wrote a paper for the same journal in which he described the equipment used by the Union Army in some detail. His conclusions were as follows:

'I shall finish with a few remarks on the apparatus I would recommend for experimental purposes. Though for actual use, I think the larger sized balloon the best; a capacity of 13,000 cubic feet would give sufficient buoyancy for experiment. I would alter, however, the shape of the envelope, as the one commonly used is the worst that could be devised for the purpose [round or pear-shaped]; in the case of a free ascent, shape matters little, as the machine must go with the wind, but when the balloon is anchored it is of paramount importance to present the least possible surface to the action of the aft. I would, therefore, give to the balloon a cylindrical form, and to the car a boat shape, and I believe that with the decreased resistance offered, such stability might be obtained as to allow of ascents being made in weather that, with the old shape, would preclude their being thought of. I would also have the whole of the network and the guys of silk, for the sake of lightness. Comparatively speaking, the first cost would be unimportant, and with care they would last a long time, while, if it was thought desirable, common cord might be used for ordinary ascents, and the silk ones brought out only in case of great altitude being required. A very thin wire would enable telegraphic communications to be kept up, if necessary, with the ground, and an alphabetical instrument would place the means of doing so within anybody's reach. The cost of an apparatus, perfect in every respect, would be about £500, and one for experimental purposes might be got up for much less. The officer in charge of it would require to have practical experience, but his assistants might be men taken from the ranks, and a few hours would make them sufficiently acquainted with their duties. The management of a balloon would seem to be a simple operation, and in perfectly calm weather when everything goes well, so it is; but to feel confident under adverse circumstances, and to know exactly what to do, and how to do it when difficulties arise, can be the result only of experience. It has been supposed that the swaying motion of a balloon when tied to the earth would occasion a nausea in some people akin to seasickness. I do not think this would be the case (with me it certainly was not so), as, if the notion were so great, fear would in all probability overcome any other feeling, and, at the same time under such circumstances, it would be useless to think of observing. I hope that the capabilities of balloons for military reconnaissances may receive a fair test, with properly prepared apparatus, as, should it be suddenly required to use them, it is quite possible that want of practice would turn what should have been a success into a failure, and the faults of the executive would be borne by the system. I am confident myself, that under certain circumstances, balloons would be found useful, and no one could say after all, more against them than that, like the fifth wheel to the coach, they were useless.'[21]

The following year, 1863, Grover and Beaumont, along with Henry Coxwell, ascended from the Queen's Parade at Aldershot in the balloon *Evening Star*, which was inflated with coal-gas; later alighting in Milford, near Godalming in Surrey, where they were hospitably entertained by the local vicar. Ascents were also made from the grounds of the Royal Arsenal at Woolwich, which, after due consideration, the Ordnance Select Committee deemed to have

Coxwell's ascent in the balloon *Mammoth* from the grounds of Crystal Palace in September 1862.

sufficient promise to be allowed to continue as a series of trials. Investigations were made by the War Office Chemist, Professor Frederick Abel,[22] concerning the generation of hydrogen and the most suitable material for balloon fabric. By 1865 it had been concluded that the expense did not justify further research at that stage, the committee being of the opinion that:

'In special cases, particularly in siege operations connected with either attack or defence, balloon reconnaissance performed by experienced officers with powerful telescopic glasses would afford most useful information, but they are not prepared to recommend the special preparation of balloon equipment in times of profound peace.'[23]

However, following the successful use of balloons in the Franco-Prussian War in 1870–71, as described earlier, a sub-committee of the Royal Engineers Committee was formed (consisting of Abel, Beaumont and Grover) to have a further look at the possibilities. A gas furnace for the production of hydrogen was constructed at Woolwich Dockyard in 1873 and it was discovered that this method would be too cumbersome for use in the field. Lieutenant Charles Watson, RE, who replaced Beaumont, worked out a scheme for aerial support to be given to an expedition against the Ashanti, along with devising a portable gas apparatus which used sulphuric acid and zinc. This fell down on cost grounds. In 1875, the use of steel cylinders to transport gas was first proposed, but not developed further at that stage. Experiments with free and captive balloons were once more carried out at Woolwich Arsenal in 1878 under the command of Captain R.P. Lee, RE and Captain J.L.B. Templer, 2nd Middlesex Militia (later the 7th Battalion King's Royal Rifle Corps), who had his own balloon, *Crusader*, filled by coal-gas. In fact, from 23 August 1878, Templer was even granted 10 shillings (50p) a day flying pay for services as an instructor – though only on actual flying days.

James Lethbride Brooke Templer.

The Times reported ascents made by Templer in *Crusader* and also the smaller balloon, *Pioneer*. It noted that Templer had lately been carrying out private experiments in *Crusader*, studying the prevailing winds to enable him to predict 'very nearly' the course his balloon would pursue, 'which will probably be turned to advantage in future campaigns.'[24] He was described as:

> 'Tall, powerful, dark, of aspect stern and forbidding, not always popular with superiors by virtue of his disregard of regulations and impatience with official delays and obstructions, but a man who usually got his way.'[25]

It is also worthy of note that, as an officer in the militia, rather than being a regular, and in his early 30s, James Templer could devote more of his time to the rather esoteric subject of military ballooning instead of being forced to consider a career pattern in the Royal Engineers, which would have perforce demanded that he undertake a broader range of postings. The sum of £71 (from an initial allocation of £150) was spent on the balloon *Pioneer* – the envelope of which was made from specially treated and varnished cambric – which took to the air for the first time on the same day that Templer was awarded his flying pay. This compared very favourably with the £1200 suggested by Coxwell in 1873 as the price of a balloon for service in the Ashanti War. *Pioneer* was taken to the Easter Review of Volunteers at Dover by Templer and Captain Henry Elsdale, RE,[26] in 1879, (in which year the unit was established as the Balloon Equipment Store) and to the Volunteers Field Day at Brighton in 1880. The balloon was filled from the nearest gas works. Elsdale sat in the basket while Templer travelled in the towing wagon. On 24 June 1880 came the earliest recorded use of a balloon detachment on manoeuvres at Aldershot, which was repeated in 1882. Experimental work was directed at the type of gas used, suitable fabric for the envelopes, improving the technique and practice of filling balloons and the whole question of transport. 'A thoroughly sound and reliable fleet'[27] of five balloons was established, including *Sapper*, *Heron*, *Fly* and *Spy*, with a few officers and men trained to use them. *Heron's* envelope was made from goldbeaters skin, (an explanation of the manufacture of goldbeater's skin will be found in Appendix 2) while *Sapper's* was of silk treated with linseed oil; in the construction of the latter, Templer was assisted by Lieutenant J.E. Capper, RE, who had just completed the Army Engineering Course at Chatham and was awaiting a posting to India with the Bengal Sappers. He was recruited by Templer because of his mathematical ability, but his tough and forceful character impressed the older man.[28] Capper himself later commented, 'I was permitted to help, as even then I believed in the military future of balloons. We designed and made the first military balloon in England.'[29] He will feature in this account again. In 1882 the store was moved to Chatham, and a small factory, depot and school of instruction were established there.

Meanwhile, Templer had experienced just how dangerous aerial activity could be; on 10 December 1881 he invited Walter Powell, the MP for Malmesbury, and James Agg-Gardner, the MP for Cheltenham, for a flight in the government-owned balloon *Saladin*. They departed Bath and headed towards Dorset:

'Crewkerne was presently sighted, then Beaminster. The roar of the sea gave the next indication of the locality to which the balloon had drifted and the first hint of the possible perils of the voyage. A descent was now effected to within a few hundred feet of earth, and an endeavour was made to ascertain the exact position they had reached. The course taken by the balloon between Beaminster and the sea is not stated in Captain Templer's letter. The wind, as far as we can gather, must have shifted, or different currents of air must have been found at the different altitudes. What Captain Templer says is that they coasted along to Symonsbury, passing, it would seem, in an easterly direction and keeping still very near to the earth. Soon after they had left Symonsbury, Captain Templer shouted to a man below to tell them how far they were from Bridport, and he received for answer that Bridport was about a mile off. The pace at which the balloon was moving had now increased to thirty-five miles an hour. The sea was dangerously close, and a few minutes in a southerly current of air would have been enough to carry them over it. They seem, however, to have been confident in their own powers of management. They threw out ballast, and rose to a height of 1500 feet, and thence came down again only just in time, touching the ground at a distance of about 150 yards from the cliff. The balloon here dragged for a few feet, and Captain Templer, who had been letting off the gas, rolled out of the car, still holding the valve line in his hand. This was the last chance of a safe escape for anybody. The balloon, with its weight lightened, went up about eight feet. Mr Agg-Gardner dropped out and broke his leg. Mr Powell now remained as the sole occupant of the car. Captain Templer, who still had hold of the rope, shouted to Mr Powell to come down the line. This he attempted to do, but in a few seconds, and before he could commence his perilous descent, the line was torn out of Captain Templer's hands. All communication with the earth was cut off, and the balloon rose rapidly, taking Mr Powell with it in a south-easterly direction out to sea.'[30]

Despite extensive search operations by naval and commercial ships from England, France and the Channel Islands, Powell and the balloon were never seen again. No doubt George Usborne, in common with other educated and technically-minded citizens in Queenstown, would have kept abreast of these developments as reported in the English and Irish press.

Early Life in Queenstown
In 1880, George was appointed to the Queenstown Coastguard and served there for three years. Then, in December 1883, he joined Cork Harbour Board as Deputy Harbour Master, becoming Pilot Master in 1893 and eventually Harbour Master in 1922. He was Honorary Secretary of the lifeboat management committee for forty years. The May 1920 *Lifeboat Journal* reported that on:

'20 April 1920, Admiral Sir Reginald Tupper, KCB, Commander-in-Chief Western Approaches, presented to Captain Usborne the Thanks of the Committee Management inscribed on Vellum, and the Silver Inkstand which had been awarded to him for his services during thirty-six years as Honorary Secretary of the Queenstown Station, which has now been closed.'

He retired from his position as harbour master in May 1925 owing to ill health and died two months later. His obituaries in the Irish press praised his long career of public service and noted that he had carried out his work with the *Irish*

The Cork Harbour Board meets on 10 October 1917, Captain George Usborne is seated in the centre of the photograph, in uniform. (*Port of Cork*)

John Gilbert, Patrick's Quay, Cork, 1886. Watercolour on paper 21 x 31cm. Crawford Art Gallery, Cork.

Rear Admiral C.V. Usborne.

Times to his usual high standard, commenting favourably upon his, 'utmost zeal and efficiency', and the *Cork Examiner* recording that he was, 'a very upright and kindly gentleman, who made innumerable friends amongst those who had the pleasure of his cultured and refined acquaintance'. George Usborne was very proud of his years of service in what he regarded as the safest harbour in the United Kingdom at all times. He recalled that he had seen the largest ocean steamers of nearly every line flying the British flag enter and leave the harbour at all stages of the tide, in all weathers, both day and night, and had never known a casualty occur, except through carelessness or some grave error of judgement.

Neville had two older brothers. Philip Osbert Gordon was born on 27 February 1879, in Folkestone. He was a Royal Engineer and later Director of Public Works in Uganda. He died in 1915 in Calcutta. Then there was Cecil Vivian, born on 17 May 1880, in Queenstown, who preceded Neville into the Royal Navy. He specialised in gunnery, and later in mine warfare, inventing the apparatus which led to the introduction of Paravane mine protection. During the Dardanelles campaign he took a flight to inspect the minefield laid in the narrow waters and was shot down by an over-enthusiastic British gunner – luckily without injury. He was promoted to captain in 1917; he was senior British officer at Salonika and later commanded the Naval Brigade on the Danube. He held a succession of staff appointments and important commands, including the battleships *Malaya* and *Resolution* after the war, and rose to the rank of vice admiral before he retired in 1933. He was recalled for service in World War Two and retired once more in 1945. Cecil died in January 1951. His obituary in *The Times* prompted a letter from a former companion in arms, who wrote as GOS and who praised the elder Usborne's drive, persuasive manner, energy, ingenuity, sympathy and good administration.[31]

In the 1880s and 1890s, during the period when Neville and his brothers were growing up, Queenstown was prospering as never before or since. It was the terminus for the main railway line from Dublin. The transatlantic liners called, going and coming to deliver and pick up passengers and mail, and the harbour was full of sailing ships inward bound from China, India, Australia

The Esplanade, Cobh, formerly Queenstown. (*via Allen Crosbie*)

and New Zealand. Life for the professional classes in Queenstown in the 1880s and 1890s was more leisured and pleasant than at any time since. The children of such families were always privately educated. The Usborne family lived at Dunlea, and later at Carndonagh. Neville's niece, Vivian Mary, later recalled:

> 'I remember the sirens of the huge liners hooting as they left port, when, aged three or four, I went to stay in the house on the hill overlooking the harbour.'[32]

The Cork Opera House was flourishing, and provided both light (Gilbert and Sullivan) and classical operas, and symphony orchestras came there for a season. Queenstown had its own Musical Hall. There was a pack of beagles on the island and major hunts on the mainland, and a lot of good shooting on the marshland round about. Only the wealthy would have possessed guns. Queenstown accommodated Cork businessmen, the families of the officers on the Royal Naval ships and the dockyard, and most of the families of the army officers stationed on Spike Island. The Admiral was the most important local dignitary.[33]

Developments in Naval Technology
The second half of the nineteenth century was also a time of great technological change with regard to warships, though technological progress was by no means welcomed by all. The great engineer, Isambard Kingdom Brunel, complained of the Admiralty's attitude to innovation during the Crimean War in the following terms:

> 'They have an extraordinary supply of cold water and capacious and heavy extinguishers… . But they have an unlimited supply of some negative principle which seems to absorb and eliminate everything that approaches them… . It is a curious and puzzling phenomenon, but in my experience it has always attended every contact with the Admiralty.'[34]

Steam propulsion in line-of-battle ships of the Royal Navy was introduced with HMS *Sans Pareil* in 1851 and the ninety-one gun HMS *Agamemnon* the following year (the first to be designed and built from the keel up with installed steam power). In 1860, HMS *Warrior* was launched, the first major warship to be built entirely of iron, which was followed by HMS *Royal Sovereign* in 1864, the first turret-armed battleship and the only one with a wooden hull. The Whitehead torpedo, which was invented in 1867, came to be regarded as a very

HMS *Devastation*.

great threat to the world's navies, particularly after the development of small, fast, torpedo boats, which could potentially sink a more ponderous battleship; the first of these in RN service was HMS *Lightning* in 1877.

In 1871, HMS *Devastation* created something of a sensation; it had no sails and relied solely on its 800 hp engine for propulsion; it had turrets fore and aft for a pair of muzzle-loading, rifled, 12-inch guns, which could train through 280 degrees – the main armament therefore being on top of the hull rather than within. The sailors were less than pleased with their accommodation, however, as when asked by a journalist what it was like below decks, the reply came that it was like living in, 'rat holes with tinned air.'[35] It is to be hoped that this was improved by the introduction of the first RN ironclad with electric lighting, HMS *Inflexible* of 1881.

Further Progress in the Air
While Neville was a babe in arms, a series of significant events in respect of lighter-than-air aviation took place in France. Firstly, in 1883–84, the Tissandier brothers, Gaston (1839–1906) and Albert (1843–1899), designed, built and flew the first dirigible powered by electricity. The envelope had a capacity of 37,400 cubic feet (1058 cubic metres) and was 92 feet (28 metres) long, with a maximum diameter of 30 feet (9.10 metres). The basket was fitted with a propeller and a small electric motor of less than 2 hp (1.48 kW) powered by a zinc-carbon battery. It made its first ascent from Auteuil, with the inventors on board, on

The Tissandier brothers' airship.

8 October 1883 and flew for about twenty minutes over the Bois de Bologne. A second ascent was made the following year, flying across Paris to Marolles-en-Brie.[36] The *Irish Times* reported on the event:

> 'Another interesting experiment in aerial navigation was tried on Friday by the brothers Gaston and Albert Tissandier; in shape their balloon resembles that of M. Giffard. The motive force is furnished by a Siemens dynamo which moves a screw. After leaving its moorings the balloon was carried by a strong west wind to the Seine, when its occupants set the screw in motion and caused it to remain almost stationary. It was then allowed to go with the current. After this it several times made headway against it. It was noticed that while the screw was working, the reporters, who followed in a carriage, could easily keep pace with it, but when the motion stopped and the wind was allowed to have its own way, they were immediately left far behind.'[37]

On 8 August 1884, French Army Balloon Corps Captains, Charles Renard (1847–1905) and Arthur Krebs (1850–1935), took off from the French Army balloon establishment at Chalais-Meudon Park, in the electrically-powered (batteries and 8 hp (5.92 kW) electric motor) dirigible, *La France*, which had a capacity of 66,000 cubic feet (1868 cubic metres). It had a very large, two-bladed propeller at the front of the bamboo, canvas-covered car and at the rear, a rudder and an elevator. The envelope was 165 feet (50.29 metres) in length, had a maximum diameter of 27 feet 6 inches (8.38 metres) and was made from

Charles Renard and Arthur Krebs.

varnished Chinese silk. It was the first aircraft in history to return to its starting point against the wind, making a return trip of twenty-three minutes, covering 5 miles (8 km). The pilots described their trip as follows:

'At four o'clock on a particularly calm afternoon the balloon, set free and having a very low ascensional force, rose up slowly to the height of the surrounding plateaux. The engine was put into motion and soon, under its impulse, the balloon increased its speed, faithfully obeying the slightest action of its rudder.'[38]

La France at Chalais in 1884.

They steered for Villacoublay, and over the town executed a broad turn and proceeded back to Chalais at a height of about 1000 feet (304 metres). They commenced their descent above the landing field:

'During this time we had to go backwards and forwards several times in order to keep the balloon over the landing point. At a height of 250 feet (76 metres) we dropped a rope, which was seized by men on the ground and the balloon was brought back to the same meadow from where it had left.'[39]

In the words of the correspondent writing for the *Irish Times*:

'The apparatus is described as a balloon pointed at both ends like a whaleboat, and holding the usual supply of gas. Below is a net containing, in addition to the officer who attended the valve and the other who steered, certain electrical accumulators, which supplied a motor, employed to set in motion a screw propeller by which the balloon, so far as we can make out, is not only driven in space, but also to some extent guided in the same way that a ship is directed in its true course by means of a rudder.'[40]

Renard informed the press that his flight was just the start of a revolution, not only in aerostatics, but also in warfare, with armies being flown vast distances across trackless wastes to relieve beleaguered cities such as Khartoum – which was at that time much featured in the daily news and was eventually relieved (but not by air) in January 1885, just two days after the death of General Gordon. He also predicted aerial services for passengers and mails. Several further successful flights were made over the course of the following year.

Then, in 1885, Gottlieb Daimler produced the world's first practical, petrol-driven, internal combustion engine, which could be developed as a power unit with a power to weight ratio suitable for propelling vehicles on land, sea and in the air. The original model had been invented eight years before by Nikolaus Otto. The year also brought the establishment of a permanent military balloon arm in Germany with the creation of the *Preussische Luftschiffer-Abteilung* at Berlin-Schöneberg. A few years later a Military School of Ballooning for the Bavarian Army was set up at Munich and a Balloon Corps was founded in Vienna.

Nor was the potential of military aviation ignored by the writers of popular fiction. In 1886, inspired by the feat of Renard and Krebs, the famed author of science fiction, Jules Verne, published *The Clipper of the Clouds*, which described the use of dirigibles as forces for good and evil. Another French author and illustrator, Albert Robida, wrote in 1887, *La Guerre au Vingtième Siècle (War in the Twentieth Century)*, which foresaw a sudden devastating strike from the air by aerial torpedoes launched from aircraft powered by electricity.[41]

The Royal Engineers Balloon Section

Meanwhile, returning to the British Army's aviation activities in June 1883, Major Lee, RE, and Lieutenant Francis Trollope, Grenadier Guards, were sent to Paris to visit the balloon exhibition and report on what they saw. Then, in September 1884, the centenary of ballooning in England was celebrated in the grounds of the Artillery Company, at Finsbury in London, by the ascent of several balloons and a lecture from M. de Fouville, President of the *Academie de Aérostation*, Paris. While this was going on the Royal Engineers were also developing their aeronautical skills by preparing for a deployment overseas. A significant development was the introduction, in 1884, of steel cylinders which could store hydrogen under compression and so transport supplies of the gas for use in the field. Balloons could now be inflated in ten or fifteen minutes. One of the most difficult problems to overcome was the design of a valve secure enough to prevent the leakage of hydrogen.[42] A balloon section, with three balloons, *Heron*, *Spy* and *Feo*, ten NCOs and sappers, commanded by Major Elsdale, RE, with Lieutenant Trollope, accompanied a substantial army expedition under the command of Major General Sir Charles Warren, consisting of some 4000 infantry, cavalry, artillery and engineers, to Bechuanaland in November 1884. The aim was to assert British sovereignty and, 'To deal with Boer raiders and to pacify the country.'[43] A local chief, Montsiou, was taken up for a flight and observed:

> 'If the first white man who came into this country had brought a thing like that and, having gone up in it before our eyes, had come down and demanded that we should worship and serve him, we should have done so. The English indeed have great power.'[44]

Sir Charles Warren was taken aloft in *Heron* in April 1885 at Mafeking and was impressed by the view of the surrounding countryside that could be obtained. It was discovered that the lifting capacity of the balloons was impaired the higher above sea level they operated. It was also noted that the conduct and ability of ground staff was vital to the success of aerial operations.[45] Moreover, it was shown that a detachment of only ten men was too small for the effective working of the equipment.[46]

A Royal Engineers mobile balloon section.

Major Templer led a section of eight NCOs and men, as well as the three balloons, *Scout*, *Fly* and *Sapper*, which travelled to the Sudan (or the Soudan – as it was termed in the contemporary newspapers) in February 1885 (following the death of General Gordon at Khartoum) as part of the protection for a military railway construction project. The materials taken also included 120 cylinders of hydrogen, a compressor, searchlights, and signalling equipment.

An artist's impression of a military balloon being inflated in the Sudan in 1885.

Camels were used to transport the gas cylinders. No doubt the heart of one of the expedition's staff officers, Major George Grover, RE, was gladdened by this demonstration of this aeronautical progress, albeit some twenty years after he had first proposed it. One particularly noteworthy event occurred on 25 March, when Lieutenant R.J.H.L. Mackenzie, RE, remained aloft for seven hours in the balloon *Scout* during a route march, towed by a mule carriage in the convoy, with a further guide rope attached to a mounted horseman, messages to the ground being passed down via the latter:

'When the convoy was ready to move, the balloon, still two hundred feet up, was made fast to a cart in the centre of the square. It was rather difficult to avoid jerking the cords which held it, and thus running the chance of breaking them; but extreme care was taken when crossing any rough pieces of ground, as it would not have been unpleasant for the occupant of the car if he had suddenly found himself floating quietly towards the mountains, miles beyond the reach of any friends. Communication was kept up with the balloon by means of written messages, and it was not long before a letter came down telling us that the enemy were still pursuing the stampeded camels down towards the sea and killing them as soon as they got up with them. The force reached the zaribas at last, unmolested, when the balloon was hauled down and packed up, the gas being as far as possible saved for future use. Thus the first ascent may be chronicled as a success.'[47]

Mackenzie was therefore the first British airman to carry out his 'force protection' duties in the presence of the enemy, namely the Mahdi's Dervish warriors. The *Irish Times* reported that:

'The convoy with the captive balloon were in no way molested, which can scarcely be wondered at if the rebels were as astonished by the strange spectacle as have been the natives of Suakin. The native gossips here are all agog at the startling phenomenon and the bazaars throughout the day have been in a perfect ferment upon the subject. Even now they have not apparently satisfied themselves as to the origin and uses of a war balloon.'[48]

However, the expedition's senior Royal Engineer, Colonel Edwards, remarked:

'The detachment deployed was numerically too weak for the duty and it is absolutely necessary that the men should be thoroughly drilled and instructed in handling the balloon in a moderate breeze. On 2 April we were obliged to supplement the detachment with men from the Royal Engineer companies, who had never worked a balloon before, consequently they were unable to keep it steady.'[49]

It was noted that the effect of the balloon on the morale of the enemy was such that the aerially escorted convoy was free from any attack, whereas the two previous ones had met with considerable opposition. On the following day, *Scout* accompanied a convoy of 1200 camels, escorted by the Berkshire Regiment; not a camel was lost. *Fly* later went further up-country and was used with success for reconnaissance. Templer was mentioned in dispatches for his actions during the expedition in the engagement at Hasheen. He also had an eye for the main chance. On his way back to England he noticed a couple of traction engines lying at Suakin, apparently ownerless. He decided that they would be a useful asset and laid claim to them by the simple but effective method of chalking, on the boilers of both, the address, 'The School of Ballooning, Chatham', to which they were shipped in due course, along with a fine marquee, which later saw much service as the RE Officers' Mess when at balloon training camps.[50]

Back in England, experiments were made with artillery spotting, aerial photography and with towing the balloon wagons by the newly acquired traction engines. The experiences in the field in 1885 proved that a balloon detachment should be supported by at least thirty sappers to work the balloon

Major Templer (second left) stands proudly atop one of the traction engines which he had acquired.

A Royal Engineers balloon being filled with hydrogen in the field.

properly. Detachments also took part in camps, one of which was at the artillery practice ground at Lydd in Kent, where members of the public often showed some interest, but rather less comprehension. An officer once spent some considerable time explaining military ballooning to a lady visitor; when he had finished she said that she thought she understood everything, but had one question, 'How do you breathe inside?'[51] Remarkably, much of the cost of maintaining the Balloon Establishment had been met by the enthusiastic and reasonably wealthy Templer, out of his own pocket. He bought some ground at Lidsing, a few miles from Chatham, where a pit was dug in the chalk of sufficient depth to take a large balloon and keep it completely secure from the wind. This anomalous financial arrangement was rectified by the War Office in 1887, when ballooning activity was split into two parts, the military flying side under Major Elsdale and a civilian manufacturing section under Templer, the whole being named the School of Ballooning. Templer was gazetted major and given a salary of £600 a year.

The establishment was as follows:

1 Officer-in-Charge
1 Instructor in Ballooning

Balloon Detachment:
1 Lieutenant
1 Sergeant
15 Rank and file (corporals and below)

The Balloon Factory:
1 Military mechanist
1 Gas maker
1 Storeman
1 Driver
10 balloon-making hands (including women)

Specialist transport was to be provided, but without horses. These were to be drawn from the Army Service Corps along with general service wagons.[52] A balloon train consisted of a balloon wagon with hauling down gear, three wagons to carry forty-four gas cylinders each, an equipment wagon with spare balloon envelopes and stores, and a water cart. All the wagons were fitted with draw bars so the entire train could be towed by a traction engine.[53]

A balloon flown by Lieutenant Bernard Ward, RE, took part in the Aldershot Summer Manoeuvres in 1889, receiving the approbation of Lieutenant General Sir Evelyn Wood, VC, after a successful night attack made on the basis of the aeronaut's report. Sir Evelyn later remarked that it was likely that balloons would henceforward play an important part in military campaigns of the future. He also advocated that the Balloon Establishment should be relocated from Chatham to Aldershot.[54] At a parade held in honour of the German Emperor, Ward 'marched past' at a height of 300 feet (91 metres), towed by a wagon.[55]

Naval Developments

Royal Naval matters were also progressing. The Naval Defence Act of 1889 gave naval architects the opportunity to concentrate on producing standard designs for different classes of ship as Lord Salisbury's government provided sufficient funding (£21.5 million) to order ten battleships, nine first-class cruisers, twenty-nine second-class cruisers, four third-class cruisers and eighteen torpedo gunboats. Ships were to be designed around their weapons rather than have them fitted into the hull as an afterthought. A countermeasure to the torpedo boat was also conceived with the laying down of the first torpedo boat destroyer, HMS *Havock*, in 1893. The balance of advantage was again altered by the introduction of a gyroscopic control mechanism for torpedoes in 1896.

Chapter Two

From the 1890s to the start of Neville's Aviation Career

Naval Service

On 14 April 1897, Neville came fourth in the competitive exam held by the Civil Service Commission in London for entry as a cadet in the Royal Navy. He scored well in Arithmetic, Algebra, Geometry, English, French, Scripture, Latin, English History and Geography, gaining 1614 marks out of a possible 2150. His lowest marks were in handwriting.

The previous year, on 28 August 1896, the first petrol-driven dirigible (an airship that could be steered as opposed to a balloon which travelled where the wind took it), powered by a 2 hp (1.48 kW) engine, had undertaken its maiden flight, Dr Karl Wöelfert's *Deutschland* in Berlin. This was an important moment in aviation history – an aircraft had flown which could not only be steered, but had a power unit light enough to be carried aloft with ease and

Wöelfert's *Deutschland* at Templehof in 1896.

Schwartz's dirigible at Templehof in 1897.

with development potential. Sadly, on 4 June 1897, Wöelfert, who was born in 1852, and his mechanic, Knabe, were killed in an accident on the *Deutschland*, when the engine vaporiser set fire to the envelope, causing an explosion of the gas within; so becoming the first dirigible fatalities. Also in 1897, the Hungarian engineer, David Schwarz (1852–1897), built a rigid dirigible with both frame and envelope constructed entirely from sheet aluminium only 0.008 inches (0.02 millimetres) in thickness – the *Metallballon*. It was 156 feet (47 metres) in length and its volume was 130,500 cubic feet (3693 cubic metres). It was powered by a Daimler 12 hp (8.88 kW) engine driving three propellers. In appearance it resembled a fat pencil stub. It took off on 3 November for its maiden flight from Tempelhof in Berlin and circled several times, but descended rapidly and broke up, fortunately without injury to the crew. The following year, 1898, the first pilot to be shot down by enemy forces was Sergeant William Ivy of the US Signal Corps Balloon Section. He was flying in Cuba during the Spanish–American War and, while observing the Spanish positions on San Juan Hill, he came under fire. The balloon's envelope was holed and splashed into the water, fortunately for the aeronaut; he lived to tell the tale and to fly another day. [Author's note: It was not until 1 August 1907 that the Aeronautical Division of the US Army Signal Corps was formed, the first dirigible being No 1, which took to the air for its maiden flight on 4 August 1908.]

Further Naval Developments

The Royal Navy, in the last decade of the nineteenth century, had undergone immense technological changes in the previous fifty years – the transition from sail to steam propulsion; the change from solid iron cannon balls to shells filled with high explosive; the development of rifled and breech-loaded guns; the change in position of the location of the main armament from batteries mounted inside the hull to turrets mounted on the upper deck, with the consequent greatly increased arc of fire; the introduction of armour plate to protect ships' hulls, and the most vital and vulnerable machinery contained therein; the replacement of wood in the construction of ships by iron and steel; and, as previously noted, the invention of the torpedo and small vessels to launch these, which could pose a formidable threat to the largest battleship; the introduction of torpedo boat destroyers as a countermeasure; armoured cruisers for the protection of commerce around the world; lighter cruisers as scouts, and the development of homogeneous classes of warships which could operate tactically as a fleet. Soon to come were the sea mine, the submarine and aviation. To match all of the above, tactical doctrine and the training of officers also needed modernisation, which did not always find favour with senior officers who still hankered after the age of sail.

Naval Training in HMS *Britannia*

Usborne entered the training ship HMS *Britannia* in May 1897. This was just a few years before it was replaced by the Britannia Royal Naval College, the

Britannia & *Hindustan* on the River Dart in the 1890s.

foundation stone of which was laid in 1902. An old three-deck, ship-of-the-line, had been moored in the Dart estuary since 1863, being joined (by means of a bridge between them) by the two-decker, *Hindustan,* in 1864, though the first *Britannia* was replaced by a larger and more modern vessel in 1869.

In 1897 the ship was under the command of Captain the Hon A.G. Curzon-Howe, 'a dignified aristocrat of the old school'[1] who had the reputation of being one of the politest and most gentlemanly officers in the navy. Mrs Curzon-Howe also lived on board with their small son and was loved by the boys for the kindness she showed to them.[2] The second in command was Commander Christopher Cradock, who was always immaculately dressed, with a pointed, neatly-trimmed dark beard, which reminded the boys of Sir Francis Drake.[3] He was also a popular Master of Beagles and would die a gallant death against hopeless odds at the battle of Coronel in 1914. Both were fine role models for a cadet to follow.[4] The Naval Instructor, the Reverend N.B. Lodge, was remembered as the best teacher one cadet, who would have an illustrious career, ever had.[5]

Few records remain from Neville's time there, with results for only two of his four terms having been retained in the college archive:

Term	Study	Seamanship	French	Conduct
1	V Sat	V Good	V Sat	V Good
2	Sat	V Good	Sat	V Good

The staff of HMS *Britannia* in 1898.

Classes would have included navigation, astronomy, topographical and mechanical drawing, the understanding of steam and steam machinery (described by one cadet as, 'the steam picket boat and other such oily delights'),[6] and a considerable amount of mathematics; in what would have been a spartan existence, 'in which boys learnt to sail, navigate, command and, above all, be commanded.'[7] The cadets slept in hammocks slung below deck in the fashion of Nelson's seamen. A cold saltwater wash on deck marked the beginning of a long working day, which began with a bugle call at 0630 and ended with lights out at 2130, devoted to inspection, meals, classes and exercise – including gymnastics, boating, games and swimming. The cadets were referred to by their progression through the four terms as 'New', 'Three', 'Sixer' and 'Niner'. Usborne was fortunate to experience sea time on *Britannia's* tender, HMS *Racer*, a handsome barque-rigged sloop of 970 tons, which had arrived in 1896, and took the third and fourth terms' cadets on cruises in the English Channel to improve their seamanship, engineering and navigation skills. He would also have been present during Queen Victoria's Diamond Jubilee celebrations in June 1897. The procession in London allowed for the participation of 100 cadets and those

Cadets at *Britannia* in the 1890s.

As a cadet Neville would have had sea time on board HMS *Racer*.

who were not chosen for this were taken to the Review of the Fleet at Spithead. In the term ahead of Usborne was Cadet A.B. Cunningham (later Admiral of the Fleet Viscount Cunningham of Hyndhope, KT, GCB, OM, DSO), who later recalled that the review took place on a brilliantly fine morning, followed by an afternoon of lightning, thunder and torrents of rain. The Royal Yacht, *Victoria and Albert*, passed through the fleet, arrayed in line after line, with ships' companies cheering and bands playing:

> 'What a brilliantly fine day, all the ships dressed overall with flags and painted in the old-time colouring of yellow masts and funnels, white upper-works, black hulls and salmon-coloured waterline, divided from the black by narrow white ribands. The senior cadets, in the *Racer*, manned yards as the Queen went past.'[8]

That evening the cadets, who were accommodated on board the old stores ship, *Wye*, changed out of their best uniforms and white gloves, and, refreshed by a saltwater bath on deck, spliced the main brace and drank the Queen's health with a glass of 1848 port.[9]

Discipline was strict, but there were instances of bullying of younger cadets by their seniors, though in the years following the Jubilee these were much less than in the decade before.

Splice the Main Brace
– cadets celebrating the
Diamond Jubilee in 1897.

Bullying had not been stamped out in 1897–98, but it was not severe; an expression of the element of sadism with which many boys seem to be endowed in their youth.[10]

Indeed, Captain Curzon-Howe showed his attitude to bullying right away when he ordered three bullies to be flogged before all the assembled ship's company and cadets. It is reported, however, that he also had to deal with over-protective mothers, as in the case of one who wrote to him asking that he make sure that her son wore his drawers in cold weather, a wise precaution perhaps, but not, it may be thought, a normal part of a captain's duties.[11]

Be that as it may, a future admiral noted that this regime was likely to suppress independence and initiative in, 'our future naval officers'. The most notorious example of this had been on 22 June 1893, off Tripoli, when HMS *Victoria* was rammed and sunk by HMS *Camperdown*, resulting in the deaths of the C-in-C Mediterranean Fleet, Vice Admiral Sir George Tryon, twenty-two officers and 336 ratings. The admiral had given an order for two columns of ships to turn towards each other, which was a tricky and hazardous manoeuvre; the captains of the two leading battleships carried out the order without questioning its desirability and, when the collision seemed inevitable, did not react swiftly enough without a direct countermanding order from the admiral, by which time it was too late. Tryon remained on the bridge as his flagship sank, and was heard to murmur, 'It's all my fault.' The executive officer of HMS *Victoria* was fortunate to escape unscathed, as indeed was the Royal Navy, as the officer concerned was Commander John Jellicoe (1859–1935). (Jellicoe subsequently became Admiral of the Fleet and an Earl, holding many major naval appointments between 1905 and 1917, and will feature more than once in this story.) At the subsequent court martial of Rear Admiral Markham, who was aboard HMS *Camperdown*, he was asked, 'if he knew it was wrong, why then did he comply with the fatal order?' He replied that he thought, 'Tryon must have something up his sleeve – a triumph of hope and obedience as compared to logic, experience and initiative.' The court found Tryon to blame, but accepted that it would be fatal for the navy to encourage subordinates to question those set in authority over them.[12]

It should be noted, however, that in the 1890s, efforts were being made to modernise the tuition given in *Britannia*; for example, reforms were instituted by Captain A.W. Moore in 1895, giving his lieutenants much greater direct responsibility for the cadets' welfare and progress. A near contemporary of Usborne was the distinguished naval airman, Vice Admiral Richard Bell Davies, VC. He recalled the curriculum at Dartmouth as having:

'Remained unchanged for very many years, and consisted almost entirely of mathematics and seamanship; we had our full measure of the myriad names of the standing rigging, little of which specialised knowledge was to be of any use to my later career.'[13]

A few years earlier, at the start of the 1890s, a cadet writing as 'Navilus' was of the opinion:

'On board HMS *Britannia*, one day is very much like another, which, though somewhat monotonous, has the advantage (if it be one) of making the time fly fast.'[14]

Another cadet, William Henry Dudley Boyle, who would become Admiral of the Fleet, and also the 12th Earl of Cork & Orrery, later wrote:

'The education given to us was almost entirely technical, or directed to that end; and, though it is true that English literature figured in the curriculum, as during our four terms there we never got beyond Southey's, *Life of Nelson*, in this it hardly extended our horizon.'[15]

Yet another gives a much more favourable and positive view:

'The elite of the Navy, in its various ranks and ratings, was on hand to guide us, with a lieutenant in general charge of each term and a naval instructor taking his class in trigonometry and navigation throughout. These instructors kept control and imparted knowledge in a manner I have never known excelled. From a varying acquaintance with arithmetic, algebra and Euclid, we were introduced to plane, and later to spherical trigonometry, advancing to celestial navigation. After four terms of three months, they sent forth boys who could not only solve spherical triangles and prove the formulae they employed, but who could also work a ship's reckoning by the sun. We learned French and drawing from civilian teachers, steam from an engineering officer and we looked to the chaplain for the weekly lesson in scripture. But we had already been well grounded in that subject, a high standard being demanded in the entrance examination. Brisk petty officers attached to each term, the very salt of the earth and sea, were perhaps our widest and most shrewd counsellors on board. Others of the same rating taught us seamanship in a delightful model room and showed us how to row or sail.'[16]

Neville would have been present at an end of term ceremony in 1897 or 1898 when the famous admiral, who was giving away the prizes, made the usual stirring speech about the glorious history of the Royal Navy and the many

POCKET MONEY.

Cadets receiving their pocket money.

victories won against the old enemy. As he came to a climax he beseeched the cadets never to forget St Vincent and Trafalgar in particular, thumping his fist into his other palm for emphasis, at which the French were firmly put in their place. The rousing speech did not go down too well with the four French officers, attending as guests of the captain, nor with the cadets who sat in embarrassed silence; it was, 'a melancholy frost.'[17] He may also have received some most irregular, but doubtless very enlightening, extra-curricular education, as more than one cadet noted that the daughter of the canteen manager was prepared to raise her skirts for interested onlookers for the sum of one penny.[18] Perhaps *Britannia* did not provide a fully-rounded education, but she certainly had her unique selling points.

Sea Training

From September 1898 to March 1902, Neville Usborne served as cadet midshipman (from 15 August 1898), progressing from 'wart' to 'snottie' and sub-lieutenant (promoted 15 March 1902). His first ship was the Majestic Class battleship of 14,900 tons, launched in 1895, HMS *Prince George*. (This was the last RN battleship class to have twin side-by-side funnels, the first to have design uniformity, and the first with fully enclosed 12-inch gun turrets protecting the gun breeches and shell handling machinery.) Then came the Canopus Class battleship, HMS *Canopus*, of 12,950 tons, launched in 1897 (which set the

The late Victorian Royal Navy; a Lieutenant with Midshipmen and a Cadet.

pattern for pre-Dreadnought
battleships), with detached duties
in Torpedo Boat No 96, of 130
tons, launched in 1893; the sail
training ship HMS *Cruiser* of
1130 tons (built as a wooden screw
sloop in 1852 and converted to
sail in 1872 to give young officers
and seamen experience handling
a square rigged ship – the last
squadron of naval ships to put
to sea under canvas was in 1899)
and the store ship HMS *Tyne*
of 3650 tons, launched in 1878.
Most of his service during these
years was in the Mediterranean
and around the British Isles. He
kept two meticulously written

HMS *Prince George*.

HMS *Cruiser*.

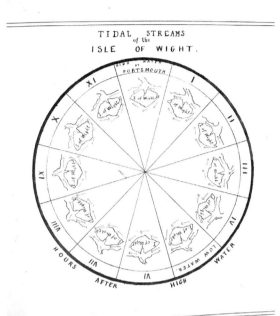

Three pages from Midshipman Neville Usborne's Logbook, showing the great care he took with his handwriting and sketching. (*via Sue Kilbracken*)

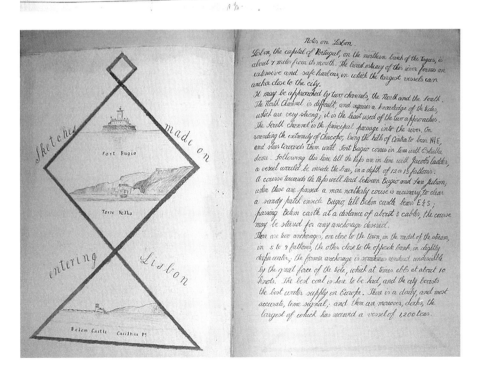

and beautifully illustrated logbooks – so his handwriting must have improved under naval tutelage. Technical drawing was not neglected; the pen, ink and watercolour illustrations were both decorative and analytical in nature. Completing the log was a compulsory part of a midshipman's training; it was inspected regularly by a supervising officer and by the captain.

The log records a visit to Lough Swilly and then to Belfast Lough in July 1899, as part of the Channel Squadron under the command of Vice Admiral Sir Harry Rawson. HMS *Prince George* was one of twenty-seven warships taking part in naval manoeuvres. There was considerable interest in the local newspapers, *The Northern Whig* and the *Belfast Evening Telegraph*:

Vice Admiral Sir H.H. Rawson.

'Never before was there such a formidable fleet of war vessels in Belfast Lough as that which now lies off Bangor.'[19]

The object of the manoeuvres, according to the Admiralty, was:

'To obtain information as to the most advantageous method of employing a considerable body of cruisers in conjunction with a fleet.'[20]

A secondary objective was:

'To throw some light on the relative advantages and disadvantages of speed and fighting strength, and the working of destroyers and torpedo boats.'[21]

Thousands of spectators descended on the seaside resort of Bangor to view the warships from the shore and also to take passage on pleasure boats offering trips around the fleet. A two-hour cruise from Donegall Quay, Belfast, on the Barrow Steam Navigation Company's 'Fine Paddle Steamer', *Manx Queen*, was advertised at 1/6 (seven and a half pence). The warships were described in detail in the newspapers, it was revealed that HMS *Prince George*, completed in 1896 at a cost of £885,037, displaced 14,900 tons, carried four twelve-inch and

HMS *Canopus*.

twelve six-inch guns, engines which could develop 12,000 horse power, had a complement of 757 and was commanded by Captain Sir Baldwin Wake Walker, RN, Bart. Young Neville Usborne noted in his log that visitors came aboard after Divine Service on Sunday, 23 July. The following day was much less enjoyable no doubt, as it was spent in coaling ship, a back-breaking and messy business shifting an average of seventy-three tons per hour, three of which Neville spent in the hold at the sharp end of the toil. After several days of further drills and evolutions, the fleet weighed anchor on 29 July and proceeded to sea to, 'clear for action and commence hostilities against B Fleet.'[22] The fleet must have made a magnificent spectacle painted in the old colours: red boot-topping, black sides, white upper works, and yellow masts and funnels. It would be another four years before the general order was given to paint all ships grey to reduce their visibility (apart from destroyers, which were to be black in home waters and white in the Mediterranean).

In late 1899 he was posted from the *Prince George* to join *Canopus*, which was commissioning for the first time, and was allowed to proceed by packet ship in order to have time for home leave. In Usborne's case the packet ship was the Orient Line's SS *Oroya* of 6057 tons, on its regular passage from Australia to England, in which he embarked at Gibraltar on 20 November. During his time serving on *Canopus* he received two cash prizes of £10 and £3, awarded to junior officers afloat for proficiency in French and German.

Greenwich and Excellent

He left the ship for the RN College, Greenwich, in March 1902, with a highly satisfactory report from Captain H.S.F. Niblett, being graded very good in respect of General Conduct, Ability and Professional Knowledge, noted as having temperate habits, winning praise for a good colloquial knowledge of French, German and Italian, and being described as physically strong, zealous, very able and promising. At Greenwich, he took his oral seamanship examination. This took the form of a gruelling grilling, which could last for several hours, from a board composed of two captains and a commander. He passed with 912 marks out of a possible 1000 and was awarded a first-class certificate, which meant promotion to acting sub-lieutenant. Life at Greenwich in those days was described as follows:

'The sudden transition to the college at Greenwich (from service at sea), in close proximity to London, with considerable freedom and increased pay, proved too much for the majority, who laid themselves out to have a good time. Of course there were some level-headed ones who worked hard, and others, more gifted than their companions, who absorbed the necessary knowledge and yet managed to find time to enjoy themselves, but these were a minority. The college never got the return it should have had for all the trouble taken over sub-lieutenants' education.'[23]

It would appear that Usborne was either clever or studious (or both), as, over the next fifteen months, there was further study and examination in navigation (parts I and II)[24] and pilotage, proficiency in which was examined at the Hydrographic Department in the Admiralty building in Whitehall. The course then migrated to the Royal Naval College, just inside the dockyard gates at Portsmouth, for the gunnery course at Whale Island and the torpedo course at Devonport. The experience was described by one of Usborne's contemporaries, who had entered Dartmouth in 1897, just a term before him, but who was a member of the same course, as follows:

'We lived here, went down each morning to the *Excellent* steps, and were ferried across the harbour to Whale Island – otherwise HMS *Excellent*, the Alma Mater of naval gunnery – for the day's work. Here everything possible was done to make miserable the lives of the sub-lieutenants. We were chivvied and bullied. Maybe we deserved it; but I cannot believe it was necessary, or that it did us any good. Being shouted at on parade, or for some minor fault, merely made me feel mutinous. I was glad to get away from the detestable place on 13 March 1903, with a second-class in gunnery, and a certificate awarded at the end of our courses stating that I had conducted myself with sobriety, but that my general conduct was not satisfactory. This smudge on my character was quite unjustly bestowed, but fully in keeping with the general atmosphere that then prevailed at Whale Island, which was harsh and inhuman. I believe my bad certificate was due to the following incident. At the end of the examination we had to return all the leather equipment and gaiters with which we had been issued to a hut on the parade ground. After a good lunch about six of us set out to do this. We found the hut locked and nobody inside, as there should have been. Not wishing to be delayed and to miss the boat to the mainland, we threw the gear in through the open window. One of the party, making insufficient allowance for a good lunch, broke a window, while an inkpot was upset and the hut generally in a mess when the storekeeper returned. So all of us were served out with these unfavourable certificates. I afterwards heard that, with the exception of myself, they all complained and managed to get them altered. I never heard of this, so my certificate as originally written is one of my proudest possessions. We next went to the *Vernon* for a six weeks' course in torpedo. Here conditions were far more human. The instruction was good; we learnt a lot.'[25]

Usborne gained first-class passes apart from Part I navigation, in which he scored a second-class pass. He was awarded the Ryder Prize of £10 for this achievement.[26]

Developments in Military Ballooning in the 1890s and early 1900s

While Neville was learning his trade, a permanent Balloon Section and Depot RE had been formed in May 1890, with appropriate provision being made in the Army Estimates, moving from St Mary's Barracks, Chatham, to the south camp in the Royal Engineer Lines at Aldershot in 1891. It now numbered three officers, three sergeants, and twenty-eight rank and file, with Templer having been promoted to lieutenant colonel and appointed Officer-in-Charge of Ballooning. It was about this time that an early army aeronaut was reproved for being without helmet, sword, sabretache or spurs whilst on duty, none of which would have been either necessary or sensible by way of flying kit.[27] In the words of a former officer-in-charge of the Balloon Establishment:

'This may be regarded as the termination of the experimental stage and the recognition of balloons as a necessary adjunct of the army.'[28]

Military balloons were now classified into five types according to their capacity: A class: 13,000 cubic feet (368 cubic metres), V class: 11,500 cubic feet (325 cubic metres), T class: 10,000 cubic feet (283 cubic metres), S class: 7000 cubic feet (198 cubic metres) and F class: 4500–5000 cubic feet (127–142 cubic metres). Steady improvements had also been made to the rigging, nets, valves

Balloon transport in 1890, showing a balloon wagon, two of the three tube wagons and an equipment wagon. Major C.M. Watson, RE, is in command.

and other accessories. A new pattern of gas cylinder had been introduced, of greater capacity and efficiency.[29]

Another aspect of early army aviation was the man–lifting kite. Major B.F.S. Baden-Powell, Scots Guards, the brother of the founder of the Boy Scouts, developed a kite for reconnaissance and persuaded a sapper to be taken aloft by this means on 27 June 1894. His kites were used during the Boer War for observation and photography. Later, the Texan, Samuel Franklin Cody, was employed by the War Office to experiment with observation kites on Woolwich Common and as a kite instructor in the Balloon Section of the Royal Engineers at Farnborough. If being in the wicker basket of a balloon felt vulnerable, then the prospect of dangling from a kite a few hundred feet in the air above a battlefield must have been a proposition for only the very brave or the most foolhardy.

The Royal Engineers in 1893. Lieutenant H.B. Jones is in the basket. (*Museum of Army Flying*)

A balloon and kite
winch with a kite.

[Author's note: Major B.F.S. Baden-Powell (1860–1937) made his first balloon
ascent in 1881. In 1894 he was attached to the Balloon Section at Aldershot,
and made numerous ascents over the next decade and more. He joined the
Aeronautical Society in 1880, becoming Honorary Secretary in 1896, founding
the *Aeronautical Journal* in 1897 and being appointed President in 1902. On 27
June 1894, he was the first to be taken aloft by a man-lifting kite. These were
later used during the Boer War for reconnaissance and photography. In 1908 he
was the second Englishman to fly with Wilbur Wright.]

An article appeared in the *Strand* Magazine in 1895, which gave a very detailed
and interesting description of the work of the Balloon Section:

> 'The next European war will be a strange and fearful thing; everyone seems
> pretty sure about that. Writers of fiction with strong imaginations and a
> smattering of military science are constantly producing forecasts of this
> fascinating subject. We learn that Mr Maxim's guns will be very much to
> the fore; probably also, Mr Maxim's embryonic flying machines. Then
> we hear of messenger dogs, swarms of poisonous flies, and, above all, –
> in a dual sense – war balloons, whose mission will be to drop charges of
> dynamite and things of that kind upon all and sundry whom it is advisable
> to destroy.
>
> 'All this leads up to the fact that we have a full-blown School of
> Ballooning at Aldershot, under the direction of Colonel Templer, whose
> name for many years has been associated with advanced military science,
> especially as regards the war balloon. The school at Aldershot is at present

established in the Stanhope Lines, where large buildings have been erected on what was, a few years ago, nothing but a dangerous swamp. Colonel Templer is assisted in his very interesting work by Sergeant-Major Greener; and the accompanying group shows the entire staff of the first division of the Balloon Section when in the field, i.e. these men work the balloon.

'Without exception, these men are enthusiasts in their work, and, although they are associated with what may be described as the most interesting and novel branch of the service, they themselves are by no means inflated. At any rate, there is very little doubt that the British taxpayer got his quid pro quo – and perhaps a little more – in return for last year's ballooning grant, which was rather less than £3,000.

'Colonel Templer generates his own gas from diluted sulphuric acid and granulated zinc. The lifting power of the hydrogen generated this way is much greater than that of ordinary coal-gas, but then its cost is much more. When manufactured, the hydrogen is compressed at '100 atmospheres' pressure and stowed away, so to speak, into huge Siemens steel cylinders, each averaging about 90lbs in weight. Ten of these elongated tubes are placed, for conveyance to the field of battle, upon admirably contrived wagons, usually drawn by horses; of course, under

A group photo proudly displaying a sign reading Balloon Section. (*The Strand Magazine* – Charles Knight)

Inflating a war balloon. (*The Strand Magazine* – Charles Knight)

certain conditions, the gallant Colonel could utilize the baggage train, of which he is so great an advocate.

'It takes, as a very simple calculation will immediately show, two wagon loads of gas to inflate a balloon of 10,000 cubic feet capacity, such as shown in the accompanying illustration.

'Here we have the working staff, with two lieutenants in command of the section, the wagon and its team, and lastly, the inevitable crowd of curious onlookers, with the still more inevitable sprinkling of the small boy genus, without which no operation of the kind would be complete.

'The man standing upon the car affixes one end of a screw nozzle to the mouth of a gas cylinder, while another of the engineers places the connecting tube to the nozzle of the balloon. The man on the car then gently turns on a very nicely constructed valve, which permits the compressed gas to leave the cylinder only at a very moderate rate. The balloon inflated, we will suppose that Lieutenant Hume and a brother officer are told of the duty of reconnoitring the enemy's position. The two officers take with them a map of the surrounding country, on the scale of two inches to the square mile. Of course, they are provided with field glasses, and the moment they discern the enemy and are able to gauge his strength, they make certain notes upon the map, using for this purpose pencils of various colours; one colour denotes cavalry, another infantry, and so on.

'In the next picture we see that everything is ready; the crew are on board, and the men who are holding the giant captive are awaiting the order to "Let go". The moment this order is given the immense aerostat shoots straight up like a rocket, but pressure is gradually brought to bear on the connecting rope, and, when at an altitude of several hundred feet, the upward course of the huge machine is checked, and it sways gently to and fro, while the skilful officers in the car anxiously scan the magnificent prospect of country far below them. The moment any definite information is obtained as to the enemy's movements, the map spoken of above is marked according to such information and then placed in a canvas bag to which a ring is attached in such a way that it glides swiftly down the rope to the ground, where a mounted orderly is in waiting. The orderly immediately gallops off with the very latest intelligence to the general in command.

'The British war balloon has long since ceased to be manufactured from silk – though this material is even now generally used by professional parachutists and aeronauts for their "envelopes". After many experiments,

Awaiting the order to 'Let Go'.
(*The Strand Magazine* – Charles Knight)

however, a perfectly impermeable material has been manufactured from ox-gut by a series of secret processes.

'It is an interesting fact that in the manufacturing shed at Aldershot, women are employed in the making of the balloons, which are for the most part of a capacity equal to 10,000 cubic feet, and have, when fully inflated, a lifting power of something like 700lb.

'There are at present in the storeroom at Aldershot, thirty-two fully equipped balloons, ready at an hour's notice to go on active service; and what is more, if, in actual warfare, they are found as useful as they have been in manoeuvres, their actual value will not have been at all overestimated.

'The envelope of the balloon is enclosed in a network of very strong cord, which is fastened below the nozzle of the balloon to a stout hoop that supports the car. The cord is manufactured by a justly-celebrated firm of rope makers in the North of England, from hemp specially grown in sunny Italy; and although it is so light that a section 100ft long does not weigh a pound, and it is only about ¼in. in diameter, it will stand a strain of 500lb. without breaking. I have myself seen this cord practically tested by Sergeant-Major Greener on a dynamometer. The car of the war balloon accommodates a couple of men, and it is made of very strong wicker work. It is 2ft 3in. deep, the same in width, and 3ft 6in long. This car is fastened to the hoop above by very strong ropes; and of course for reconnoitring purposes, it is supplied with a grapnel, a captive rope, a photographic outfit, and many other articles that are carried in the common or Crystal Palace variety of balloon.

'In the next illustration is seen the most direct and valuable mode of communication between the officers in the car of the war balloon and the forces below. I refer to telephonic communication. In the picture it will be seen that a light wagon carries the necessary electrical plant. On the occasion of my own visit to the scene of operations, I watched an orderly gallop up to this wonderful piece of portable mechanism, and he roared into the cart as it were, "Any fresh information?"

'The officer, with a truly astonishing quickness, gained most important news, receiving a reply which ran as follows: "There is a large body of cavalry on your right flank, behind the hill, deployed ready to charge the supports." This message came in an amazingly sharp and articulate voice – a veritable viva-voce message from the clouds.

'The accompanying reproduction shows the Aldershot war balloon "*Talisman*" reconnoitring at such an altitude as to command the entire radius of country over which the manoeuvres are being conducted. It will

A portable receiving station of the aerial telephone. (*The Strand Magazine* – Charles Knight)

War balloon directing cavalry. (*The Strand Magazine* – Charles Knight)

be noticed that on the windward side the balloon is rather flat, instead of convex; this indicates that there is a vacuum, so it is coming down to be refilled. The body of cavalry seen is being wholly guided by instructions received from the "*Talisman*".

'The system of reconnaissance by pencil-coloured maps dropped from the balloon at present holds the field against photography; but it must not be assumed that the camera is a wholly futile ally on the battlefield. As a matter of fact, most successful and valuable pictures are constantly obtained, showing in most beautiful detail the nature of the surrounding country and the obstacles to be encountered. You must remember, though, it takes at least half an hour to photograph, develop and dry the negative, and print a proof; from which it is obvious that information given to the commanding officer by this means is a little stale, as it conveys to him rather where his opponent was, than where he is at the moment.

'When the officers in the balloon have procured all the information possible regarding the movements of the enemy, the war balloon is brought down, and is towed into some sheltered valley by the men of the balloon section, as is seen in the last photograph reproduced here; then, of course, the balloon is placed under sentry protection. Not that much protection is needed, save, perhaps, from the derision of the small boy genus before

The towing party at work. (*The Strand Magazine* – Charles Knight)

referred to. I distinctly remember seeing a balloon towing party followed by a troop of gamins, who, far from being impressed by the huge machine, gave tongue from time to time and implored the men to, "tike it 'ome".

'Such is the work of the captive balloon. There are times, however, when Sergeant-Major Greener and other officers release the captive and travel to different parts of the surrounding country at a speed of perhaps forty miles an hour. As one might imagine, however, this speed is hardly noticed by the occupants of the balloon.

'At the Aldershot School of Ballooning, selected officers go through a course of instruction at appointed seasons; and altogether, we may feel assured that we are well to the fore, as a nation, in the science of belligerent aeronautics.'[30]

On 1 April 1897, Lieutenant Colonel Templer became the first superintendent of the Balloon Factory, directly responsible to the War Office, at a salary of £700 per annum, as it was now recognised officially for the first time. His own title had, until then, been Instructor in Ballooning, which failed to do full justice to his position and duties. This period also brought about the publication of the first comprehensive service guide, the *Manual of Military Ballooning*, which was compiled by Captain B.R. Ward, RE. Free run ballooning became a popular part of the courses which were held for officers, not only in the Royal Engineers, but also from other arms and a selected few from Staff College. By this means aeronauts could learn to control and land a captive observation balloon in the event of it breaking away from its cable. It was also looked on as a skill which might come in useful in providing transport out of a besieged location. The normal drill on a free run was to plot the course taken by means of Ordnance Survey or Bradshaw railway maps. On landing, the balloon would be deflated and packed into its basket, a telegram would be sent to Aldershot and the aeronauts would return by train with the basket travelling in the guard's van.

In October 1897, *The Times* featured a column titled *Military Ballooning*, which described at some length the recent activities of Captain G.M. Heath, RE, and his balloon section supporting the Horse and Field artillery as they exercised on the gunnery ranges at Oakhampton and Lydd. The writer commented that the large size of contemporary armies and the extensive areas of country which they occupied rendered reconnaissance from the air ever more useful. He added that most observational flights were crewed by two aeronauts, one mounted in the netting to manage the equipment and the other in the wicker car, therefore able to devote his entire attention to observing, recording and sketching. The

Surveying the enemy's country. (*The Strand Magazine* – Charles Knight)

potential vulnerability of balloons to enemy fire was discussed and dismissed as being not as great a problem as might be supposed. The question of the dirigible balloon was also raised, but the problem of a suitable means of steering in all but the lightest of winds was regarded as admitting that there was no easy solution.[31]

In 1899 an international declaration was made, operative for a period of five years, following the First Hague Peace Conference, the Hague Convention. One of its provisions was to prohibit the launching of projectiles or explosives from balloons or any other kind of aerial vessel.

The Army used balloons for observation, field sketching of enemy positions, artillery spotting purposes and also as communications relay stations by heliograph in the Boer War between 1899 and 1900, with 1st Balloon Section, Major H.B. Jones, RE, providing notable service at Magersfontein, Kimberley, Paardeberg and Pretoria; 2nd Balloon Section, Major G.M. Heath, RE (later Major General Sir Gerard), at the siege and relief of Ladysmith and 3rd Balloon Section, Brevet Major R.D.B. Blakeney, RE, (later Brigadier General) at the relief of Mafeking. Some thirty balloons were sent to South Africa, including the *Duchess of Connaught* and the *Bristol*. Such was the requirement that the existing balloon establishment had to be reinforced at short notice by the recall of personnel with previous experience.[32] The Commander of the British

A contemporary artist's impression of the 1st Balloon Section being deployed in the Boer War in 1900.

Forces, Field Marshal Lord Roberts, VC, appreciated the efforts of the Balloon Sections, 'the captive balloon gave great assistance by keeping us informed of the disposition and movements of the enemy.'[33] The Boers were rather less impressed, though it could have been worse. They feared that balloons would be used for the aerial bombardment of the Boer capital, Pretoria. The Balloon Factory had indeed worked out a general scheme for bombing from the air, but this was not taken any further. The Boer leader, General Cronje, commented tersely; 'The British were greatly assisted by balloons.' A more detailed survey was made by Colonel Arthur Lynch, who was Australian-born of an Irish father and a Scottish mother, and who was serving with the Boer army. On 27 March 1902, he gave a lecture in Paris entitled, *Du rôle des ballons militaires anglais dans la guerre de l'Afrique du Sud.* He paid tribute to the expertise of the Balloon Sections; 'I take this occasion to say that the English take pride in themselves, and perhaps not without reason, that they possess the best balloon service of all the armies of the world.' Then he added, 'the balloons have been of great value to the English on several occasions. Observations made by balloon often enabled the English to note exactly the position of a battery, a laager, an encampment, or some fortifications; or even troop movements made in preparing for a major attack.' He noted that aerial observation greatly increased the accuracy and effectiveness of artillery fire, much to the annoyance of the enemy, who saw the balloons as, 'a symbol of the scientific superiority of the English'.[34]

[Author's note: Lynch (1861–1934) had a remarkable career, gaining engineering, philosophy, science and medical degrees during his education in Melbourne, Berlin, Paris and London. He first went to South Africa as a war correspondent and then persuaded President Kruger to appoint him to the rank of colonel in the Boer Army. He served with distinction with the 2nd Irish Brigade, which, if truth be told, was rather a motley band of diverse nationalities. In late 1900, he visited the USA to plead the Boer cause and befriended the future president, Theodore Roosevelt. On his return to the United Kingdom he was elected as the MP for Galway (from where his family had originated). On presenting himself at the Houses of Parliament he was arrested, tried for high treason, and condemned to death on 23 January 1903. After the intercession of President Roosevelt, the King granted him a free pardon. He continued with his eclectic range of studies and also became the MP for West Clare in 1909. In 1918, following useful war work, he was appointed to the rank of colonel in the British Army. After the war he returned to medicine and authorship.]

The Boers did make attempts to shoot down the balloons, but they did not succeed, despite perforating envelopes on occasion and wounding an aeronaut once. A balloon could sustain a number of bullet holes while retaining much of its effectiveness and was easy to repair. This experience no doubt contributed to the later debate as to whether or not airships could survive on the battlefield. The goldbeater's skin envelopes also stood up well to hard use and retained their gas well. Teams of oxen or mules towed the balloon wagons in this campaign, which was often a slow and frustrating process, even though Templer was in South Africa as the Director of Steam Road Transport in 1900, where his traction engines did much other useful work.

While Colonel Templer was engaged in South Africa, his duties at the Balloon Factory were carried out by Acting-Superintendent Brevet Lieutenant Colonel J.P.L. Macdonald, RE (later Major General Sir James), who had prior experience of the role when he was left in charge at Chatham in 1884–5, when Templer and Elsdale were serving in the Sudan and Bechuanaland respectively. When Macdonald was selected to lead the expedition to China in 1900, his successor as Acting-Superintendent was Major F.C. Trollope, RE, who had been second-in-command in Bechuanaland.

Another section was sent to China, with the balloons *Tugela* and *Teviot*, commanded by Captain A.H.B. Hume, RE, to support the International Relief Force for the siege of the Legations in Peking (On the conclusion of activities in China it became the Experimental Balloon section at Rawalpindi in India.)[35] and yet another to Australia under 2nd Lieutenant T.H.L. Spaight, RE, for

A balloon being deployed in Antarctica by members of Captain Scott's expedition in 1902.

the Commonwealth inauguration in January 1901. Two balloons were supplied to Captain Scott for his Antarctic expedition in the *Discovery*. The third mate, Lieutenant Ernest Shackleton, RNR, was sent to Aldershot for a short ballooning course. In February 1902, at what would later be named Balloon Bight in the Bay of Whales, on the Ross Ice Shelf, a balloon was inflated and anchored by a wire pegged into the ice. Shackleton assumed that he would be the first Antarctic aeronaut; however, Scott pulled rank and insisted on going up before him. Shackleton went next and ascended to 650 feet (198 metres), from which height he took a number of photographs. Dr Edward Wilson declined the offer of a flight, as he thought it was far too risky an enterprise:

> 'Some twenty or thirty hydrogen cylinders were laid near, the fixings attached and the balloon filled. The captain, knowing nothing whatever about the business, insisted on going up first and, through no fault of his own, came back safely. The whole ballooning business seems an exceedingly dangerous amusement. There is one man who is supposed to know all about it, who has had a week's instruction.'[36]

The growth of the Balloon Sections between 1899 and 1901 was marked; with the provision in the Army Estimates rising from three officers, thirty-one NCOs and men, to eight officers, 173 NCOs and men.[37] Templer took up his role of superintendent once more in the middle of 1901. In December of that year he travelled to Paris, where, among other luminaries, he met Alberto Santos-Dumont and Colonel Charles Renard. Perhaps inspired by his fellow pioneers he devoted much time and effort over the next few years to promoting the dirigible balloon. His subsequent report to the War Office, dated 2 January 1902, stated:

'I am of the opinion that we are well ahead of them [the French] in all matters appertaining to captive balloon work. At the same time, the dirigible balloon has now, by the prowess of M. Santos-Dumont, been so advanced that I [shortly] will be in a position to recommend that certain experiments be carried out in dirigible balloon work by this department.'[38]

The contemporary historian of British military ballooning, Colonel Watson, agreed, writing in 1902:

'The question of dirigible balloons has to be taken up, as it will never do for England to be left behind in the path of progress. But there is no reason why, if funds can be allotted for the purpose, the Balloon Factory at Aldershot should not produce a dirigible balloon as good, if not better, than that which can be made in any factory on the Continent.'[39]

The Army Estimates for 1902 contained an enhanced requirement for six Balloon Sections of twelve balloons each, five operational and one cadre. In

1903, the Balloon Sections had 150 officers and men, and thirty-six horses. The commanding officer from April 1903 was Lieutenant Colonel John Capper, CB, RE. As the first field officer in command in peacetime since 1889, his appointment put, 'new life into the branch'.[40] He soon made his mark by recommending that officers and men going aloft should wear kit that was practical and serviceable, with particular reference to the undesirability of belts, revolvers and spurs.[41] In June, he was also appointed as Secretary to the new Committee on Military Ballooning, which had the remit of reporting generally upon, 'the extent to which it is desirable to attempt to improve and

Lieutenant Colonel John Capper.

develop military ballooning', bearing in mind the recent operational experience and also taking account of progress in other countries. One of the members of the committee was Brevet Lieutenant Colonel H.H. Wilson, DSO, (1864–1922) who was born in Co Longford and would later, as Field Marshal Sir Henry Wilson, be assassinated by the IRA.

The committee interviewed some of the balloon officers who had served in South Africa and representatives of the artillery. Three senior officers spoke warmly of the aeronauts' contribution, Lieutenant General Lord Methuen, Major General A.H. Paget and Rear Admiral H. Lambton (who had been responsible for the naval gunners at Ladysmith). Progress in the rest of the world was surveyed and it was noted that while there had been ongoing research in France, a dirigible had not been produced at Chalais–Meudon since *La France* in 1884; the expertise in Germany with regard to kite balloons was considered, though no mention was made of Count Zeppelin.

The Rise of the Zeppelin

The first flight of the LZ1 rigid airship, which was 420 feet (128 metres) in length, 38 feet (11.54 metres) in diameter, with a capacity of 400,000 cubic feet (11,320 cubic metres), developed by the now-retired German army General, Count Ferdinand von Zeppelin, (based on the original designs of David Schwarz) had taken place on 3 July 1900, from Friedrichshafen near Lake Constance (Bodensee) before a crowd of 12,000 spectators. Construction had

LZ1 in its shed on Lake Constance.

begun some two years earlier in June 1898 in a hangar resting on ninety-five floats on the lake. It was a quite revolutionary engineering concept on a massive scale, a rigid structure of vertical rings held in place by longitudinal girders, with bags or cells containing hydrogen suspended within the framework under its fabric outer cover. Over the next few months it made two more flights, only one of which could be said to have been very successful. The LZ1 was a crude, heavy design, which could lift a payload of just 660lbs (299kg), and which was difficult to control and manoeuvre. The sliding weight in its keel for trimming the airship in flight was a particularly ponderous conception. A newspaper reporter commented that all von Zeppelin's ideas:

> 'While extremely interesting, have undoubtedly proved conclusively that a
> dirigible balloon is of practically no value.'[42]

Dr Hugo Eckener (1868–1954), who would later have a huge role to play in the Zeppelin story, was a little more positive in his report for the *Frankfurter Zeitung* about the second flight on 2 October:

> 'Amid cheers, it rose calmly and majestically into the air. It hovered over
> the lake, making small turns about its vertical axis. It also turned slightly
> about its horizontal axis, remaining steady and calm, always at the same
> height and above the same place. There was no question of the airship
> flying for any appreciable distance, or hovering at various altitudes. One
> had the feeling that they were very happy to balance up there so nicely.'[43]

Sadly for the Count, after one further flight, with all his funds exhausted, the LZ1 was grounded and dismantled. Its top speed had been just over 19mph (32kph). The concept of a rigid airship had been proved workable, but further development was needed to make it a practical aerial vehicle.

Other Dirigibles

Privately funded experiments with small non-rigid dirigibles had achieved a degree of success in France, and indeed England. On 19 October 1901, the Brazilian, Alberto Santos-Dumont (1873–1932), and his small airship No 6, flew from Saint-Cloud, circled the Eiffel Tower and returned whence it came in under thirty minutes to win a prize of 100,000 francs offered by M Deutsch de la Meurthe of the Aéro-Club de France. Santos-Dumont and his series of fourteen small designs can truly be said to be the first practicable non-rigid airships. Later, he worried about the non-peaceful use of airships, envisaging,

Santos-Dumont and his first dirigible in Paris, 1898.

'aerial chariots of a foe descending upon England'.[44] He also predicted that the airship would be used for observing submarines below the surface of the sea and that they might drop 'dynamite arrows' on them.[45] Further progress was made by Paul and Pierre Lebaudy, together with the engineer Henri Julliot, whose first airship, the eponymous *Lebaudy*, took to the air on 13 November 1902, and a year later made the world's first cross-country flight by dirigible of 38 miles (62 kilometres), from Moisson to the Champs-de-Mars in Paris.

In 1902 came the first navigable flight in the UK by an airship, made by Stanley Spencer at Crystal Palace on 22 September. He landed safely after an hour and forty minutes in the air. It was 75 feet (23 metres) long, with a diameter of 20 feet (6 metres) and a capacity of 20,000 cubic feet (566 cubic metres). The engine was a water-cooled 3 hp (2.22 kW) Sims with a propeller of 10 feet (3 metres) in diameter. The motive power was very low and the airship could progress at a very slow rate only, and had great difficulty making any headway against even a slight wind.

It may therefore be considered that the Committee on Military Ballooning should have widened its scope somewhat and not just examined other governmental establishments. However, detailed recommendations were made as regards the future organisation of the Balloon Sections, Balloon School and

The Stanley Spencer airship at Crystal Palace on 22 September 1902. (*via Nick Forder*)

Balloon Factory. It was proposed that the latter should be re-sited to a location which would allow greater room for expansion – early possibilities which were considered included sites in the vicinity of Northampton and Rugby. Research and development objectives were identified: a dirigible balloon, an elongated balloon, man-lifting kites, small signal balloons, a mechanical winch to haul down balloons, and photographic equipment. One of the most difficult problems which it debated concerned the major weaknesses of the spherical balloon – its tendency to wobble and rotate at the end of its tether, so causing a certain amount of motion-induced sickness to the occupants, and the limitations this imposed on accurate observation as it made it rather difficult for the observer to hold his binoculars still; a wind speed of greater than 20mph (32kph) so exacerbated these that any useful work from the balloon was all but impossible. The committee's final report was submitted on 4 January 1904. It has been described as, 'the most comprehensive review of military aviation' made to that date.[46]

It should also be considered in the light of another historian's comment that:

'By 1900, education, experience and environment, had created a ruling caste [in England] whose knowledge of the revolution then taking place in armaments was limited. A very long period of peace and prosperity was ending. The Boer War announced the need to change from a colonial to a world-wide strategic concept.'[47]

Farnborough – the cradle of British Military Aviation

The new location selected was Farnborough Common, a few miles up the road from Aldershot. (This move heralded the start of a process whereby a small town in Hampshire, just outside Surrey and close to the border with Berkshire, would become one of the most renowned centres for aeronautical experiment, testing and development in the world.) A few months later Colonel Templer received a welcome boost, as his salary was increased to £900 a year. His worth was underlined in a letter to the War Office from Major General W.T. Shone, the Inspector General of Fortifications:

> 'We cannot afford at the present time to lose the services of Colonel Templer, and I would invite attention to the large sums now expended by France and Germany in endeavouring to manufacture a satisfactory dirigible.'[48]

He was also described by 'The World's First Air Correspondent', Harry Harper of the *Daily Mail*, as, 'a burly, genial figure with a walrus moustache.'[49]

The Treasury allocated the sum of £2000 to build an airship for the army; upon which Templer started work in respect of manufacturing an elongated envelope from goldbeater's skin, and investigating the design and construction of a suitable engine. To assist with familiarising some of his officers and men with the internal combustion engine, Templer bought two second-hand motor cars. These proved highly popular with foxhunting Royal Engineers, as they now had a free means of transport to their meets.[50] He also paid another visit to Colonel Renard at Chalais-Meudon, where he discovered the French Government was apparently allocating between £25,000 and £30,000 to the activities of the establishment.[51] Back at Aldershot, two envelopes had been prepared by 1904 and tests were carried out with regard to gas retention, which used up all the available funds and so work ground to a halt. The move from Aldershot to Farnborough, while it would prove beneficial in the long run, did not, of course, serve to speed up work in hand while the transfer of location was being carried out, nor indeed would the change of command from Templer to Capper.

A flavour of life with the Balloon Section in those days may be gained from the autobiography of F.M. Sykes, who, at that time, 1904, was a 27-year-old lieutenant in the 15th Hussars. (Air Vice-Marshal Sir Frederick Sykes (1877–1954) would become an important figure in British aviation and was later described in glowing terms by Murray Sueter in his book, *Airmen or Noahs*;

Filling a balloon at Aldershot in 1903.

'The Military Wing, RFC, owed much to Sykes' great abilities. He was a hard worker and bore much of the burden in those difficult times in creating a military air service for the army, which is slightly less conservative than the navy.') By permission of Colonel Capper, he was attached to the Balloon Camp for a period, under the command of Lieutenant P.W.L. Broke-Smith at Bulford, and then attended a course at Farnborough. He first flew in a very small balloon of only 4500 cubic feet (127 cubic metres) capacity. In fact it could not even lift a basket, so Sykes was taken up to 200 feet (61 metres) in a net suspended from the gasbag. He recalled:

Sir Frederick Sykes.

'We had an exciting time with the various types of balloons on field-days. We tried experiments in raising and lowering a balloon while on the move with an observer in the car, both forward, backward and laterally, so as to render it as difficult as possible for the envelope to be hit by gunfire. Sometimes, in favourable conditions, we managed to attain an elevation of 1300 feet (396 metres) with two of us in the car, and gained a splendid view of many miles in all directions. With one of us alone, a height of 1600 feet (487 metres) was achieved, and various methods of signalling were tried.'[52]

Captain P.L. Broke-Smith.

As the balloons were all spherical in shape, they had a marked tendency to oscillate in the wind in such a way as to promote motion sickness in some of the aeronauts, but not Sykes:

'When the balloon was fairly steady one could sketch the country with considerable accuracy, and in addition we did a lot of photographic work, and also practised telephoning from the air to headquarters.'[53]

Free-trailing was popular as a diversion, lowering a hemp rope and dragging it across the ground to keep the balloon at more or less an even height – though:

'Crossing telegraph wires and woods led to considerable complications, as we were completely at the mercy of the wind and a change of direction occurred at every few hundred yards.'[54]

Other exciting pastimes included:

'Pleasant but chilly night ascents, but the most enjoyable and instructive experiences were on free runs. The stillness and serenity of moving as a part of the wind at a great height above the earth gave pure delight.'[55]

The experience, though enchanting, was not without its perils:

A free balloon above the clouds.

'A sudden change of temperature often caused a balloon to descend with such velocity that it became necessary to expend much ballast to avoid being entangled in trees, hitting houses, or (in open ground) getting severe bumps. On one occasion we only escaped a collision with a passing train by letting out an extravagant amount of ballast.'[56]

Sykes believed that flying had a great future for both military and civil use, which was strengthened by: 'The practical experience of ballooning, the only form of aeronautics then in existence in England.'[57]

This was not strictly accurate, as man-lifting kiting was also practised under the flamboyant S.F. Cody. One of the aeronauts regularly taken aloft was Lieutenant Broke-Smith, describing it as:

'Reliable in practice to lift an observer to a height of 1500 feet above the ground, which was the normal balloon observation height and which could be operated in winds of 20–50mph. Reports could be made by telephone or message bag and the same cable, observer's car or basket, and limbered winch wagon, could be used for both kiting and ballooning. A drill was evolved, and the kites could be set up and flown in less than the twenty minutes taken to fill and put up a balloon.'[58]

The intrepid Broke-Smith, on at least one occasion in 1905, was raised to a height of 3500 feet (1060 metres) by this means.

Observation from the air was starting to be regarded as a necessary component of the order of battle. Balloons had proved their usefulness, but they were either tethered or were taken to wherever the wind blew them. Moreover, they were large, round targets for enemy guns. A balloon also took a long time to unpack, inflate, launch, recover, deflate and stow away on its wagon. About eight wagons were needed to transport a balloon company – which the sections had been renamed in 1905. These were usually horse drawn, though motive power was sometimes provided by traction engines.

A Cody man-lifting kite.

By 1905, the old Balloon Shed had been dismantled and re-erected at Farnborough, a new large airship shed had been constructed, as well as a substantial main workshops building and a hydrogen plant. Over the next few years, the work of the Balloon Factory included investigations into man-lifting kites, photography, signalling between ground and balloons, petrol motors, elongated balloons and mechanical towing machinery. Experimental work was carried out at Gibraltar and Malta to examine the possibility of using balloons in spotting submarines and mines. The Gibraltar detachment, commanded by Lieutenant G.F.

2nd Balloon Section at Gibraltar, 1904.

Wells, RE, conducted trials with a balloon operating off a destroyer. Due to the difficulties encountered with the weather, and its effect on the stability of the balloon at speeds in excess of 25mph (40kph), it was not judged a great success.

Willows No 1, Splott, Cardiff, on 18 August 1905. (*Via Ces Mowthorpe*)

Airship activity was not confined to the Balloon Factory. The first of several successful airships constructed by Ernest Willows (1886–1926), which was 72 feet (22 metres) in length, had a diameter of 18 feet (5.5 metres) and a capacity of 12,000 cubic feet (340 cubic metres), first flew on 5 September 1905, near Cardiff, powered by a 7 hp (5.18 kW) Peugeot motorcycle engine driving a propeller aft, measuring 10 feet (3 metres) in diameter, but with two further steering propellers on swivelling mounts in the nose of the triangular keel. Willows believed that the ability to direct the passage of an airship accurately was of the utmost importance and his work with steering propellers was based on the previous ideas of Captain William Beedle. During the course of its maiden flight, which lasted an hour and twenty-five minutes, Willow's airship attained a height of 120 feet (36 metres).

In April 1906, the Balloon Companies were absorbed by the Balloon School under Colonel Capper as Commandant, who was also appointed Superintendent of the Balloon Factory from May 1906, with a total salary of £944 a year. Capper had been a Brevet Lieutenant Colonel since 1900, being appointed to substantive rank in October 1905, with further brevet promotion to full colonel in January 1906. Capper was noted as a rigid disciplinarian who had done a good job in reorganising the Balloon Sections. He inspired loyalty and respect, and was capable of personal kindnesses to his men off parade. He was, however, much less accomplished than Templer as regards scientific and mechanical engineering knowledge. Templer retired as superintendent in 1906, but was retained for a further two years as Consultant Engineer on the development of the dirigible, at a fee of £300 per annum plus his retired pay. Templer (1846–1924) deserves to be remembered as one of the seminal figures in British aviation history. Capper praised his enthusiasm, boundless energy, optimism in the face of setbacks, kindness and dogged determination to overcome all obstacles placed in his path by his official superiors. He noted that Templer was not always popular with senior officers due to his disregard of regulations and bureaucracy, but in the end usually managed to get his own way and convince them he was right. It would appear that he fell foul in some way of Lieutenant General Sir John French, the C-in-C of Aldershot Command. A letter from French, of 19 October 1905, shows that he did not regard Templer highly as an administrator and that he had something of a prejudice against non-regular officers holding executive positions.[59] An unorthodox financial arrangement made by Templer's clerk, Warrant Officer Jolly, with a private company regarding the sale of surplus oxygen, did nothing to improve Lieutenant General French's humour.[60]

The Army's future in the air could have been considerably enhanced if a venture undertaken by Capper in December 1904 had met with official approval. While in the USA attending the World's Fair Exhibition in St Louis on behalf of the War Office, he had taken the opportunity to visit the Wright brothers at Dayton.[61] (Orville Wright's historic first flight of 17 December 1903 was described in the *Daily Mail* as having been made by a balloon-less airship.) They had just finished flying for the season, having progressed to flights of five minutes duration. Quite informally and without authority, Capper sounded out the brothers with regard to coming to England and working for the War Office. They responded that in return for a hefty fee, £20,000, they would be prepared to work solely for the British Government for four years. This sum represented about twice the yearly budget allocated by the War Office at that time for ballooning. Back in England, Capper very strongly recommended that this proposal should be taken up; negotiations did in fact take place over the next year and more, but no agreement was reached.[62] Capper wrote in his report:

'At least [the Wright Brothers] made far greater strides in the evolution of the flying machine than any of their predecessors. The work they are doing is of very great importance, as it means that if carried to a successful issue, we may shortly have, as accessories of warfare, scouting machines which will go at great pace, and be independent of obstacles of ground, whilst offering from their elevated position, unrivalled opportunities of ascertaining what is occurring in the heart of an enemy's country.'[63]

Interestingly, the Secretary of State for War, R.B. Haldane, who served in that position between 1905 and 1912, was of the opinion that the Wrights were not scientific enough in their approach to solving the challenge of sustained, powered flight. He regarded them as clever empiricists.[64] Haldane, a very able Liberal Imperialist, was noted for his arrogance and smoothness, which considerably irritated his political opponents.[65] (Richard Burdon Haldane (1856–1928), held ministerial office in both Liberal and Labour administrations. In a recent book he has been described as one of Britain's ablest war ministers, whose greatest political gift was a willingness to listen to professional advice, distil the best and facilitate its implementation.)

Neville Usborne's career between 1903 and 1908

On 15 March 1903, Neville Usborne was promoted to Lieutenant RN. He joined HMS *Thames* to enter the nascent submarine service on 24 June 1903. This was a Mersey Class 2nd class cruiser of 4050 tons launched in 1885. She was converted to a submarine depot ship in 1903. The *Thames* was fitted as a floating workshop, and was moored with the powder and quarantine hulks high in Fareham Creek, Portsmouth, because submarines were a new and uncertain weapon – HM Submarine No 1 had been launched only a few months before on 2 November 1902. It would appear that the underwater life was not appealing, as Usborne left the submarine service in 1904 to serve – from February 1904 to August 1904 – in HMS *Doris*, one of a class of nine 2nd class cruisers of

Neville served in HMS *Doris* in 1904.

5600 tons built between 1894 and 1896. His commanding officer reported that he was, 'a capable, zealous and hard-working officer.'[66] Additionally, the written approbation of their Lordships of the Admiralty was expressed for two reports submitted by Usborne on the defences of Lisbon and of Palma, Majorca.[67] It is interesting – but inconclusive – to note that HMS *Doris* was one of four Royal Navy ships supplied in 1903 with a set of Samuel Cody's man-lifting kites; pilot kite, two lifters and a carrier with controls and a basket, and intended to be launched and towed behind a ship for the purposes of reconnaissance, signalling, spotting the fall of shot, or of elevating wireless aerials.[68] (The other vessels supplied with kiting apparatus were the battleships HMS *Majestic* and HMS *Revenge*, and the armoured cruiser HMS *Good Hope*. Officers and men from the four ships undertook instructions in London in the use of the kites.) No records remain to show if *Doris* used the kiting apparatus while Usborne was a member of the crew, but if this was the case then it may well have stimulated his interest in the possibilities of aviation.[69]

In August 1904, approval was given for six months leave to go abroad to study German, during which time he was placed on the books of HMS *Firequeen*, the Portsmouth depot ship.[70]

Having been selected for qualification as a Lieutenant (T), March 1905 found Usborne at HMS *Vernon*, the RN torpedo school in Portsmouth, where the pioneer ironclad *Warrior* had arrived in 1904 as a floating workshop, power plant and wireless telegraphy school. In May 1905, he added to his skill at French (for his proficiency in this language he had been awarded the Ryder Memorial Prize as the best student of his year) with the attainment of Interpreter (Higher Standard) in German, for which a gratuity of £70 was granted. In August 1905 he gained a further note of their Lordships' approval for his services as an interpreter during a visit from the French fleet.[71] From July 1905 to April 1906 he was a Lieutenant (T) under training in HMS *Defiance* and was again described as, 'zealous and hard working.'[72]

This was a ninety-one gun screw vessel of 5700 tons, the last RN wooden line-of-battle ship, launched at Pembroke in 1861. She became the Navy's torpedo school ship in 1884 and was sold in 1931. While serving there Usborne once more came to their Lordships' attention, being praised for the experiments he carried out in connection with wireless telegraphy.[73]

From April 1906 to March 1907, he attended the Junior Staff Course at the RN College Greenwich. While there he was awarded the Trench-Gascoigne 2nd Prize of thirty guineas by the United Services Institution for an essay on a naval subject. For this he wrote a closely argued and technically detailed piece which was titled; 'What is the relative value of speed and armament, both strategically and tactically, in a modern battleship, and how far should either be sacrificed to the other in the ideal ship?' The RN's most likely probable enemy was identified as the German Navy and the factor governing the relative strengths of the two was stated as the amount of money each was prepared to spend. Usborne writes with clarity and lucidity, and supports his points with a judicious use of statistical evidence and graphical presentation. He concludes that the British fleet should aim for a policy of gradual growth, keeping well ahead of possible opponents in the matter of speed, but without in any way sacrificing gun power to this necessity. It is obvious from reading Usborne's words that he takes his profession seriously and is studying technical, tactical, strategic and political matters with interest.

Having qualified for Lieutenant (T), from April 1907 to June 1907, he served in HMS *Actaeon* – the shore establishment for torpedo training at Sheerness, its nucleus being the former twenty-six gun steam frigate *Ariadne* of 4538 tons and was rated, 'a very capable torpedo officer.'[74]

In March 1907, it would appear that an interest in aviation had developed, as he wrote to the Admiralty requesting that he might be noted for employment

Neville served in HMS *Berwick* from 1907 to 1908.

in connection with aerial navigation work should anything for officers arise in the future.[75] While awaiting something suitable, Usborne continued with his specialisation. From June 1907 to September 1908, he served as Lieutenant (T) in the County Class cruiser, HMS *Berwick*, of 9800 tons, launched in 1902, and was once more praised in his CO's report: 'A most able torpedo officer. Very zealous and hard-working. Has the knack of handling men.'[76]

As part of his duties he would have been in charge of much of the ship's electrical fittings, therefore it may be assumed that he was developing and gaining in technical knowledge all the time. His skill as an interpreter proved useful once more during 1907, when he was again thanked for services rendered during the visit of the German cruiser, SMS *Scharnhorst*. He subsequently wrote a report on the wireless telegraphy equipment of the German vessels, for which he was praised.[77] Further evidence of his desire to be involved in aviation may be seen in the application which he made in August 1908 to undertake the Army Balloon Course. This was approved, subject to a place being available on a course commencing after September 1908.[78]

Reports have survived of a Lieutenant Usborne being in charge of the Royal Navy's further experiments with Cody kites at Whale Island, Portsmouth,

A Naval kite being prepared for flight at HMS *Excellent* in 1908.

between August and October 1908.[79] However, the reports on the trials were not signed by Neville, but by his brother Cecil Vivian. They took place ashore and in a variety of warships, including the battleship HMS *Revenge*, the cruiser HMS *Grafton,* and the torpedo boat destroyers HMS *Fervent* and HMS *Recruit.* Harry Harper recorded that Cody, 'astonished the officers of that vessel by striding up their gangway in full cowboy attire, complete with an enormous ten-gallon hat.'[80] Usborne was taken aloft on more than one occasion, reporting that from a height of 1200 feet, he had a good bird's-eye view of Portsmouth Harbour, Portsdown Hills and the Isle of Wight. Exercises were also conducted with submarines and experiments with photography were made.[81] Despite favourable reports from Lieutenant Usborne, Captain Tupper of HMS *Excellent* and the Commander-in-Chief, Portsmouth, Admiral Fanshawe, the Admiralty decided to proceed no further with naval kiting in his reply to the C-in-C of 24 December 1908.[82]

It seems more than likely, given Neville's already stated interest in aviation, that he would have talked over progress or otherwise at Whale Island with his brother. Family matters were not overlooked, as in December 1908; he was the best man at Vivian's wedding, which took place in St Margaret's Church, Westminster.

Dreadnoughts and Submarines

In October 1906, HMS *Dreadnought* was completed, having been built in just one year. With her revolutionary heavy armament and steam turbines, *Dreadnought* rendered all her contemporaries obsolete. Caught napping, Imperial Germany would respond in due course with dreadnoughts of her own.

In December of the same year, SM U-1, the first German U-boat, was commissioned into the Imperial German Navy. The Royal Navy was also building up its submarine service with the B, C and D classes being designed, built, and commissioned between 1905 and 1910, each an improvement on its predecessor.

Chapter Three

The 'Golden Age' before August 1914

Naval Aviation Career before the First World War

Towards the end of 1908, or the start of 1909, Neville was appointed for work at Barrow-in-Furness in connection with construction of Naval Airship No 1. An entry in his naval record of service notes he was on the books of HMS *Vernon* for further torpedo qualifications, but also seconded to the Admiralty for special services in connection with airship construction and also for duties as an interpreter in German.[1]

The first indication of any serious interest being taken in aviation by the Admiralty was on 21 July 1908, when Captain R.H.S. Bacon[2], CVO, DSO, RN, the Director of Naval Ordnance, submitted proposals to the First Sea Lord, Admiral Sir John Fisher[3], GCB, GCVO, ADC, suggesting that a Naval Air Assistant be appointed, that the War Office should be asked to place the Superintendent of the Balloon School in contact with the Admiralty and that a rigid type of airship should be built for the Royal Navy.[4]

On 14 August 1908, a letter from the Admiralty invited Messrs Vickers, Son & Maxim of Barrow (Which, as part of BAE Systems, is still to this day a major contractor for UK Government armament work.) to tender for a rigid airship comparable to, or better than, current German airships. There is no doubt that Usborne would have been aware of the developments in lighter-than-air aviation over the previous decade, and that his skills in German would have been most useful in reading material written in the German technical and aviation press.

Progress in Germany

The reconstituted design and production team at Friedrichshafen had suffered the trials and tribulations associated with the development of any new technology. It is of interest to note that British official interest had been aroused, as in December 1905 the British consul in Stuttgart was asked to take note of events at the Zeppelin works.[5] The LZ2, which was smaller than the LZ1 and with more powerful engines, crashed on its maiden flight in January 1906 due to uncontrollable pitching movements, engine and steering failure, and was totally wrecked. Sustained flight was achieved with the LZ3 later in that year, which had horizontal stabilisers to cure the problem. Its maiden flight, on 9 October, lasted over two hours, achieving a top speed of 24mph (38kph) with eleven souls on board. In 1907, the *Daily Mail's* air correspondent, Harry Harper, who, in 1906, had been appointed the first full-time air correspondent of a national newspaper, reported:

'Out upon the gleaming surface of Lake Constance the giant craft lies hidden in its floating corrugated iron shed. Count Zeppelin's crew are at work inside making various changes suggested by successful trials. When they have finished, Count Zeppelin is confident that he will be able to sail for an unbroken period of twenty-four hours. German military experts were jubilant over the Count's latest achievements and are bringing their utmost influence to bear to induce the government to purchase the ship without waiting for further experiments. Count Zeppelin's manoeuvres with his airship during the past week have been most remarkable and have convinced everyone that the ship is the most efficient at present in existence.'[6]

In 1907, at the Second Hague Conference, the declaration prohibiting the dropping of explosives from the air was renewed, but was signed by only twenty-seven of the forty-four powers represented there and of those who would take part as belligerents in the First World War; by Great Britain, the United States, Portugal and Belgium only. The bombardment of undefended places by any means whatever was forbidden. It lapsed automatically in August 1914 and ceased to be binding when non-contracting powers became belligerents. In the meantime it served to concentrate the minds of those in government in Great Britain and would result in the establishment – the following year – of a committee under Lord Esher,[7] which will be discussed below.

On 1 July 1908, LZ4 made the first international flight by Zeppelin to Switzerland, overflying Lucerne and Geneva, setting a new world air endurance record of twelve hours. A twenty-four hour flight followed a month later at a time when the longest duration aeroplane flight in Europe was but fifteen minutes. (Though Orville Wright was soon to make a solo flight of an hour and a half in the USA.) Unfortunately, LZ4 came to grief while moored on the ground near Stuttgart. It was destroyed in a gas explosion caused by the build up of static electricity caused by the rubberised cotton gas cells rubbing against each other. Luckily nobody was injured. But from the wreckage emerged a wealth of public support in Germany. Money poured in from the rich and poor, which enabled construction of the LZ5 to begin. On 10 November 1908, Kaiser Wilhelm II came to Friedrichshafen to award the Count with the Prussian Order of the Black Eagle and to declare that he was the greatest German of the new century. In the spring of 1909, LZ5 made a long distance flight of 39 hours and 39 minutes, covering 712 miles (1150 km). The Count had become a national hero:

> 'An emblem of German pride, honour and endeavour. Shops sold marzipan Zeppelins, sweets, cigarettes, harmonicas and yachting caps. There were Zeppelin streets, squares, parks, roses and chrysanthemums.'[8]

More importantly, perhaps, from a practical point of view, the German Army bought LZ3, renaming it SMS (*Seiner Majestaet Schiff*) Z-I, and LZ5, which became Z-II.[9] A little later, in 1909, one of the army airships was flown by Count Zeppelin, Major Sperling, and a crew from the Army Balloon Corps, to Munich, followed by a detachment of cavalry, where she was reported as having dipped her nose three times in salute to the Prince Regent and a huge crowd at the city's Exhibition Hall, and then onwards over the Royal Palace, from where the Princess Maria Theresa and her daughters waved their handkerchiefs in salutation.[10] Soon afterwards, Zeppelin and Parseval airships took part in the Imperial Army manoeuvres, held on the border of Wurtemburg and Bavaria, as also did Krupp's newly invented anti-aircraft artillery.[11]

Work progresses at Farnborough under Colonel Capper

Sadly, the first and only fatal accident experienced by British Army free ballooning aeronauts occurred on 25 May 1907. King Edward VII and Prince Fushimi of Japan visited the Balloon Factory to witness a demonstration of free ballooning. The balloon, *Thrasher,* carrying Lieutenants T.E. Martin-Leake, RE, and W.T.M. Caulfield, RE, ascended and disappeared from view. Over Abbotsbury the two officers called out to a local farmer to catch hold of the trail rope, but to no avail. It came down in the sea off the Dorset coast near Bridport; neither of the officers were ever found, although the tangled wreck of the balloon was salvaged by a fishing vessel. Meanwhile, the Royal Party paid a visit to the nearby shed where important work had been progressing. It is believed that while inspecting work therein, the King personally named the bulky and impressive dirigible, *Nulli Secundus.* [The King's choice of name for the airship was reported in the highly reputable French aeronautical periodical *L'Aérophile:* '*Nulli Secundus tel serait, assure-t-on, le nom donné, sur le désire du roi Edouard VII, au nouveau dirigible Anglais; il suffit à indiquer que l'Angleterre entend bien ne pas demeurer en arrière des nations continentals dans les applications du ballon automobile.*']*[12]

Samuel Cody[13] was engaged on the design of the airscrews, engine mounting and the control surfaces for the airship being constructed there. According to Harry Harper, Cody's, 'picturesque appearance, and genial, laughing, hail-fellow-well-met manner' did not endear him to some War Office officials, but more importantly, he and Capper established a rapport and mutual respect.[14] A gondola made from a metal tube framework and covered by fabric was constructed by Cody based on plans made by Capper, replacing Templer's original idea of two basketwork balloon cars. It should be noted that Capper and Templer remained on good terms, and that he made an important contribution to the design of *Nulli Secundus*, particularly in respect of the construction of the envelope. The challenge facing the team at Farnborough has been described thus:

> '*Nulli Secundus I*, of course, had more than the usual disadvantages associated with any new and untried airship; not only had both she and her pilot [Capper] never flown before, but the whole design and construction had been carried out by a team that had never produced an airship before.'[15]

It should, of course, be noted that the same challenge faced nearly every other pioneer of either aeroplanes or airships, including Count Zeppelin, Santos-Dumont and the Wright Brothers, and indeed Harry Ferguson or Lilian Bland in Ireland. Capper tried to rectify his lack of aerial experience by taking part, accompanied at times by Mrs Capper, in a number of civilian balloon events and competitions.

The maiden flight in the brief career of British Army Dirigible No 1, *Nulli Secundus*, was from the Army Balloon Factory at Farnborough on 10 September 1907. The great shed had been doubled in length to accommodate the airship, which was a brown, sausage-shaped balloon, made from goldbeater's skin, some 111 feet (34 metres) in length, with a diameter of 18 feet (5.5 metres) and a capacity of 55,000 cubic feet (1556 cubic metres) covered with a net, with the gondola suspended below from a light framework which could hold three crewmen. She was powered by a 40 hp (29.6 kW) Antoinette engine. At first there were a few problems with the engine running hot and generating less power than required to turn the airscrews at a sufficient rate for successful, sustained flight.[16] After some adjustments, she undertook a short series of trials with two flights on 10 September, the second of which was witnessed by Colonel Templer and which concluded with a heavier than desirable descent which caused some superficial damage. No further flights took place for the

Nulli Secundus I over
St Paul's on 5 October
1907.

next three weeks as the Balloon School was programmed to take part with balloons and kites in the autumn manoeuvres. The time was spent productively in making structural alterations to the control surfaces. Two trips were made on 30 September and 3 October, which culminated in a circuit as far as Guildford and back. *Nulli Secundus* had now flown a total of about three hours and a distance of 25 miles (40 kilometres). Capper was determined to influence public opinion and so coerce the War Office into providing greater funding for the development of aviation. It may also have been the case that he was influenced by the success of Zeppelin LZ 3, which had recently made a flight of 200 miles (320 kilometres) in nine and a quarter hours around Lake Constance, and also the French Lebaudy, *La Patrie*, which, on 12 July 1907, had flown a closed loop of 40 miles (64 kilometres) around Chalais-Meudon, at an average speed of 22mph (35kph). So he determined upon a bold and spectacular flight. On 5 October, *Nulli Secundus* was flown the 50 miles (80 kilometres) to London in three and a half hours with Capper at the helm, Cody tending the engine and Captain W.A. King, the instructor in ballooning and map-reading, flying over Kensington, Hyde Park and the War Office, circling St Paul's Cathedral and landing on the cycle track at Crystal Palace, so establishing a new endurance record for non-rigid airships and ensuring huge headlines in the daily papers. Harry Harper reported on the momentous event as follows:

'In the streets, trams and all other vehicles came to an abrupt halt. London's millions just stood staring up into the sky in amazement as the airship flew low, only 500 to 600 feet above streets and houses. It was so low that people looking up could see Cody and Capper quite clearly in their small control car, and every now and then Cody would turn from his engine to lean over the side of the car and wave to those below. On the roof of the War Office members of the Army Council stood waving handkerchiefs. It was a moment of triumph.'[17]

[Author's note: *Nulli Secundus* took off from Farnborough at 10.40 am and followed the course Frimley – Bagshot – Sunningdale – Staines – Hounslow – Brentford, at a height of between 750 and 1300 feet (230–430 metres) and an average speed, with a following wind, of 24mph (40kph). She passed over Kensington Palace, Hyde Park, Buckingham Palace, Whitehall, Trafalgar Square, The Strand and Fleet Street, circling St Paul's at about 12.20 pm. From there a course was taken over Blackfriars, Kennington and Clapham Common before alighting at Crystal Palace at 2 pm.]

Capper was pleased with the way the airship had answered the controls and had steered well, both with and into the wind, overcoming the resistance of the strong breeze to make headway.[18] They were driven back to Farnborough in Cody's large touring car, in which Lieutenant Clive Waterlow had followed the airship, along with petrol, tools and the ground crew, an event which Waterlow described with some glee in a letter to his mother.[19] (Waterlow had joined the Balloon School as a 2nd Lieutenant on 18 October 1906; he would spend the rest of his life on airships until his untimely and tragic death in an accident at RNAS Cranwell in 1917, at the age of thirty-one.)[20] Three days later, owing to heavy winds and rain which had damaged and thoroughly soaked the envelope, as well as lowering the temperature of the hydrogen, so degrading its buoyancy and lift and, despite the innovative use of slipstream from the propellers to assist in drying out the envelope, the airship had to be deflated, and was taken back to Farnborough by means of horse and cart.[21]

Capper was interviewed after the flight and said that he was very happy with it; the airship had performed well and could have stayed aloft for longer. He decided to terminate the flight because of the deteriorating weather and didn't want to take risks at a stage when airship development was in its infancy.[22]

La Patrie was lost on 29 November 1907, blown unmanned from her moorings at Verdun across Northern France, Cornwall and the Irish Sea. Numerous sightings were reported in the *Belfast Telegraph*, 'to

Lieutenant Clive Waterlow RE.

the consternation of the inhabitants' of country towns and villages who, 'gathered in large numbers' to view the great yellow dirigible pass overhead.[23] She struck a hillside on the south side of Belfast Lough at Ballydavey, Holywood, Co Down, losing a propeller in the process, but ascended once more and was last seen off the Isle of Islay speeding into oblivion.[24]

During the winter of 1907/08 work began on redesigning and rebuilding *Nulli Secundus*; modifications included the replacement of the covering net by a varnished silk 'chemise', a new understructure, the addition of a reserve gasbag, a new car for the crew and engine mounting, alterations to the control and stabilizing surfaces, and a new bow elevator.

In April 1908, Colonel Templer's contract was not renewed. No longer would his stocky form be seen in the environs of the balloon shed with a snuff-box in one hand and a large coloured handkerchief in the other. A terse file note is all that has survived by way of an official tribute, 'Colonel Templer's services were dispensed with from the 1st inst – 27.4.08.'[25] He faded away and

In November 1907 parts of the Lebaudy airship *La Patrie* were left on a hillside in Co Down.

Nulli Secundus II.

has never really been given the recognition he deserves as a great pioneer of military aviation.

Nulli Secundus II first flew on the evening of 24 July 1908, and proved to be somewhat unstable and difficult to trim. Two more short flights were made in August, during which a top speed of 22mph (35kph) was reached, but she was of little value and was broken up. At some stage over the summer a party of naval personnel visited Farnborough and received some instruction in airship handling. Colonel Capper later remarked that as far as the airship's name went it actually came a bad second to the Willows 1A.[26]

The Times was much more willing to sing the praises of the team, in particular Cody, Capper and Templer, which had reconstructed *Nulli Secundus*:

'As is now known there are many airships which have been completed and are under construction. Every new vessel proves more conclusively to the unbiased mind that it is merely a question of time, practice, experiment and general development – especially regarding the construction of a light yet powerful engine – before airships will be sufficiently navigable, even in strong winds and unfavourable weather, to prove of enormous value to every civilised portion of the world. The first trial of the rebuilt *Nulli Secundus*, which took place on Cove Common last week, should certainly give every Englishman satisfaction that our experiments, though somewhat tardy, are coming to a more successful path and should encourage all who possess either foresight or patriotism or both.'[27]

The use of new technology also extended to communications, experiments in wireless telegraphy being conducted. The first wireless company of the Royal Engineers was formed in 1907 at Farnborough. Its primary task was to investigate the possibilities of military communication by means of airborne wireless sets and was, therefore, attached to the Balloon School. In May 1908, Capper, and Lieutenant C.J. Ashton RE, ascended in the free balloon *Pegasus* to a height of 8000 feet and, when aloft over Petersfield, received signals from a wireless station at Aldershot some 20 miles (32 kilometres) away and also from the battleship HMS *King Edward VII*, which was lying off Portsmouth. The British and Irish press reported in July 1908 that successful experiments had taken place near Berlin, conducted by the German army, concerning the dispatch of wireless telegrams from a dirigible.[28] As this technology involved sparks on electrical contacts it was regarded as rather hazardous when in close association with a gasbag full of hydrogen, however the Germans persevered, and within a few months were using airships equipped with wireless sets on army manoeuvres.

Also in 1908, Lieutenant E.M. Maitland – 'a brilliant, brave and gallant officer, whose personal influence on the officers and men of the Airship Service became legendary, even in his lifetime'[29] – made his first parachute jump from a trapeze suspended below a hot-air balloon at Crystal Palace, landing on the roof of a public house, from which encounter he emerged unscathed – but not so the roof.

Contemporary Media Comment

It is interesting to note that in January 1908, *Pall Mall* magazine featured the first part of a new serial story by H.G. Wells, *The War in the Air*, which included a highly coloured description of a devastating attack on a fleet of American dreadnought battleships, followed by a ruinous air raid on New York by an armada of German airships:

> 'As the airships sailed along they smashed up the city as a child will shatter its cities of brick and card. Below, they left ruins and blazing conflagrations, and heaped and scattered dead; men, women and children mixed together.'[30]

Authors in France and Germany during this period, such as Emile Driant and Rudolf Martin, also wrote of airships transporting

A cartoon from the US magazine *Puck* of January 1906.

vast armies to attack Russia or Britain and bring death and destruction on a huge scale. Others believed – employing what could only be wishful thinking – that warfare from the air would be so destructive that it would make conflict between the major powers less likely.[31]

There was a growing sense of public unease that Britain was no longer so securely insulated by the Royal Navy from the threat of invasion. A popular contemporary success in the London theatre was the play, *An Englishman's Home* by Guy du Maurier, which showed in dramatic form what might happen if England were subject to a German invasion.

Developments in Government Policy

The potential threat from the air began to shake the populace from its Victorian stance of complacent insularity.[32] Indeed, the Chancellor of the Exchequer, David Lloyd George, made Parliament aware of H.G. Wells' latest story when participating in the Aerial Navigation Sub-committee of the Committee of Imperial Defence, which had been established in October 1908 with the following terms of reference:

> 'Several of the great powers are turning their attention to the question and are spending large sums of money in the development of dirigible balloons and aeroplanes. It is probable that for countries with land frontiers immediately across which lie potential enemies, the development of airships has hitherto been more important than it is for Great Britain, and that we have been justified for this reason in spending less money than some of our neighbours. The success that has attended recent experiments in France, Germany and America has, however, created a new situation which appears to render it advisable that the subject of aerial navigation should be investigated.'[33]

The Chairman of this sub-committee was Lord Esher, who was not only a distinguished military strategist, but also had the ear and confidence of the King, Edward VII. The other members were the Chancellor of the Exchequer, David Lloyd George; the Secretary of State for War, R.B. Haldane; the First Lord of the Admiralty, Reginald McKenna; the Director of Naval Ordnance, Captain R.H.S. Bacon, RN; the Chief of the Imperial General Staff, General Sir W. Nicholson; the Director of Military Operations, Major General J.S. Ewart and the Master General of the Ordnance, Major General C. Hadden. Its aim was to deliberate what should be done about assessing future dangers from the air, how to counter them and how much money to spend on this. Written evidence principally concerning balloons and dirigibles was submitted by Sir Hiram Maxim, Charles Rolls, Lieutenant Colonel John Capper, RE, and Major B.F.S. Baden-Powell. It was decided that airships might well have some utility in the roles of reconnaissance over land and sea, as well as artillery spotting, and that hostile airships might become capable of carrying out bombing raids on the British Isles. From the minutes of the meeting which Colonel Capper attended, it would appear that he lost not only the support of General Nicholson, who strongly disapproved of aircraft of any sort, but also of R.B. Haldane, which did not bode well for the security of his tenure at Farnborough.[34] Haldane had been educated in Germany and much admired the inhabitants' efficiency and technological prowess, being particularly interested in Count Zeppelin's experiments and progress.[35] He was in favour of creating an aerial service, but he wanted progress towards this aim to be structured, measured, organised and systematic, with a scientific research and development programme directed and controlled by the government. Others disagreed and felt that in order not to fall further behind the continental powers, Britain should purchase immediately the latest available technology.[36]

Figures were released by the War Office in response to a question from Lord Montagu of Beaulieu showing a comparison of the sums spent on aviation in 1908 by several European governments. Leading the field was Germany with £135,000 from public funds, to which was added £265,000 collected by private subscription by the National Zeppelin Airship Fund. Next was France with £47,000, then Austria-Hungary with £5500 and trailing in fourth was Great Britain with £5270, £1980 of which was allocated to the army for dirigible balloons and £3290 on aeroplanes.[37] As well as being a distinguished motoring authority, Lord Montagu was very interested in aeronautics and was a founder member of the Aerial League of the British Empire, founded in January 1909. Its aim was to convince the country of the vital importance to the British Empire of aerial supremacy, much in the way that the Royal Navy had assured domination of the seas in the century following Trafalgar. He was particularly exercised by the thought of a fleet of airships striking pre-emptively at the strategic targets concentrated in London, effectively winning a future war before the army or the Royal Navy could get to grips with enemy forces.[38]

'It would be possible for dirigibles to leave the frontier stations of at least five Continental powers, all within 500 miles distance from where we are now seated, and do much damage at Aldershot, Portsmouth, Dover, Chatham, Sheerness, and other military and naval stations, without taking into account that an attempt would certainly be made to paralyse the heart of the nation by attacking certain nerve centres in London, the destruction of which would impede or entirely destroy the means of communication by telephone, telegraph, rail and road.

'Germany's plans in airships, as in other directions, are not fully known to us; nor would this be the occasion to state how such information can be obtained. But it is beyond doubt that she has, at the present moment, the best and the only fully equipped aerial fleet in the world, and one which is more than a match for all the other dirigibles in existence.

'The day is not far distant when England will have to be something besides nominal mistress of the seas. She will have to be at least equal to her neighbours in the matter of aerial defence and offence, and it is our business and the duty of the nation at large to see that the authorities are awakened in time to their responsibilities in this direction.'[39]

Moreover, a very trenchant article in *The Times* of February 1909 was highly critical of the British efforts so far in the field of aeronautics and argued forcibly for the airship:

'The war of the future is likely to be decided in no small measure by the use of scientific instruments of destruction controlled by highly trained men. That the airship in its various forms promises to become such an instrument is every day becoming more and more apparent. Progress may be astonishingly rapid, but without well-equipped laboratories, testing grounds and factories, our authorities are utterly unable to discover the merits of new ideas. We are laboriously going over the same preliminary ground which the French and Germans traversed years ago. A most important task is to bring the adult Briton to understand that there is an immediate need for an aerial defence scheme. With this end in view I would favour the holding of public meetings and lectures throughout the important centres and, better still, practical demonstrations by airships, even if we have to go abroad for the machines and the men. It is painful to report that no successful dirigible or aeroplane has yet been flown in the British Isles and that the vast majority of the people have never seen one in any form.'[40]

A subsequent article in March of the same year contended:

'In 1912 the Germans will have at least twenty-four mammoth Zeppelin airships, each capable of overseas excursions and probably speedier than any naval vessel. Our rate of production is one vessel per annum and by 1912, at most, we may have some five small-sized, slow, non-rigid airships, which compared to Zeppelins will be as antiquated cruisers to Dreadnoughts. A Zeppelin of the present-day type could reach this country in ten hours and do enormous damage in a brief space of time.'[41]

Whilst the critique of the British lack of organisation was reasonable enough, the correspondent's estimate of the German capability was over-egging the pudding somewhat. The somewhat febrile atmosphere was heightened by a rash of reports received in police stations and newspaper offices across the country – in the first few months of 1909 – claiming the sighting of mysterious flying objects, widely believed to be airships of unknown but suspicious origin. This became known as the Phantom Airship Scare and was part of a developing national phobia concerning Germans and their hostile intentions, such as the rumour that there were 80,000 soldiers of the Kaiser embedded in the country, disguised as waiters, barbers, businessmen and shop assistants.[42] It was, to a certain extent, a by-product of the Anglo-German naval rivalry and the German desire to have colonies to match those of the British Empire. The paranoia might have been better directed to an appreciation of the portents of firstly, the remarkable feat of Louis Blériot in the early hours of 25 June 1909 when he completed his crossing of the English Channel in his frail monoplane in a time of thirty-seven minutes, and secondly, the International Flying Meeting at Reims a month later, of which it was written:

'Reims marked the true acceptance of the aeroplane as a practical vehicle and as such was a major milestone in the world's history.'[43]

Yet the fixed-wing aeroplane was still in its infancy. David Lloyd George attended the Reims meeting and was impressed by what he witnessed, causing the *Morning Post* to comment:

'If Mr Lloyd George's words help to rouse the minds of his followers to the importance of the question, they will do more for the interests of the country than his stupid abuse of landlords. The Chancellor of the Exchequer says that Englishmen would soon grow enthusiastic if they saw airships in flight. In this he is quite right. As Mr Lloyd George no doubt realizes, it is the dirigible balloon that at present is the best adapted for practical uses. The terrible damage which such a vessel could work, and the tremendous moral effect its operations would produce, render it a most formidable engine of war. An attack could only be effectively met by other airships, and the English people cannot realize too soon the urgent necessity of organizing an aerial fleet. Until this is done the position of the country is one of grave and increasing danger.'[44]

There was, however, official and military awareness in 1909 of the potential threat posed by German dirigibles. The British Military Attaché in Berlin, Colonel Frederick Trench, had paid particular attention to airship development in the country; questioning his contacts, travelling around the country to view airships, visiting the factories in which they were being constructed, and keeping abreast of reports in the national, regional and technical press. He sent detailed reports to the War Office in London, noting, amongst other events, that a school for aeronauts had been established at Friedrichshafen; secret contracts had been let for the increased manufacture of hydrogen, which would be taken over by the military on the 'outbreak of hostilities' and that airship manoeuvres, including wireless telegraphy, bomb dropping and 'airship chasing', had taken place in the Rhine Valley near Cologne; which was regarded as being of particular significance as that city was, 'almost the nearest point to England'.[45] Not only did he produce these official reports, but he also wrote privately to Colonel Capper, whom he knew well. He attempted to arrange for Capper to visit Germany to have a look at the dirigibles, but encountered reluctance on the part of previously friendly contacts, which made him even more suspicious of Germany's ultimate intentions.

Back at Farnborough
Over the winter of 1908, Colonel Capper and the team at Farnborough had built another non-rigid airship, Dirigible No 2, which made its first appearance in the late spring of 1909 and was unofficially christened *Baby*. The envelope was fish-shaped, or pisiform,[46] to lessen wind resistance as compared to Dirigible No 1 and was made of goldbeater's skin; she was 84 feet (25 metres) in length and had a diameter of 24 feet (7 metres), with a volume of 21,000 cubic feet (5943 cubic metres). Capper had liaised with the National Physical Laboratory at Teddington with the testing of ebony models of possible envelope shapes in the air channel or wind-tunnel located there, having been told by the Wright brothers of the utility of such a device. One ballonet was contained inside the envelope which, to begin with, had three inflated fins to act as stabilizers. These proved unsatisfactory as they were lacking in rigidity, and were replaced after the first inflation by the ordinary, non-inflatable fixed planes. Two 10 hp (7.4 kW), 3-cylinder Buchet engines were mounted in a

Baby in May
1909.

long car driving a single propeller, and, at a later date, these were replaced
by a 25 hp (18.5 kW) REP radial engine, which was not a great improvement.
Finally, a 35 hp engine (25 kW) designed by Gustavus Green was installed.
Green (1865–1964) was the first successful aero-engine designer in Great
Britain. Over a period of seven months, from 11 May to 10 December 1908,
Baby made thirteen fairly short flights with this variety of engines and control
surface configurations. This could charitably be described as a development
programme based on the trial and error method. She proved to be very
unstable and rather slow, barely reaching 20mph (32kph); a complete redesign
was required. During the autumn, permission was obtained to enlarge the
envelope and fit a more powerful engine.

Further Official Interest
The establishment of the Advisory Committee on Aeronautics in 1909 was a
major step forward, though it had taken all of three years to come to fruition.
Early in 1906 a proposal had been made by Colonel J.D. Fullerton, RE,
supported by Colonel Templer, for the appointment of a committee consisting
of military officers, aeronauts, mechanical engineers and naval representatives to
harness the available expertise to investigate all technical matters aeronautical in
a structured and scientific fashion. A modified form of this idea was put forward
some three years later by R.B. Haldane, the Secretary of State for War. He was
particularly keen to involve the National Physical Laboratory at Teddington
and thereby, hopefully, bring the best scientific talent to bear upon the study
of flight, and give the government direct control of aeronautical research and
experiment. (The laboratory was founded in 1900 to carry out scientific tests

Captain Murray Sueter in 1915.
(*Via Peter Wright*)

for theoretical purposes and also for the benefit of British industry, in imitation of, and in somewhat belated response to, the *Physikalisch Technichse Reichsanstalt*, which had been established in Berlin since 1887. It represented a significant move away from the Victorian *laissez faire* attitude, which held that industrial activities should be the exclusive pursuit of private enterprise.) A conference was held in the room of the First Lord of the Admiralty and its deliberations were approved by the Prime Minister, Herbert Henry Asquith. The Advisory Committee for Aeronautics was set up with ten members, seven of whom were Fellows of the Royal Society. The President was Lord Rayleigh, OM, FRS and the Chairman, Dr R.T. Glazebrook, FRS, the Director of the National Physical Laboratory. [Lord Rayleigh (1842–1919) was a Nobel Laureate in 1904 and had a worldwide reputation as one of the foremost mathematical and experimental physicists of his day.] The army was represented by Major General Sir Charles Hadden, the navy by Captain R.H.S. Bacon, and the Meteorological Office by Dr W.N. Shaw. Soon, two others were added, Mervyn O'Gorman, when he took over the charge of the Balloon Factory, and 'the brilliant but unorthodox',[47] 'difficult and temperamental',[48] Captain Murray Sueter, RN.

[Author's note: Sueter was born in 1872 and, as a junior officer, showed indications of an original mind, and a considerable inventive genius in the new fields of torpedoes, submarines and wireless telegraphy. As the first Director of the Admiralty's Air Department from 1912 to 1916, he was a tireless advocate of air power and succeeded in annoying many influential senior officers. He was effectively exiled to command in Southern Italy and, following an ill-advised letter to the King in 1917, his active naval career was cut short. After the war, when neither the Admiralty nor the Air Department was prepared to offer a position to this talented maverick, he became a Member of Parliament and a thorn in the side of the establishment. He was, however, knighted in 1934 and lived to a ripe old age, dying in 1960.]

From that time on the National Physical Laboratory worked in very close co-operation with the Balloon Factory. Some of the topics considered, investigated and experimented upon included – air resistance, stresses and strains on materials, means of protecting airships from electrical discharges, the best shape for the wing of an aeroplane and the best fabric for the envelope of an airship. Colonel Capper was a significant omission; despite his obvious knowledge and enthusiasm, he was too outspoken and irascible, and had not impressed Haldane, who considered that he was a clever empiricist but was not the man to build up an Air Service as he envisaged it, on a foundation of science.[49]

The government's view of the role of the committee was expressed in the House of Commons. On 20 May 1909, Arthur Balfour asked the Prime Minister about the new committee. Mr Asquith replied:

'It is not part of the general duty of the Advisory Committee for Aeronautics either to construct or invent. Its function is not to initiate but to consider what is initiated elsewhere, and is referred to it by the executive officers of the navy and army construction departments. The problems which are likely to arise… for solutions are numerous, and it will be the work of the committee to advise on these problems, and to seek their solution by the application of both theoretical and experimental methods of research.'[50]

The Advisory Committee visited Farnborough on 5 July 1909. No records of what was discussed have survived, but at least early contact was made. It may be considered a weakness that the Advisory Committee was heavily biased towards theoretical knowledge. Where were the industrialists, the engineers, the aviators, who could have assisted with the application of the theory to reality, perhaps by using some of the empiricism so disregarded by Haldane? Writing after the First World War, the official historian approved of Haldane's methods:

'These and scores of other problems were systematically and patiently attacked. There were no theatrically quick results, but the work done laid a firm and broad base for all subsequent success. Hasty popular criticism is apt to measure the value of scientific advice by the tale of things done, and to overlook the credit that belongs to it for things prevented. The science of aeronautics in the year 1909 was in a very difficult and uncertain stage of its early development; any mistakes in laying the foundations of a national air force would not only have involved the nation in much useless expense, but would have imperilled the whole structure.'[51]

Enter Mervyn O'Gorman

In October 1909, the Balloon Factory and Balloon School at South Farnborough, which had been under one control, were separated, with Capper as commandant of the school. The superintendent of the factory appointed, on a salary of £950 a year, was Mervyn Joseph Pius O'Gorman, who became universally known as O'G:

Mervyn O'Gorman.

'A witty Irishman of flamboyant courage and imagination who had already attained eminence as an authority on suction gas engines, and was consultant engineer in the firm of Swinburne, O'Gorman, and Baillie. Sporting a gold-rimmed monocle, fiercely brushed-up moustache, long cigarette holder, and immaculate dress, he was, at thirty-eight, a man of brilliant and strong character, he made warm friends as readily as bitter enemies; a thruster with a penetrating outlook founded on degrees in Classics and Science at University College, Dublin, and a post-graduate honours course in electrical engineering at the City and Guilds Institute of London University – yet withal, an artist.'[52]

The selection of O'Gorman fitted perfectly with the desire of R.B. Haldane, as expressed in Parliament, to appoint a, 'practical man, a civilian and an engineer'[53] and had been made on the recommendation of Lord Rayleigh. It was believed that he was better suited than Capper to work closely with the scientists serving on the Advisory Committee for Aeronautics and also at the National Physical Laboratory. It was also thought that as a civil servant he would be free of the malign influence which senior military and naval officers, opposed to aviation in any shape or form, could (and did) exert on colonels and captains. *Flight* Magazine welcomed the appointment:

'Important changes have, as our readers are aware, taken place in connection with the control of the various departments associated with military aeronautics, the outstanding departure having been the appointment of a civilian, Mr Mervyn O'Gorman – a well-known consulting engineer and automobile expert – to the post of superintendent of the Military Balloon Factory. Hitherto, Colonel Capper succeeded, out of his indomitable energy, in looking after this large and important work in addition to his proper duties as commandant of the Military Balloon School, which in wartime provides the balloon companies that are attached to the fighting forces. How one man could ever be expected to run a factory, design dirigibles, aeroplanes, and other such machines, in addition to instructing soldiers in the art of aerial warfare, is somewhat of a mystery, but Colonel Capper made an attempt that has gone a long way towards laying the foundation of what we hope will in time develop into the finest military equipment in the world. Now that the two departments have been separated, each should progress apace; it is, as we have mentioned, only necessary to look from the roadside to see that developments have already taken place since Mr Mervyn O'Gorman's accession to the office of superintendent of the factory.'[54]

There is no doubt that 'O'G' was one of the most important figures in the development of aviation in Britain, and set it on a path of sound science and engineering. Not only was he talented himself and filled with an abounding energy, he had the gift for choosing good subordinates and gaining their loyalty. One of the most successful of his recruitments was F.M. Green, who became chief engineer in January 1910.

The Royal Navy's First Airship

Meanwhile, in February 1909, the Committee of Imperial Defence had recommended that £35,000 should be spent on a rigid airship project for the Royal Navy in order to ascertain what its full potential might be; as had been done a few years before in respect of experimental submarines, while the army should concentrate on non-rigid airships for which £10,000 was allocated, and that the development of aeroplanes should be left in the hands of private enterprise.[55] This was a triumph for Captain Bacon, who had been under the direct instructions of the First Sea Lord, Admiral Sir John Fisher, whose aim had been to secure this funding. It also represented a degree of success for General Nicholson, as some of the impetus for army aviation was kicked into the long grass. Haldane would bide his time. The naval airship order was announced in parliament by Reginald McKenna, the First Lord of the Admiralty, in March 1909:

'The question of the use of dirigible airships for naval purposes has been under consideration for some time and it has been decided to carry out experiments and construct an aerial vessel.'[56]

It was noted in the report of the Committee of Imperial Defence that captive balloons and, to a lesser extent, kites, had for many years formed a part of the regular equipment of all modern armies. Great progress with regard to dirigible balloons, particularly in France and Germany in recent years, was remarked upon. With regard to the future use of dirigibles in naval warfare, reliability; ease of mooring; endurance; speed relative to surface vessels; sufficient crew accommodation to allow relief personnel to be carried; a wireless telegraphy set and navigational facilities, were considered as essential. It was added that accurate sights had been obtained by officers at Barrow, using a German bubble artificial horizon device fitted to an aeronautical sextant. The principal use was advocated as scouting and fleet protection at a much lower unit cost than a 3rd Class cruiser or a destroyer. The utility of an airship for dropping explosive devices was considered as unproven. The future use of fixed-wing aeroplanes was also thought to be unproven, particularly with regard to mechanical reliability, carrying capacity, the ability to operate at height and to fly in unfavourable weather. It was also thought that the endurance of aeroplanes would be affected by the physical strain on the 'driver'. Future combat between airships and aeroplanes was also considered, it being decided that there was no concrete proof at this point as to which would prevail.[57]

On 7 May a tender from Vickers was accepted.

A construction shed was built at Cavendish Dock, Barrow-in-Furness, and it was agreed that the design would be by a consortium of naval officers and Vickers engineers. It must have seemed a very promising career path to Neville Usborne, being taken out of the midst of his generation of officers to take part in a project supported by the First Sea Lord. As well as Murray Sueter, who was in command, and Usborne, the third member of the naval team in the early days was Chief Artificer Engineer A. Sharpe, RN. They were joined later by Commander Oliver Schwann, RN, as Assistant Inspecting Captain of Airships, Lieutenant C.P. Talbot, RN, and Engineer-Lieutenant C.R.J. Randall, RN. The Vickers technical team was controlled by Charles G. Robertson, the Marine Manager at Barrow, who had no prior, 'experience of aeronautics, nor of the light structural work involved'.[58] One of his senior assistants was the mathematician, H.B. Pratt, who calculated the airship in its final configuration was not strong enough to bear the load that would be imposed on it; his advice was ignored. There was little technical knowledge available; therefore construction was very much on trial and error lines. It was a highly ambitious project, with a length of 512 feet (155 metres) and a beam of 48 feet (15 metres); it was as large as any of the Zeppelins constructed so far. Its frame was made of forty transverse twelve-sided rings, each connected by twelve longitudinals. Beneath the frame was a triangular keel with an amidships cabin. Inside the framework were seventeen

HMA No 1 under
construction at Barrow.

gasbags filled with hydrogen and which had a total gas capacity of 700,000 cubic feet (19,810 cubic metres), each had two valves (of Parseval design) at the top, one automatic, the other manual. They were manufactured by Short Brothers of rubberised fabric imported from Germany. The framework was to be fabricated from an entirely new and untried aluminium alloy, Duralumin, which offered the strength of steel at one third of the weight, and which had been developed in Germany and introduced only very recently. Vickers had considerable difficulty in working it. Originally, the internal bracing wires were also made from Duralumin, but repeated breakages during construction meant they had to be replaced with steel. The silk outer skin, which was waterproofed using an aluminium-based dope, was silver grey on the upper half and yellow below; in order to make the topside as far as possible a non-conductor of heat and so minimise the effect of the sun's rays on the expansion of the gas, while encouraging the conduction of heat underneath to facilitate the equalisation of temperature between the gas and the surrounding atmosphere. Streamlining was employed with the main body being cylindrical, tapering towards the somewhat blunter nose and tail. Four stabilising fins (two vertical and two horizontal), two sets of quadruplane rudders and two sets of triplane elevators were mounted at the stern. The control surfaces were not hinged, but used Short's Reversible Patent Aerocurve, which flexed. There was a further elevator under the bows and another rudder to the rear of the aftermost of the two underslung cars, made from mahogany sewn with copper wire and which were connected by a gangway. The original idea was for a long-range scouting and gunnery direction platform to assist the main battle fleet, equipped with wireless telegraphy (WT) which was as much in its infancy as aviation. There was some discussion concerning the possibility of arming the airship with 'locomotive torpedoes.'[59] From an early date, officers of the Royal Navy had been interested in the possibility of using aircraft to deliver torpedoes. This was recorded in Air Publication 1344, *History of the Development of Torpedo Aircraft*:

'In the early part of 1911 many discussions concerning the use of torpedo aircraft took place amongst our Naval Officers, Captain Murray Sueter, RN, Lieutenant N.F. Usborne, RN, Lieutenant Hyde-Thomson, and Lieutenant L'Estrange Malone, RN, were amongst those who were particularly interested in this subject. It will be remembered that at that time aircraft were entirely in their infancy; they could hardly carry a passenger, and the idea of carrying a large weight was almost incomprehensible; their use as a weapon was only vaguely discernible. The rigid airship *Mayfly* was at this time being constructed at Barrow, and the naval officers under Captain Sueter, RN, employed on this work, frequently discussed the prospects of torpedo aircraft. The possibilities were vividly represented by the late Commander N.F. Usborne, RN.'[60]

Captain Murray Sueter, who was described subsequently as, 'a brave new warrior of the machine age who had gone, with enthusiasm, from working on submarines and torpedoes, to flying machines and motor vehicles,'[61] was appointed Inspecting Captain of Airships, to oversee the design and production of the airship, and so assembled a team of technically minded and promising officers.

The aviation press reported on 30 July 1910:

'Secrecy at Barrow. EXTRAORDINARY care is being taken at Barrow-in-Furness to ensure that no details with regard to the big naval dirigible under construction there shall leak out. The shed is closely guarded by Marines and only those employed on the work are allowed to enter. It is said that recently a man was found inside the barricade, and, on being taken to the police court, was sentenced to two months imprisonment, although it was not suggested that he was a spy.'[62]

A report has survived covering the period from 26 September 1910 to January 1912, when Lieutenant Usborne served under Sueter. He was appointed to HMS *Hermione* for Naval Airship No 1. *Hermione* was a small 2nd Class cruiser which was intended to act as a sea going depot ship for the airship, which was going to be named *Hermione*, but is better remembered now by the nickname bestowed upon it – *Mayfly*. HMS *Hermione* proceeded from Portsmouth to Barrow in September 1910 under conditions of great secrecy – as indeed was all work in the airship shed. Sueter made a significant entry in the ship's logbook on 25 October:

'Airship Officer of the Day is to keep herein a careful record of all work carried out in connection with the airship. Lt Usborne is to generally supervise what is entered to ensure that the record is accurate.'[63]

Sueter's later report stated:

'He has conducted himself with sobriety and to my entire satisfaction. A very zealous and capable officer, he has worked hard in making himself an expert in aeronautical work and has considerable knowledge in this line. I have strongly recommended Lieutenant Usborne for promotion. He was selected as captain of Naval Airship No 1.'[64]

According to a contemporary and more senior officer, Usborne made many useful technical contributions. Indeed, he applied for Aeronautical Patent 6150 'Dirigible Airships' in 1910, which concerned a system to conserve, as a buoyancy aid, the water vapour given off in the process of the combustion of petrol and air.[65] Commander E.A.D. Masterman went on to write:

'He would then have been about twenty-seven years of age, close on his half-stripe as Lieutenant Commander RN. It is no exaggeration to say that of that collection of officers, many of whom were brother torpedo men, his was the outstanding personality. Nothing was decided without his advice and few things undertaken of which he disapproved. His was the knowledge, slight though it now appears, for undertaking the construction of a rigid airship larger then any existing, his the brain and the ingenuity in overcoming unforeseen obstacles and his the drive which he continually brought to bear on Messrs Vickers when the firm demanded time to set matters going and on anyone else connected with the progress of the great experiment. He was the expert and revelled in so being.'[66]

What was he like? Masterman stated:

'In appearance he was rather below normal size, a slightly prominent nose, blue eyes, sandy coloured hair and very forcible expression. He hardly ever spoke without emphasis. He had a dominating personality with a vital spark, most difficult to withstand in argument. Not sparing of others, but himself prepared to do as much, or more, than he demanded of them. He was interested in spiritualism, socialism and new thought, music and motor bikes. He was abstemious in his pleasures, very self-disciplined, lived for work, talked, thought and dreamt airships, kept himself very fit. He indulged in 'height training', climbing to high parts of the shed or scaffolding and making perilous walks.'[67]

Lt Cdr N.F. Usborne about 1913 or 1914.

Developments elsewhere while Naval Airship No 1 was under construction

In April 1909 the Parliamentary Aerial Defence Committee was formed to exert pressure upon the government to improve the measures and resources provided for the aerial defence of the nation. An early result of its effectiveness, but not necessarily its sound judgement, was announced in June 1909:

'AIRSHIPS FOR THE NATION.

'In connection with the combined efforts of the *Morning Post, Daily Mail*, and the Parliamentary Aerial Defence Committee to provide the nation with the beginning, at least, of a fleet of airships, we summarise the chief items of the information which has been made public regarding the projects in hand. The new *Clément-Bayard* airship, on which the Parliamentary Committee has secured a month's option, is to be about twice the size of its predecessor. According to Mr Arthur Du Cros, MP, the Secretary of the Committee, the length of the envelope will be 300 feet, and the cubic capacity about 227,500 cubic feet. This should provide for the carrying of twenty-five passengers, but during the trip which it is proposed to make from Paris to London, probably only six will be on board, consisting of M Clément, Mr Arthur Du Cros, and the crew of four. This, however, is not definitely settled, except so far as relates to the crew, which will include the pilot, two helmsmen – one for the elevating planes and one for the rudder – and the engineer. Instead of a single engine and propeller, as in *Clément-Bayard No I*, the new vessel will have two propellers, one on each side of the hull, and each will be driven by a motor of 220 hp. Sufficient petrol can be carried to enable the airship to travel 700 miles, and it is capable of ascending to a height of 6,000 feet. The vessel is still only in sections, but the work of completing her is being pushed on as fast as possible and it is hoped that she will be ready to make the trip to London at the end of August. Since he made his first trip in the original airship last October, it has been a cherished wish of M Clément to be the first man to visit London from abroad by airship. Although he had not contemplated remaining with his vessel in Great Britain for more than a few days, in view of the offer from the proprietors of the *Daily Mail* to provide a shed for the accommodation of the airship, he has readily acquiesced in the suggestion that he should remain for a month, so as to give as great an opportunity as possible for Members of Parliament and government officials to make themselves thoroughly acquainted with its possibilities. On one day, too, the general public will be enabled to see the airship, for the Aerial League have arranged with Mr Arthur Du Cros to have it on exhibition for that period. With regard to the shed for the airship, towards the cost of which the *Daily Mail* have so generously supplied £5,000, Mr Herbert Ellis has been entrusted with the work of designing it, and he has visited France in order to make himself acquainted with the sheds already erected there. M. Clément's own shed is constructed of galvanized iron lined with cork, so as to keep the temperature fairly even both in summer and winter. He suggests that the dimensions of the building should be 300 feet long, 90 feet high and 75 feet wide. With regard to a site for the shed, the War Office have had under consideration the question of providing this, and both Farnborough and Salisbury Plain have been suggested as possible locations, but it is hoped that a suitable piece of land may be obtained nearer London.'[68]

The *Daily Mail* in fact raised £6000 for the construction of an airship shed at Wormwood Scrubs, on land provided by the War Office and a private donation of £5000, in what might be described as a fit of misguided, patriotic enthusiasm, had enabled the ordering and purchase of an airship from the French Clément-Bayard Airship Co.

On 19 February 1910, in the House of Commons, the Secretary of State for War, R.B. Haldane, made the customary speech introducing the army estimates for the forthcoming year. He took the opportunity to clarify the government's policy with regard to aviation:

'I want now to say a word about dirigibles and aeronautics. The aeronautical department at the National Physical Laboratory got to work almost at once after it was set up last year, and since then it has been found necessary to increase its staff, and the work at Teddington is in full swing. We have also reorganised the construction department at Aldershot, which used to be under the care of Colonel Capper, who did remarkably good work. We want Colonel Capper's great abilities, however, for the training of officers and men at the Balloon School, and for the work which he has hitherto done we have got hold of a man of great capacity and high eminence, Mr O'Gorman, who is very well known in connection with the construction, not only of motor engines, but other subjects connected with motoring. Mr O'Gorman has now organised a construction department at Aldershot. The next step we propose to take – and we have already decided on its lines – is to substitute for the present corps a regular aeronautical corps, such as exists in Germany, separate from any other corps in the army, devoted to aeronautics. The Balloon School will become the training school for that corps. I am convinced that until we get everything perfectly clear we shall only make very slow progress. The results of the investigations of the committee presided over by Lord Rayleigh are now being used for the designs we are now engaged upon. At present we have one small dirigible at Aldershot, designed by Colonel Capper, (*Baby/Beta*) which so far has been doing well, and two more are coming from France. There is the *Clément-Bayard*, the negotiations for which have been undertaken by the Aeronautical Committee of the House, and, if they are satisfactory, it is not impossible that the War Office may purchase it. There is also the Lebaudy, which, through the patriotism of the *Morning Post*, has been offered to us. It is coming over before long. We are also working on designs of a large dirigible of our own (*Gamma*) which I hope will be completed, certainly commenced, in the course of the financial year. Then, of course, there is the great naval dirigible, which is rapidly approaching completion at Barrow, and which, I believe, will be launched in the summer. As soon as we have made ourselves masters of the lessons which these teach, we shall go on working at the construction of other dirigibles and shall be in a position of having a fleet. The whole subject is in its infancy. I am never alarmed by reading about the progress of other nations in this respect. Already much of the material possessed by foreign nations is being found to be unsatisfactory, and I have not very much fear that if we put our backs to it we shall find ourselves ahead.'[69]

It was reported in *The Times* of 7 April 1910, that Lieutenant Neville Usborne, 'who had been superintending the construction of the naval dirigible,' had travelled from Barrow to Paris and would return in the *Clément-Bayard* airship, taking charge of navigation as soon as the vessel was over British soil. In May it was noted that he was still in France attending the trials.[70] Furthermore, Captain Bacon warned him that when crossing the Channel on no account should any mock attacks be made on any of His Majesty's ships they might fly over.[71] Sadly, delays to the programme foiled this plan, no doubt to Usborne's great disappointment, as he had first been given the Admiralty's permission to travel to France in connection with the airship project as early as September 1909.[72]

On 16 October 1910, the first airship flight from France to the UK was made by Baudry's *Clément-Bayard II* from La Motte-Breuil to Wormwood Scrubs, some 246 miles (398 km) at an average speed of 41mph (64kph). The craft had a length of 251 feet (76 metres), a diameter of 43 feet (13 metres) and a capacity of 247,200 cubic feet (7000 cubic metres), being powered by two 120 hp (90 kW) Clément-Bayard engines. A photograph of the airship's arrival graced the front cover of *Flight* Magazine of 22 October 1910 with the caption:

'PARIS TO LONDON BY AIRSHIP.—The arrival of the *Clément-Bayard* airship at Wormwood Scrubs on Sunday last. Note the sand ballast being thrown out in order to check too rapid a descent in landing. The military helpers are seen in the distance in readiness to receive the airship immediately it arrives within reach.'

The *Clément-Bayard II* lands at Wormwood Scrubs.

The airship thereafter was a complete disaster; it had already made more than forty ascents in France, the envelope leaked badly and an argument over payment with the manufacturers ensued. Eventually, half of the originally agreed price of £25,000 was paid. She was dismantled and taken to Farnborough, never to fly again. Had she done so she would have been re-named *Zeta*.[73] The War Office had announced to the House of Commons certain requirements which it desired *Clément-Bayard II* to meet. These throw light on what was then considered to be the ideal airship for military purposes and are reproduced in Appendix 4.

Not to be outdone, a rival newspaper, the august *Morning Post*, organised in its columns a National Fund which raised £18,000 to acquire a second French airship, from Lebaudy-Frères of Soissons, announcing the success of this venture on 21 July 1909 and described as, 'a real war-type of dirigible, than which no more up-to-date model exists throughout the world.'[74] (Paul and Pierre Lebaudy, together with the engineer Henri Julliot, had been building airships since 1902, including the first dirigible supplied to the French Army in 1906, to which three more had been added by 1909, including *République*, which was the first to be used by the French Army on manoeuvres.)

The *Morning Post Lebaudy* first flew in France in August, at which time Colonel Capper and a *Daily Mail* journalist, Hamilton Fyfe, were up in her.[75] When she arrived on 26 October 1910, she was the largest airship to have been seen in Britain to that date; being 337 feet (102 metres) long, with a diameter of 39 feet (12 metres), a capacity of 353,000 cubic feet (9990 cubic metres) and was powered by twin 135 hp (100 kW) Panard engines, which gave a top speed of 34mph (55kph). In fact helpful winds on its Channel crossing, with a crew of seven, enabled it to average 36mph (58kph). One of those on board was Major Sir Alexander Bannerman, RE, 'a stout, moustached, dyed-in-the-wool

The Lebaudy airship arrives at Farnborough on 26 October 1910. (*Via Ces Mowthorpe*)

officer'[76] who had succeeded Capper at the Balloon School a fortnight earlier, despite knowing little about airships or aeroplanes, but possessing, 'a certain amount of practical experience in ordinary gasbag ballooning,'[77] and an absolute belief that attack from the air would be a hit and miss affair, with the likelihood that not one bomb in 10,000, from a height of 5000 feet (1524 metres), would hit a battleship.[78] In the opinion of one aviation historian:

> 'The War Office attitude was demonstrated still further in its treatment of the purely military Balloon School. Colonel Capper retained his post until he became due to promotion from brevet to substantive rank on 7 October 1910. The War Office refused to let him continue as commandant at this higher rank, but instead downgraded the post to that of major, and appointed Major Sir Alexander Bannerman as his successor.'[79]

Colonel John Capper (1861–1955) became the Commandant of the Royal School of Military Engineering at Chatham, so removing an air expert with a worldwide reputation from direct involvement in military aviation. He served throughout the First World War as a Corps Chief Engineer, Divisional Commander and Director General Tank Corps, attaining the rank of major general and a knighthood.

The Lebaudy was no more successful than the *Clément-Bayard II*. Unbeknown to the authorities at Farnborough, the designers had increased the height of the airship, with the result that as it was being walked into its specially built shed, the envelope caught on the roof and suffered a serious tear. (This is described in full in Appendix 5.) Repairs (and alterations to the shed) took several months. When it flew again in May of the following year, with a French test crew in control and Major Bannerman in attendance, all went well at first, with Cody and Geoffrey de Havilland circling around the airship in their aeroplanes. But after about an hour in the air it proved to be unmanageable, and it descended and crashed out of control, tearing down telegraph poles and uprooting railings in its path, and in front of a large crowd which had come to watch the spectacle, luckily without killing or badly injuring anyone.[80] After another Franco-British argument the airship was scrapped. So ended: 'A sad and ridiculous chapter in British aeronautical history.'[81] R.B. Haldane may well have been tempted to say, 'I told you so' as the two debacles certainly vindicated his view of a measured scientific approach as opposed to buying something foreign off the shelf just because it was there.

A purely civilian enterprise had much greater success, as on 4 November 1910, E.T. Willows and Frank Gooden made the first crossing of the English Channel by a British aircraft in the Willows No 3 *City of Cardiff*, which was

120 feet (36 metres) long, 23 feet (7 metres) in diameter and with a capacity of 32,000 cubic feet (905 cubic metres). Departing from Wormwood Scrubs they crossed to Douai, where they force-landed. The airship was deflated and repaired at the Clément-Bayard works and then flew to Paris on 7 January 1911, where it undertook a number of passenger-carrying flights:

'The Willows Trip to France.

'In view of the way in which foreign aviators are treated when they happen to land on British soil, it is instructive to note the treatment meted out by our neighbours across the Channel when a Britisher happens to land there. On Mr Willows coming down at Corbehem, near Douai, in order to discover his whereabouts, he was rather surprised when three gendarmes mounted guard over his ship, and an officer demanded the payment of about £30 Customs duty. Matters were eventually smoothed out by the Aero Club of France, who explained that the incident arose simply owing to the fact that notice had not been given to the Customs authorities, who were bound to act as they did. The airship was brought out from the *Daily Mail* garage at Wormwood Scrubs on Friday afternoon, and, with Mr E.T. Willows piloting her, assisted by Mr W. Gooden in charge of the engines, a start was made at 3.25 pm. Steering straight across London, the aeronaut then made for Bexhill, and at 6.35 the English coast was left behind. Two hours later the French coast was in sight. At 10 o'clock the vessel was taken to a height of 5,500 feet, in order to enable Mr Willows to steer by the stars, as the clouds prevented him picking out the places passed over. Later, the weather became very foggy, and at 2 o'clock in the morning Mr Willows decided to bring his craft down. Mr Willows had no idea where he was, but when the two aeronauts had got the machine on

Willows No 3.
(*Via Patrick Abbott*)

the ground safely anchored they found a peasant and sent him off to the village to get help. The framework of the car was somewhat damaged in the landing. M Breguet, whose flying ground at La Brayelle is not far off, motored over to render what aid he could to Mr Willows, and afterwards, when making a second visit, he flew over in his aeroplane. Mr Willows had intended, after repairing his machine, to complete the journey to Issy, and a large crowd gathered there on Sunday afternoon to welcome him. The weather conditions, however, changed in the meantime, so that Mr Willows deemed it advisable not to go on. He therefore had his balloon deflated, packed up and sent to Issy by rail, where it found a temporary home in M Clément's dirigible shed.'[82]

Willows himself was hopeful that the government would support his efforts by ordering an airship from him. The venture had at least raised his public profile and increased his expertise in airship handling. He was reported in the press as commenting, 'Of course, I have obtained experience which would be of great value in training men in the handling of small dirigibles and by this means the best results are obtained afterwards in the handling of the larger class. This, I think, is the lesson to be learned from the numerous disasters to the Zeppelins.'[83]

Meanwhile, the army's airship men had been making some progress. The unsuccessful *Baby* had been transformed into the Dirigible IIa, soon renamed *Beta*, which had been completed in February 1910. It is worth noting that in this month a survey noted that there were twenty-six airworthy airships in the world, fourteen in Germany, five in France, two in Italy, and one each in Great Britain, Austria-Hungary, Belgium, Russia and the USA.[84] *Beta's* envelope was that of the *Baby* increased in length by 20 feet (6 metres) and it now had a volume of 35,000 cubic feet (990 cubic metres). The car was composed of a long frame, having a centre compartment for the crew and engine. The 35 hp (26 kW) Green engine was retained in an improved form, driving two wooden two-bladed propellers by chains. *Beta* was fitted with an unbalanced rudder, while the elevators were in the front of the frame. A contemporary account described it as being many times larger than its predecessor, having the appearance of a fish and being coloured dead chrome-yellow from end to end. The reporter judged that it appeared to be thoroughly under control from the moment of its ascent, throughout an hour-long flight in the vicinity of Farnborough until it returned to its shed, which no doubt would have gratified the aeronaut in charge, Colonel Capper, assisted by Captain King, Mr Green and Mr McQuade, the Works Manager.[85] Further test flights were made in March by Captain Carden and

Beta – the pilot's seat and controls. (*Via Nigel Caley*)

Lieutenant Waterlow, which encouraged thoughts of a longer voyage.[86] In this they were successful. On 3–4 June 1910, they flew to London and back during the hours of darkness, with a crew consisting of Colonel Capper, Lieutenant Waterlow and Mr T.J. Ridge of the Balloon Factory, taking about three and a half hours for the round trip; the first night flight:

'The ascent was made at 11.40 pm and the course was set by the stars. When the main London and South-Western railway line was reached, the airship followed the metals until the Brooklands motor track at Weybridge was reached. Then a straight line to St Paul's was taken, the Thames being crossed three times in its windings. The first crossing at Thames Ditton, the second near Hurlingham and the third near Battersea Park. The dome of St Paul's was circled and the return journey, with a following wind, was made at top speed, between 25 and 30 miles an hour. The main London to Portsmouth road was struck at Hounslow and proved a splendid guide to the aeronauts, who followed it through Staines and Sunninghill to Farnborough.'[87]

The flight was followed on the ground by the Balloon Factory's Chief Draughtsman and Chief Mechanical Engineer in a motor car – but so rapid was the progress made by *Beta* that they lost sight of the airship not long after it departed from Farnborough Common. Harry Harper was offered a flight in *Beta* one afternoon:

Beta I in 1910.
*(Museum of
Army Flying)*

'Clad in a suit of overalls which had been lent me, I was given the task of keeping the log of the trip, being provided with an official logbook for the purpose, and a stub of pencil.

'The engineer crouched in a tiny seat just behind his noisy motor. We other two, the skipper and myself, were poised perilously on a little railed platform, which had two or three boards stretched across a metal frame to form its floor. There was no support of any kind to grip at save a couple of flimsy handrails which, as soon as the engine began running fast, vibrated so much that one could scarcely hold them. The platform too shook violently, and the whole affair was distinctly intimidating.'[88]

As Harper tried to keep his mind on the task of entering engine data, height and course, his hands, face and the pages of the logbook became covered in a thin film of oil blown back from the engine. Worse was to follow:

'We began to encounter a gusty, bumpy wind. The little airship began to make bad weather of it, like a small yacht in a rough sea. Up she went at the bow and then down again with a sickening lurch. Then she would roll and give a sort of uneasy wobble. All the time I was clinging for dear life to that bleak exposed platform, trying to prevent myself looking down apprehensively through the cracks in the floorboards.'[89]

He noted that he was very glad to return to earth, that he had managed to complete all the log entries required and that *Beta* made a good landing despite the bumpy conditions.

Gamma – the control position. (*Via Nigel Caley*)

Beta was followed by *Gamma*, which first took to the air for a 50 minute flight on 2 February 1910 in the capable hands of Capper and Waterlow. Her rubber-proofed fabric envelope had a capacity of 75,000 cubic feet (2122 cubic metres), with an 80 hp (59 kW) Green engine in the extended car driving swivelling propellers, the gears and shafts of which were made by Rolls-Royce. The engine drove the propeller shafts direct, one from each end of the crankshaft, allowing a top speed of 30mph (48kph). The engine gave some teething problems to begin with, but in March, Captain Carden and Lieutenant Waterlow carried out a series of successful test flights.[90] *Gamma* was badly damaged in a spring gale while moored out at Farnborough, but she was fully repaired, so leading to the following report in June 1910:

Gamma or *The Yellow Peril* in 1910. (*Museum of Army Flying*)

'*Gamma* Out Again. Having had the damage sustained during the recent gale repaired, the army airship *Gamma* was out for a trial run on Saturday afternoon. Piloted by Lieutenant Broke-Smith, RE, with Lieutenants Cammell and Reynolds, and Mr Green, as crew, the dirigible manoeuvred successfully over Farnborough Common for forty minutes. The only incident was the stampeding of some horses belonging to the Oxford University Territorials, which were apparently frightened by the whirr of the motor as it passed over them.'[91]

Not long afterwards, the airships received a visit from King George V and Queen Mary, which was described as follows:

'Army Airships Inspected by the King and Queen. On Monday afternoon, during the time HM the King was at Aldershot, the two army airships, *Beta* and *Gamma* were taken out and cruised over from Farnborough. The former then returned to her shed, where she was closely examined by His Majesty, who rode over from the camp. The Queen, who had motored over to Farnborough to see the dirigibles, also had the mechanism of *Beta* explained. *Gamma* had some little engine trouble, and descended at Crookham, but later returned to the balloon factory. On Wednesday afternoon both airships were out, *Gamma* cruising over the vicinity of Guildford, while *Beta* started off from Farnborough in the direction of Bournemouth.'[92]

Beta made another visit to London in July, this time in daylight, crewed by Lieutenant Broke-Smith, Lieutenant T.J. Ridge of the London Balloon Company, RE (Territorials), and Sergeant Ramsey, RE. (This was the first Territorial Force air unit and was in existence for five years from 1908 until 1913. Ridge was also the assistant superintendent of the Balloon Factory.) This time navigation was by map and compass, and slow progress was made against a stiff headwind. An average height of 1500 feet (457 metres) was maintained and the conditions were smooth, apart from cross currents encountered over the Thames valley. Once over the city, large crowds stared upwards at the graceful sight as *Beta* passed over the City of London, the Strand and the Houses of Parliament. The return trip was accomplished at a speed of 35mph (56kph) and, as there was petrol to spare, a detour was made to fly a circuit over the Royal Pavilion at Aldershot, being watched from the windows by King George and Queen Mary. On landing back at Farnborough, the airship's crew were greeted by cheers from the crowd assembled on the common.[93] Later, *Beta* had a minor mishap, making a forced landing near Andover due to a broken crankshaft. The inherent safety of the airship was demonstrated, as a safe descent was made into a field near a farmyard. Farnborough was speedily advised of the difficulty, and spare parts and mechanics were dispatched by motor car. Soldiers were summoned from nearby Tidworth and *Beta* was transported to a local foundry, where repairs were effected during the night, so allowing *Beta* to proceed to Bournemouth the next day.[94] Not long afterwards permission was given, with some reluctance, in case that it would frighten the troop horses, for both aeroplanes[95] and airships to take part in the army manoeuvres of September 1910, to be held on Salisbury Plain. Instructions were issued:

'As this is the first occasion on which aeroplanes and dirigible balloons have been employed in this country for military work, their employment is largely a matter of experiment; and as the science of aerial navigation is still in its infancy, unreal conditions, which would not obtain in war, must be observed for the safety of the aeronauts and their machines.' [96]

Given the propensity of troops of the BEF in August 1914 to fire off volleys of musketry at any passing aircraft without waiting to ascertain if it was friend or foe, this was probably timely advice. *Beta's* contribution to the manoeuvres was recorded thus:

'*Beta* at the Manoeuvres. On Saturday afternoon the army airship *Beta* returned to Farnborough after a week's scouting in connection with the manoeuvres at Salisbury. On the previous Monday she sailed over to Salisbury, commanded by Colonel J.E. Capper, RE, and scouted for the "enemy" during the afternoon. A slight mishap with the engines kept her "confined to barracks" on Tuesday, but on Wednesday, Thursday, and Friday, practically the whole of Somerset, Dorset and Wiltshire were covered during reconnoitring operations, going as far west as the Bristol Channel, in all about 1000 miles, and the observations taken are reported to be most accurate.'[97]

Though *Beta* was officially neutral, not being part of either the East Land or West Land forces, Capper and his crew were able to watch the troops of both the divisions, to bring despatches, and to communicate with Lieutenant General Sir Horace Smith-Dorrien, KCB, KCMG, DSO, the C-in-C of Aldershot Command. [Smith-Dorrien was more open-minded than many senior officers; he was sure that 'aerial machines' would play an important part in future wars and stated at a meeting of the Aldershot Military Society, on 22 February 1910, that, 'we soldiers must take every opportunity of studying all there is to be learned on the subject'.] The airship passed over the headquarters' staff, where the officers were able to exchange information and convey from the car of the dirigible a sketch-map of the position of the forces as seen from the airship. *Beta* spent several nights moored out in the open, under the shelter of trees or in quarries. Mobile support was provided by one of the old ballooning gas trains drawn by a traction engine. On one occasion she was in the air for seven and three-quarter hours without landing, carrying a crew of three. She has been described as; 'The first truly efficient British service airship.'[98] Some senior officers were impressed, General Sir John French, 'spoke of the keen practical attention with which all far-seeing military authorities had taken up aviation'.[99] Others were much less so, the Chief of the Imperial General Staff, General Sir W.G. Nicholson, GCB, ADC, RE, who although a talented administrator and a sapper himself, 'was of the opinion that aviation was a useless and expensive fad, advocated by a few cranks whose ideas were unworthy of attention'.[100] [By 1911 it should be noted that Nicholson had changed his opinion and acknowledged that aircraft would play a part in the next war, 'whenever it may come'.] A national Sunday newspaper did not mince its words:

'The trouble at the War Office with regard to aviation is not Major Sir Alexander Bannerman, it is essentially due to the presence at the War Office of an engineer officer of exalted rank, who is not merely frigid towards aviation, but is even violently opposed to the idea that it has any military value. It is unfortunate that a man with such ideas should happen to be in a position in which he is able to place obstacles in the way of every suggested forward step.'[101]

General Nicholson's was a voice and personality of great influence in Whitehall, and was singularly intolerant of anyone whose views opposed his. Nor were some of the naval hierarchy any more keen on establishing command of the air, as an anonymous admiral commented; 'I do not say we do not wish to do so, but I think we will be forced to do so.'[102]

They would be even less enthusiastic about sharing any co-operation on matters of aviation with the army.

Meanwhile, the French army had also staged its annual manoeuvres in the autumn of 1910, making use of eight fixed-wing aircraft of various types and four airships, *Liberté*, *Clément-Bayard*, *Colonel Renard* and *Zodiac*. One of the airship pilots of those halcyon days before the war recalled:

'There were many adventures in the days of the early army airships, but there were no serious accidents and there was no loss of life. Engine breakdowns were not unusual and other failures occurred, such as the propeller chains snapping, the elevators jamming, valves sticking, or fittings coming adrift owing to vibration. Very frequently defects were remedied in the air, whilst the airship drifted free; this sometimes necessitated one of the crew crawling out along the frame, or onto an outrigger, to effect adjustments.'[103]

Sometimes the drifting plan could be a little dangerous, as on one foggy day when *Beta*, having just regained the use of her engine, very narrowly avoided coming into collision with the spire of Salisbury Cathedral. On another occasion, as they passed noiselessly over a cricket match, the batsman stared upwards at the airship and lost his middle stump to the bowler who was concentrating on the matter in hand. Broke-Smith also reflected on the methods adopted when a forced-landing was required; the airship would alight in a sheltered spot, protected from the wind and weather, the grapnel being hooked onto a handy hedge or tree, and assistance would then be summoned from Farnborough. The technique of emergency landings became regarded as a matter of routine.

On 4 October, Colonel Capper addressed a meeting of the Women's Aerial League with an illustrated lecture on airships and aeroplanes. He expressed considerable dismay regarding what he saw as the apathy of Britain as regards the conquest of the air, when compared to the drive and enthusiasm shown on the Continent and in America. He believed that aerial expertise was vital to national interests and urged the women of Britain to wake their men up to, 'the realities of the matter, as men would do anything for the women.' He predicted that in future, aerial navigation would be common and that all wars would begin with the conquest of the air, which might result in making war so terrible a proposition for the population that peace would be the outcome.[104]

Also in October, the War Office announced that the air branch of the army would be expanded and that the Balloon School would be reconstituted. Flying in heavier-than-air machines would be included and officers from all arms would be encouraged. In November the Secretary of State for War, R.B. Haldane, visited Farnborough and was taken for a flight in *Beta* by Captain Broke-Smith. The minister arrived dressed as for Parliament in his top hat and had to be persuaded that this was not really appropriate flying gear and put on a borrowed flat cap instead.

Later in the year it was decided to purchase a new 110,000 cubic feet (3113 cubic metre) envelope for *Gamma*, as the one in use was proving to be rather leaky. It was ordered from the Astra Airship Company in Paris. Flying began early in the New Year of 1911 and it was reported that:

'The army airship *Beta* made her reappearance on Tuesday last and carried out the first of a series of instructional trips in the neighbourhood of Farnborough. Captain Broke-Smith was in command, and he was accompanied by Major Sir Alexander Bannerman, Commandant of the Army Balloon Factory. A trip of some twenty-two miles was made, during which the little airship behaved splendidly. These trips will be continued at every available opportunity during the coming spring and summer for the purpose of instructing various officers in the science of aerial navigation.

'On Monday Mr Cody was out, and made several trips with passengers, including Major Sir Alexander Bannerman and Lieutenant Cammell. In one of these trips he chased after the *Beta* and succeeded in getting past her.

'On Tuesday the airship was under the control of a non-commissioned officer, whose work was supervised by Lieutenant Waterlow.'[105]

The report the following week contained an item of greater significance for the future use of airships, *Beta,* on the night of 27–28 January, was flown by Clive Waterlow, with Captain H.P.T. Lefroy, RE, manning the wireless apparatus:[106]

'*Beta* and Wireless Telegraphy. During the instructional cruise made by *Beta* on Saturday last, communication was kept up with headquarters at Farnborough by means of wireless telegraphy. The trip lasted for over

Beta was fitted with a wireless apparatus in 1911.

an hour, and, taking a southerly course, the airship was steered to within a few miles of Portsmouth before turning and making a wide westerly detour via Andover on the return journey to Farnborough.'[107]

Lefroy and Lieutenant R.A. Cammell had already undertaken wireless experiments while free ballooning in the *Andes* from Cove Common to Leatherhead in August 1910.

The success was slightly tempered by the fact that owing to the noise and interference, the engine had to be stopped to enable signals to be received. Lefroy recorded his thoughts on the experiment in his logbook:

'Petrol pipe on engine burst when half a mile from the Balloon Factory. I at once informed ASX (Aldershot wireless telegraphic station) of this and told him to try and let me know when the engine was not running. He at once started up, and I got very loud signals and read: All your signals good but ... and then the engine was off again and I lost the rest. Quite impossible to hear signals (when engine running so close) without any special device, such as soundproof helmet – could not even hear the test buzzer and barely hear the spark-gap; returned to factory and landed safely about 5.10 pm.'[108]

By February messages were being transmitted and received from *Beta* up to a range of 30 miles (48 kilometres). Not long afterwards the first Airship Pilot's Certificates were issued on 14 February 1911 by the Royal Aero Club. The holder of No 1 was Lieutenant Colonel Capper, No 2 was Captain P.W.L. Broke-Smith, No 3 was Lieutenant Clive Waterlow, No 4 was E.T. Willows and No 8 was Captain E.M. Maitland.

HM Airship No 1 Makes Her Debut

On 9 May 1911, Neville Usborne was elected a member of the Royal Aero Club of the United Kingdom (which had been founded in 1901 with the aim of 'encouraging aeronautics', and of which *Flight* magazine was the official organ, supplied weekly to members). Two weeks later Airship No 1 was taken from its shed by a ground party of 300 sailors in the early hours of 22 May, for handling and mooring trials. The logbook noted:

'At 4.18 am, airship clear of shed. Warped out to mooring post using capstan; capstan seized after a few minutes, hauled out the remainder of the way by hand, with assistance of propellers and of *Hermione*'s steam cutter. Secured to head of mooring post by bow wire, nose of ship close up

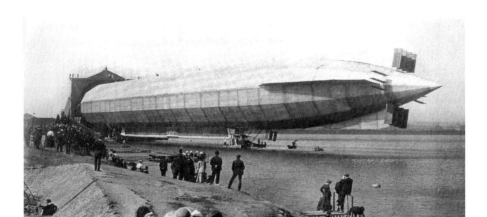

HMA No 1 brought out for first time on 22 May 1911. (*Huston Collection*)

to head of post. Wind light and variable. Ship riding lightly, but slewing through about sixty degrees relative to pontoon. Attempted to check this by securing the forward hauling down ropes. During one yaw of airship heard the flange of the channel bar (round which the port hauling down rope was secured) crack cast off hauling down ropes.'[109]

Extracting the airship from her exceedingly narrow shed was no easy matter and was described as being like drawing a cork from a bottle.[110] She was moored to a 38 foot (11.54 m) mast erected on a pontoon in Cavendish Dock. This was the first time a rigid airship had ever been made fast to a mast. By 10.00 am the wind had freshened and the slewing motion had become more intense:

'Started forward motor and used it intermittently to check the surge forward by running propellers astern. Used twenty feet on bow mooring wire to keep ship clear of yardarms, swinging increased greatly in violence, heavy jerks being experienced, but seeing no damage beyond slight straining of the bow framing. The forward motor overheating, the steam boat was used to keep the ship astern by a long grass line to the after gondola. The use of the motor was reserved for especially bad yaws.'[111]

Further measures were taken at 1.30 pm:

'Removed windscreen on mooring post, effect apparently very beneficial. Hung a boat's anchor, shackle of cable and 12 x 6 in projectiles from stern

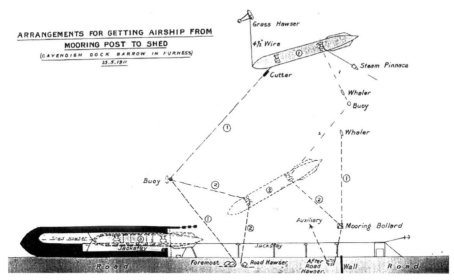

A diagram illustrating the procedure required to manoeuvre HMA No 1 back into its shed.

of pontoon to check it slewing, effect very good. Bossed airship close up to mooring post, yawing much reduced. Removed yards from mooring post.'[112]

The onlookers included *Flight* Magazine which announced; 'At last our leviathan of the air has emerged from its hiding place into the full light of day.' The author was in awe of the airship's size:

'Think of it! It would almost exactly fill St Martin's Lane from end to end and from side to side. It can carry twenty-two persons and has cost to date the sum of £41,000. More than an acre and a half of continental fabric was employed in the construction of the envelope, and the hydrogen, compressed in cylinders, was brought from the Knowles Oxygen Co's works at Wolverhampton by the train load at a time. Its constructors are the great firm of Vickers Ltd. The outer covers and gas ballonets were made by Messrs Short Bros, and the airship is fitted with their patent valves and rudders.'

The sailors' performance was also appreciated:

'One of the most striking sights in connection with the launch was the sudden appearance of sailors on the very top of the envelope, where there is a prepared gangway and access to which is obtained by means of a rope ladder through the centre of the envelope itself.'[113]

Vigilance during the hours of darkness was maintained with the aid of a searchlight which played upon the massive hull. The logbook noted on 23 May:

'Ship riding easily with very little yawing. Ran each engine thirty minutes, changing air tanks. Took in sixteen gallons of fresh water. Forward girder of transverse frame 14 slightly buckled; partly deflated bags 6 and 8 to bring them to same degree of fullness as bag 7, and to relieve above girder.'[114]

Further comments made the next day included:

'Ship riding easily, yawing very slight. Wind gradually decreased to Force 3. Took in 8000 cubic feet of hydrogen from bottles placed in cutter. Crew cleaning ship and undergoing instruction in starting up motors, trimming system, etc. Cast off steadying boats, the wind freshening and the boats causing much bumping of the gondolas and straining of hull.'[115]

The trials were successful in that the airship withstood winds of up to 45mph (72kph). Moreover, engine tests were conducted, and a considerable amount of handling experience and data was collected by the nine officers on board, their only complaint being that they had not been allowed to smoke! The Chairman and Directors of Vickers wrote to Captain Sueter on 24 May 1911 to congratulate him on the achievements so far:

'I am exceedingly pleased to receive your letter of this date, stating that we have established a world's record in building an airship which has successfully withstood the heavy gale of last night while moored in the open. The Chairman and Directors take this opportunity to heartily congratulate you on the successful launch of the ship, and likewise on the splendid well-thought-out arrangements made by yourself, resulting in her being so safely and satisfactorily moored. At the same time, it was felt that the heavy breeze during the first night after the launch must have given you a somewhat anxious time. I thank you on behalf of myself and our experts for your very kind observations which are, you can rest assured, greatly appreciated. Will you kindly permit me to place on record how very much we esteem the hearty collaboration of your good self and

your staff in the building of the first airship for the British Navy, and
to state how confident we are that a considerable amount of the success
which has been achieved is due to the invaluable assistance so readily
rendered at all times by yourself, your officers and your men.'

Yours sincerely,

J. McKechnie[116]

For obvious reasons the company was very keen to develop the best possible
relationship with the Royal Navy in general and with Murray Sueter in
particular; it was just as anxious as Sueter that the airship being constructed at
Barrow would merely be the first in a lucrative line of repeat contracts. Sueter
made repeated attempts to convince the First Lord of the Admiralty, Reginald
McKenna, that this should be the case, but was advised that the First Sea
Lord, Sir Arthur Wilson,[117] was very much against airships, believing that they
could easily be destroyed by a 'squib' fired by pistol from an aeroplane at close
range, or by means of a fishing line and hooks raked along the gasbag.[118] Indeed,
somewhat dishearteningly, he received more than one letter from Rear Admiral
Sir John Jellicoe, the Controller of the Navy and Third Sea Lord, during this
period, alerting him to the fact that others in high authority at the Admiralty
did not believe in airships.[119]

[Author's note: Wilson (1842–1921) won the VC at the battle of El Teb in
1884, but was not by nature inclined to favour technical progress, for example,
describing the early submarines as, 'underhand, unfair and damned un-English'.

Sueter praised Fisher and Jellicoe highly for their support, but had little time
for most of the other Sea Lords. He also felt that three First Lords of the
Admiralty had been particularly 'air-minded', the competent McKenna (1908–
1911), the mercurial Churchill (1911–1915) and the philosophical Arthur
Balfour (1915–16). On the other hand, Churchill, though a supporter of Sueter
and his dynamism, was not blind to his faults, writing to the First Sea Lord,
Prince Louis of Battenberg on 12 December 1912, 'Captain Sueter requires
supervision.'][120]

On 25 May, preparations were made to return the airship to its shed; the first
attempt at 5 am had to be abandoned due to the wind picking up. The crew tried
again in the afternoon, when the wind had abated:

'Airship slipped from mooring post; drifting towards northern bank
of dock. Steamboat made fast a line to starboard bow of airship to haul

her to northward, but could make very little impression. By using warp, forward propellers and the steamboat hauled airship clear. Airship then hauled over towards shed, using warp and propellers, rudders amidships. The airship's bows were hauled close in to the entrance of the shed, but with the wind being from her port bow to her port beam, considerable difficulty was experienced in getting the airship in line with the shed. The thwarts, specially strengthened, of the steadying boats, to which the shore hawsers were secured, started to pull out; spars were improvised from the shore hawsers to the heels of gondola struts, which averted the collapse of the boats and letting go of the hawsers. The force of the wind on her port side caused the ship to heel fifteen to twenty degrees to starboard. The stern of the ship was eventually, with much difficulty, hauled in line, and the ship secured to the jackstay, guys from the top of the ship got hold of, and the ship righted. The ship was then hauled along the jackstay into the shed, slight difficulty being caused by one or two jackstay outriggers being carried away. Airship housed in shed 3 pm, total damage, a hole in the forward gondola by wooden distance pieces of steadying boat.'[121]

But it soon became clear that HMA No 1 was overweight and incapable of static flight, even with the power provided by a pair of 200 hp (148kW) 8-cylinder Wolseley engines driving a pair of four-bladed propellers to port and starboard, and a twin-bladed propeller to the rear. Gross lift was estimated to be 19.665 long tons (44,048lbs/19,980kg), with the weight being 19.589 tons

Mayfly at Cavendish Dock. (*VSEL; now part of BAE Systems*)

(43,876lbs/19,902kg), not including fuel or crew. The resulting disposable lift of 0.076 tons (77.22kg/170.24lbs) was utterly negligible. The options were to insert another bay and increase the lifting capability, or to lighten ship. The latter was chosen, the external keel and many other items were removed – including the water recovery apparatus, the mooring chain and the anchor! The disposable lift was thereby increased to 3.21 tons (3,261kg/7,190lbs), which would be enough for trial flights and training.

Murray Sueter paid tribute to Usborne's work in this connection: 'The late Commander Neville Usborne also schemed out a very efficient water-recovering apparatus by cooling the exhaust gases of a petrol engine. I believe he was the first in this country to experiment in a practical manner in this direction. In this way we regained in water a very high percentage of the petrol consumed by cooling – over a large surface – the high-temperature exhaust gases from the petrol motor.'[122]

Sueter reported to the Admiralty on 20 August that he had refused to accept the airship from Vickers, stating:

'On Thursday I balanced the airship when floating freely in air in the shed and suggested some alterations. On Saturday evening I again balanced the airship in the shed and found that we could reach 500 feet altitude with the airship, but would only have some 150lbs of ballast for discharge in fore gondola. This I considered inadequate and refused to accept the airship. The framework, as altered, supports the gondolas in the air without any sign of the girders buckling. At a conference with Messrs Vickers representatives this morning, I stated that the Admiralty requirements by specification were one ton petrol and one ton ballast with the ship trimmed properly. Messrs Vickers are now considering what to do. It is not proposed to accept the airship until the lift by specification is obtained.'[123]

Another problem as a result of the delays and alterations was that the airship now needed to be inflated with 'new hydrogen'. Sueter concluded his report by asking if the Admiralty would pay for this, or should the extra cost of some £150 be charged to Vickers, who was now making it quite plain to him that the company was, 'considerably out of pocket'.

The aviation press reported as follows:

'Our Poor Naval Airship. In spite of hopes that the naval airship might have been given another airing, she is still kept most religiously inside the shed at Barrow, and rumour has it that, as a result of a visit of the Advisory Committee on Aeronautics, the great envelope of the airship will be cut in half and considerably lengthened in order that she may carry more weight. Apparently she is not quite capable of lifting the twenty tons for which she was designed, and either the buoyancy will have to be increased, or the weight will have to be cut down.'[124]

On 24 September 1911, she was taken out of the giant shed again, tail first. Just as the nose was clearing the hangar doors, a strong gust of wind caught the massive airship and rolled *Mayfly* virtually on her beam-ends. Shortly after righting herself, the hull of the airship abruptly tore apart forward of the rear car. Her back was broken – overstressed without the stiffening and support of the keel. HMA No 1 was a wreck, and became the subject of much negative publicity about being a waste of an eventual total of £100,000 of taxpayers' money:

'It scarcely needed the lesson of the collapse of Naval Dirigible No 1 to demonstrate the elementary fact that the big dirigible is a failure. We had learnt that from the experience gained with the *Morning Post Lebaudy* and the almost equally unfortunate *Clément-Bayard*, so that we can scarcely feel surprised at this latest catastrophe. On this side of the Channel the dirigible has been, not to put too fine a point upon it, an utter failure; and on the Continent it has been very little better in spite of the long voyages

HMA No 1 lies with its back broken at Barrow in September 1911. (*Ces Mowthorpe Collection*)

under favourable conditions which have been accomplished. Before the aeroplane became the highly efficient organism it is today, it was natural that the lighter-than-air type of flying machine should have attracted a great deal of attention from those who were seeking dominion over the air. The type of craft evolved was admittedly crude and cumbrous, but it was the best we could do, and at any rate it was capable of making ascents, and in good weather, of being navigated to a set course instead of being at the absolute mercy of the lightest air that blew. The school which believed in the gasbag as the airship of the future held, and rightly, that experiment and research might quite possibly lead to the evolution of a type which should be capable of safe navigation in all but the worst of weather conditions. But they had not reckoned with the rapid rise of the heavier-than-air type – a rise which has resulted in the complete overshadowing of the airship by the aeroplane. So completely has the one outbid the other for supremacy, that we might almost say that the dirigible of anything like the dimensions of the unfortunate naval craft which was wrecked on Sunday, is discredited and obsolete. We do not blame the naval authorities for building this vessel. It must be remembered that she was laid down two years ago, when it was impossible to say wherein lay the future of flying. Continental powers were experimenting with airships of similar type, and to have held our hands while possible rivals were attempting to build up aerial navies would have been folly of the worst description. But things have progressed apace in the period that has elapsed since the navy embarked upon airship construction, and no amount of prescience could have foretold that aerial science would stand where it is today. Now that the lesson has been so drastically driven home, it may be hoped that our authorities will keep in mind the excellent maxim of the card-player relative to the cutting of losses. They have been generous in their allocation of money for the building of this experimental craft. It has proved a failure and the money has been wasted, albeit through no fault of anyone. It is just as necessary today, as it was when it was decided to build the Vickers craft, that we should keep up with the rest of the nations. They have practically abandoned the gasbag, and are concentrating all their energies upon the development of the military aeroplane. Therefore, we trust that our own authorities will rise to the needs of the situation, and alter the direction of their experimental work.'

The writer went on to add:

'We have been careful to confine our condemnatory remarks to large craft, because we are not convinced that the lighter-than-air type is altogether without possibilities, but if it has any future at all, we believe that it lies in craft of less ambitious dimensions than those of the unwieldy Zeppelins and Lebaudys. Certainly, while the latter have been leaving their bones dotted over the face of Germany and France, the smaller vessels of the *Beta* and *Gamma* type have achieved some small measure of success. It may, therefore, be advisable to go on experimenting with them for a time, though we confess to being more than a little sceptical even with regard to that.'[125]

Fortunately there were no fatalities, most of the crew had managed to dive overboard as the airship reared and plunged. The report of the Court of Inquiry into the accident, which was presided over by Vice Admiral Sir Doveton Sturdee, CMG, CVO, no longer exists. It has been noted that Sturdee had no previous experience of aeronautics and that his first remark on seeing the wreck of the airship was, 'Ah! The work of a lunatic!' But then, which reasonably senior officer had any relevant knowledge at that time apart from Templer or Capper? It could not be expected that the navy would have welcomed the army delving into its affairs, however sensible such an idea might have been. In fact two years before, on 2 August 1909, R.B. Haldane replied in the House of Commons to a request for greater inter-service aeronautical co-operation by saying that he could not, 'see what the distinguished soldier who is at the head of the balloon school of construction has to do with the work of the Admiralty in constructing a rigid dirigible. The Admiralty will only be too glad to see him if he has anything to say to them, and he will be only too glad to give the Admiralty any information he can; but I do not see any material connexion between the two different pieces of work at the present moment'.[126] A statement which is quite breathtaking in its complacency and imbecility, given that the Balloon School was the only other governmental repository of knowledge and experience of the operation of lighter-than-air craft over the previous thirty years. Nor was the Advisory Committee for Aeronautics, established in 1909, ever asked by the Admiralty to examine the details of the design.

The First Lord of the Admiralty, Winston Churchill, censored publication of Sturdee's findings at the time and all known copies of the report have been lost or destroyed, so the precise findings are never likely to be discovered. It is known, however, that the court found structural weakness to be the cause of the accident, which was hardly a revelation. A recommendation was made to the First Sea Lord, Admiral of the Fleet Sir Arthur Wilson, VC, Bart, that no more rigid airships should be constructed for the Royal Navy. On a more positive note, Usborne was praised for his conduct in showing good judgement at a critical moment and in trying to minimise the danger of the situation by deflating some of the gasbags.[127] Lieutenant Talbot was also commended for his gallantry in rescuing some of the crew from the aft gondola. Usborne remained in Barrow with the care and maintenance party until the great airship frame was broken up. He was less successful when he made an application to the Admiralty for the time spent at Barrow prior to his formal appointment to HMS *Hermione* from 26 September 1910, being considered as time served in a ship of war at sea (which would have enhanced the period of service reckoned for pay and promotion purposes). This was refused by their Lordships.[128] The Admiralty having lost interest in rigids for the time being, in January 1912 the Airships Section disbanded. Sueter was placed on the half-pay list and his brother officers were ordered to report for general service. HMA No 1 was certainly not a success, but the story is not one of total failure, as valuable knowledge had been gained. The facts of this are spelt out in some detail by Sueter, who, not surprisingly, also drew some less favourable conclusions with regard to the official response to the *Mayfly's* mishaps:

'With this airship we learnt to handle large volumes of hydrogen gas, specialized in outer cover and gasbag fabric work; in carrying out at Barrow, and with the help of the National Physical Laboratory, a long series of tensile tests in warp and woof of a large variety of fabrics. Also a large number of osmosis experiments were carried out to determine the rate of leakage of hydrogen through various gasbag materials, and entry of air. We found slightly more nitrogen leaked in than oxygen. These seam tests and permeability tests were all most instructive. We studied the loss of lift through large variations of temperature. Also, with the good and always ready help of the NPL, when Dr Richard Glazebrook was the able director, the stability of various aluminium alloys, such as Duralumin, vibration tests with this metal etc, were investigated. Nearly all the work with the *Mayfly* we found of the greatest value in building up the small airship fleet that Admiral Lord Fisher required in the war to assist in countering the German submarine menace. After the wreck of the *Mayfly*, I begged every Sea Lord to continue airship development, but without success. All airship work was closed down. To wait and profit by the experience gained in developing a new weapon by another nation is always a tempting policy to those in authority. Some said, why not

Rear Admiral
Jellicoe and
Captain Hugh
Watson aboard
the Zeppelin
Schwaben in
1911.

wait, like we did with the submarine? France developed this underwater weapon of warfare – we stayed our hand until we were forced to come in. Then we soon caught the French up. Let Germany waste money in this costly airship business. We could soon catch her! Fortunately, we did not go to war with France whilst we were playing the waiting game with submarines. But with airships, the Sea Lords of the Admiralty permitted a potential enemy country to develop a weapon that we did not possess ourselves. Surely this was an unwise policy, and when war did break out with Germany in 1914, we had no rigid airships for working with the fleet and keeping the North Sea under aerial reconnaissance.'[129]

Nor indeed were all senior naval officers totally blind to the potential of airships and aviation. Sir John Jellicoe took it upon himself, in November 1911, to go to Germany and take a flight in the commercial Zeppelin, *Schwaben*, accompanied by the Naval Attaché in Berlin, Captain Sir Hugh D. Watson, RN. Jellicoe subsequently discussed his findings with the First Sea Lord, but to no immediate effect.[130]

More Successful Flights by the Army

Once more the army had been using its small airships with some success while the navy struggled. In March 1911, the Secretary of State for War, R.B. Haldane, made a statement to the House of Commons in connection with the recently published army estimates, which included this comment: 'The balloon factory, really the dirigible factory, has been completely reorganised and has got a very efficient civilian staff of experts under a gentleman well known in aeronautics [Mervyn O'Gorman]. Considerable changes have been made and new machinery introduced, by which three times the output of hydrogen will be obtained.' He looked forward to the addition of further dirigibles to the army's present strength of two, *Beta* and *Gamma*.[131]

Of O'Gorman's time at Farnborough it was later written:

'The same sort of credit belongs to the conduct of the balloon factory under Mr Mervyn O'Gorman, who had charge of it during that very crucial period from the autumn of 1909 to the summer of 1916. When he took over the factory, he found at Farnborough, one small machine shop, one shed for making balloons, and one airship shed. The workers were about a hundred in number, fifty men and fifty women. Seven years later, when Lieutenant Colonel O'Gorman was appointed to the Air Board as consulting engineer to the Director General of Military Aeronautics, the hundred had swollen to four thousand six hundred, and the buildings situated on the forest land of Farnborough had increased and multiplied out of all recognition. This development was made necessary by the war, but it would have been impossible but for the foresight which directed the operations of the period before the war. The factory, working in close co-operation with the Advisory Committee and the National Physical Laboratory, very early became the chief centre for experimental aviation with full-sized machines.'[132]

On 1 April 1911, the Air Battalion of the Royal Engineers was formed, to take over from the Balloon School at Farnborough, 'to which will be entrusted the duty of creating a body of expert airmen. The training and instructing of men in handling kites, balloons and aeroplanes, and other forms of aircraft, will also devolve upon this battalion.'[133]

An officer, who could be selected from any regular arm or branch of the service, was required, on joining the battalion, to go through a six months' probationary course (including two months kiting and ballooning) and if, during this period, he showed no aptitude for the work, then he had to return to his unit. On satisfactorily completing the probationary period, he would be appointed to the Air Battalion for a term of four years (inclusive of the time of probation), and would be seconded from his regiment. Certain qualifications were applied. These were fairly demanding: (a) special recommendation by commanding officer; (b) possession of aviator's certificate; (c) previous experience of aeronautics; (d) rank not above that of captain; (e) medical fitness for air work; (f) good eyesight; (g) good map-reader and field sketcher; (h) unmarried; (i) not less than two years' service; (j) under thirty years of age; (k) good sailor; (l) knowledge of foreign languages; (m) taste for mechanics and (n) light weight (under 11 stone 7 pounds). The warrant officers, non-commissioned officers, and men, were to be drawn from the Corps of Royal Engineers.[134]

In command was Major Sir Alexander Bannerman, RE, who owed his appointment to good connections with the general staff. He would not even have described himself as the country's foremost aviation expert or exponent. It consisted of two companies, No 1 (Airship) at South Farnborough, commanded by Captain E.M. Maitland, Essex Regiment, of whom it was said that he was, 'as quiet as a Quaker and as considerate as a hospital nurse,'[135] and No 2 (Aeroplane) at Larkhill, under the command of Captain J.D.B. Fulton, RFA, which, by the summer, could field five or six flyable aeroplanes. The battalion establishment was for fourteen officers, twenty-three NCOs, 153 men, two buglers, four riding horses and thirty-two draught horses. It can be seen therefore, that by the formation of the two companies, that it was as yet undecided as to whether airships or aeroplanes would develop into the most effective war machines.[136] Maitland had under his command the two airships *Beta* and *Gamma*, several free balloons and a flight of man-lifting kites. There was quite some debate at this time concerning the status of pilots; it was Maitland's firm conviction that the pilot should always be in charge of the airship or aeroplane and not have a system, as advocated by some, of non-commissioned pilots under the command of commissioned observers – thus creating a subservient relationship much like that of chauffeur to master. In the Imperial German Air Service the latter method prevailed.

A general aeronautical policy also had to be decided upon and set out. The War Office was faced with something of a dilemma in this respect. Both Germany and France were at a greater stage of advancement in military aviation; France favoured the fixed-wing aircraft as the way ahead, whereas Germany showed a greater inclination to the airship. Which was correct? Neither the politicians, civil servants, nor military men, had sufficient knowledge or experience to be certain as to the best way forward. In comparison to the Air Battalion, France had upwards of 170 aeroplanes and several airships, while Germany had twenty to thirty military aeroplanes and about twenty airships.

In May 1911, *Beta* suffered a slight but embarrassing accident; Clive Waterlow was in command and had been instructed to investigate a report from other pilots that *Beta* was difficult to land:

'*Beta* Bags a Telegraph Pole. At the conclusion of some practice flights at Farnborough on the 18th inst., the army airship *Beta* had a trying experience, although fortunately came through with "flying" colours. The airship was not quite low enough for the soldiers to grab the tow rope, and in consequence it dragged across the ground for some distance. In crossing the Farnborough Road the rope got entangled round a telegraph post, which it succeeded in pulling out of the ground. No other damage was done however, the airship landing safely shortly after.'[137]

Waterlow very sensibly recommended that to rectify this problem, more engine power should be maintained on approach to increase the airflow and thereby give greater effectiveness to the elevator.

Not very long afterwards the Army Council issued provisional regulations for the guidance of the Air Battalion. It was to be regarded as supplementary to the cavalry:

'The new unit is regarded by the Army Council as one of the most valuable means of obtaining information at the disposal of the commander of an army. It will not, however, replace other means of acquiring information, such as cavalry and agents, but will be used in conjunction with such services. The Air Battalion is to be so distributed that the units may not only be placed in the best positions to obtain information, but to co-operate with the other arms, and especially with the cavalry, in this all-important service.'[138]

Airship crews were given specific advice:

'The presence of troops, if in the open, can be observed in clear weather at an altitude of 5000–6000 feet, within a radius of four to six miles from the aeroplane or dirigible. When nearer the earth objects will be rather more easily distinguished, but are a shorter time in view, and the area is restricted. Dirigibles will be exposed to considerable danger from artillery fire when lower than 4,500 feet or within a range of 5000 yards, and from rifle or machine-gun fire when at a height of less than 3500 feet, or at ranges under 2000 yards. For transmission of intelligence from dirigibles, wireless telegraphy, signalling, or carrier pigeons can be used.'[139]

Very sensible advice was also given to troops on the ground:

'In deciding whether it is advisable to open fire on airships the probability of escaping observation if fire is reserved is to be considered. Special observation parties of men skilled in distinguishing between friendly and hostile craft might be detailed to watch for the enemy's machines and give warning to the artillery and machine-gun commanders, who will be prepared to fire much in the same manner as against moving targets on land.'[140]

Some very interesting information for the airmen was contained at the foot of the same report:

'On Tuesday, Colonel Seely, in the House of Commons, informed Mr Ashley that the whole question of extra pay to be granted to officers of the Air Battalion was receiving consideration.'[141]

Gamma had been fitted with her new French envelope. In the summer she was reported as making a number of flights in support of the London Balloon Company and RE Territorials, including some as early as 3 am (to take advantage of the light air often to be found in the pre-dawn hours), adding:

'At many of the journeys, the London Balloon Company have assisted the Regular Air Battalion in the handling of the airship, some useful airship experience being thus gained for the first time.'[142]

Then a few days later:

'Very early in the morning of Wednesday last week the army dirigible, *Gamma,* was brought out of its shed, and with Lieutenant C.M. Waterlow in charge, and Captain E.M. Maitland, Lieutenant T.J. Ridge, and a mechanic on board, it cruised for some considerable time over Aldershot Camp and district at heights ranging up to 1000 feet. The alterations which have been carried out during the process of overhauling appear to be giving every satisfaction.'[143]

It was noted in September:

'*Gamma* Visits Guildford. The army airship, *Gamma,* with a crew of six, including Captain Broke-Smith, Captain Maitland, and Mr Mervyn O'Gorman, made a prolonged flight on Tuesday morning last, circling Guildford and returning to Farnborough by way of Farnham, Crondall, and the Long Valley. The flight lasted one and a half hours, and the distance covered was forty miles.'[144]

And:

'*Gamma* Has a Night Out. Lubrication troubles putting both her engines out of action led to the army airship *Gamma* having an exciting time on the 14th inst. She was caught by a heavy wind just at twilight and driven across the Hog's Back, but was safely brought down in a clearing not far from Farnham. She was undamaged, and, being moored under the lee of some trees, she remained out in the open all night while the Engineers of the Air Battalion put the engines right. Although a strong wind was blowing on the following morning, Lieutenants Waterlow and Fox took charge of the airship and succeeded in getting it back safely to headquarters at Farnborough.'[145]

In the same issue another correspondent wrote with some foresight:

'Shortly afterwards, we observed a huge sausage-like shape above us, and identified it as *Gamma* from Farnborough. It sailed round the ground at about 700 or 800ft, and then went straight off in the direction of home. One could not help thinking what an easy mark it would make for a gunner,

The airship sheds at Farnborough, with the Royal Aircraft Factory in the foreground. (*Via Nigel Caley*)

even if two or three times the distance away. It seemed very steady, but rather slow.'[146]

And finally:

'*Gamma* at Salisbury. On 22 September last, the army airship *Gamma* made a successful flight from Farnborough to Salisbury Plain, via Basingstoke and Andover. Piloted by Captain Broke-Smith and Captain Maitland, with a crew of six, including Mr Mervyn O'Gorman, a halt was made in front of the hangars on Larkhill, Salisbury Plain, for lunch. Starting again at two o'clock, the return journey was made in one and a half hours, the outward journey having taken fifteen minutes longer. The total distance covered during the flight was 110 miles.'[147]

Meanwhile, in France, airships and aeroplanes had taken part in the annual army manoeuvres for the second year running, and aviators gained recognition as the 'fourth arm' alongside the artillery, cavalry and infantry.[148]

As the year drew to a close a further successful experiment was made:

'Ripping the Army Airship. In the envelopes of dirigibles, as of balloons, there is a panel of fabric so cemented to the main body of the material as to enable it to be ripped off by pulling a cord. In ballooning, the ripping panel is used during the last stage of descent in order to destroy the buoyancy, and to prevent the rebound after the car first touches the earth. In the use of dirigibles this practice is of course not followed as a rule, but as it might be necessary, in emergency, to rip before touching earth,

A view of *Gamma*'s car which shows the engine and swivel propellers.

it was determined at the Army Airship Factory to see if the proceeding was feasible, and likely to result in much or little damage to the machine. The airship *Gamma* was employed for the experiment, and the conditions were such as to have enabled the crew to leave the ship by sliding down the trail ropes. The envelope immediately collapsed when ripped, and the airship fell to the ground, but subsequent inspection showed that only stays and wires that could be easily replaced had been damaged by this somewhat drastic trial.'[149]

The Committee of Imperial Defence Deliberates

In the middle of November the Prime Minister, H.H. Asquith, requested that the Committee of Imperial Defence:

'Should consider the future development of aerial navigation for naval and military purposes, and the measures which might be taken to secure to this country an efficient aerial service.'[150]

He had been influenced to some extent by general public disquiet with the government's aeronautical policy when compared to the efforts of France and Germany. The *Mayfly's* costly mishap had not improved the position.

During 1911, a feeling of dissatisfaction, 'had been growing concerning the inferiority in aerial strength of the country as compared with our continental neighbours'. The criticism grew in volume and weight until the cabinet felt that some steps should be taken to see whether or not the existing system could be improved.[151]

As ordered by the Prime Minister, the membership of the sub-committee was particularly strong. The chairman was the newly ennobled Viscount Haldane, the Secretary of State for War. Other members included Winston Churchill, First Lord of the Admiralty; Lord Esher, a permanent member of the Committee of Imperial Defence; and Colonel Seely, the Under-Secretary of State. Included among the service members were Vice Admiral Prince Louis of Battenberg, the Second Sea Lord; Lieutenant C.R. Samson,[152] despite his junior rank, for his technical expertise; Major General C.F. Hadden, Master-General of the Ordnance; and Brigadier General David Henderson of the General Staff. Mervyn O'Gorman represented the Army Aircraft Factory, while Sir R. Chalmers, Permanent Secretary to the Treasury, completed the membership. (Henderson[153] (1862–1921), would become the Director General of Military Aeronautics in 1913 when the War Office at last came to recognise the importance of aviation, and of whom Lord Trenchard said, 'he was the founder and father of the Air Force.') There was debate and uncertainty within the sub-committee concerning the utility of airships in future military and naval operations, which was mirrored in the changes of mind in the fertile brain of Winston Churchill. In December 1911, he stated to the sub-committee that he would require a good deal of converting before he could acquiesce to a policy of building dirigibles.[154] By April 1912, he had become convinced that airships seemed likely to become, 'an indispensable adjunct of the fleet'.[155] Early in the following year he engaged in a lively correspondence and debate with the First Sea Lord, Sir Arthur Wilson, which concluded, somewhat waspishly, as follows:

'In these notes I have endeavoured to merely supply you with the facts and arguments as they are at presently known to us, and I do not wish to be taken as expressing a decided opinion in favour of airships compared to aeroplanes. In thanking you again for your paper, may I remark that it will give my colleagues and myself much pleasure to receive at any time helpful criticisms and any information or suggestions on these difficult air problems that we are now faced with.'[156]

In some quarters of the Royal Navy it was believed that the First Lord's enthusiasm for air power was actually of positive benefit:

'It was common gossip amongst junior officers, no doubt with very little foundation, that the Sea Lords had gladly given the forceful young First Lord a free hand over air matters in order to divert him from interfering with the Grand Fleet.'[157]

It was decided that a technical sub-committee, chaired by Seely, should examine the whole question of airships, and would result in the commissioning of a fascinating investigative mission for Sueter and O'Gorman which will be described later.[158] The main recommendation of the full sub-committee's report would be ready within three months and, as will be seen, would have far-reaching consequences for both Army and Royal Navy aviators.

Not everyone agreed with the stately progress with regard to aeronautics as favoured by Haldane; an alternative view was expressed by Viscount St Aldwyn, who, as Sir Michael Hicks-Beach, had served as Lord Salisbury's Chancellor of the Exchequer at the end of the nineteenth century:

'My Lords, all my official experience as ex-Chancellor of the Exchequer would induce me to refrain from pressing the War Department in regard to anything that would involve unnecessary expenditure. But I do think that in this matter there has been very slow progress indeed. The noble viscount appeared to me to be waiting for some design of perfection in this matter. Now that has never been the policy of the Navy, and quite rightly too. I remember ships built on designs which were considered reasonably good in order that we might be provided with what at any rate was the best that could be obtained at that time. I would venture to tell the noble viscount opposite that I am afraid under present circumstances, if we should unfortunately be involved in war, we should be quite unprepared with regard to appliances of the kind which have been the subject of discussion. I do hope, therefore, that the War Office will take care that there is some provision in respect of aviation without waiting for some possible design in the future which may not be attained until it is too late.'[159]

The policy of the government up to this time was well summarised in a report of the Technical Sub-Committee of the Standing Sub-Committee of the Committee of Imperial Defence, dated 30 July 1912, which boasted of assuming the position of the ostrich:

'Up to the end of the year 1911 the policy of the government with regard to all branches of aerial navigation was based on a desire to keep in touch with the movement rather than to hasten its development. It was felt that we stood to gain nothing by forcing a means of warfare which tended to reduce the value of our insular position and the protection of our sea power.'[160]

Neville Usborne's Flying Career Resumes

It would appear that Usborne's career did not suffer because of his close association with HMA No 1. In February 1912 he was elected as one of the first Associate Fellows of the Aeronautical Society along with Captain Murray Sueter and fellow airship pilot, Lieutenant Clive Waterlow, RE. They were in august company as others elected by the same ballot included Frederick Handley Page, Horace Short and E.T. Willows. The Aeronautical Society had been created in 1866 for the purpose of increasing knowledge of aeronautics, and marked the beginning of the establishment of a systematic record of aeronautical study and achievement in Britain. It obtained a Royal Charter and so added Royal to its title in 1918.

From his naval record of service it would seem that Usborne was posted to HMS *Victory* for the first three months of 1912. This may have been a holding appointment, or perhaps a short course at the School of Navigation.

On the evening of 4 March 1912, the Aeronautical Society held a meeting at the Royal United Service Institution at which Lieutenant Waterlow of the Air Battalion, Royal Engineers, read a paper entitled *Military Airships*, in which he surveyed the current position of airships in the British Army. The audience included his superior officers Major Bannerman and Captain Broke-Smith. He deprecated the fact that the Royal Aero Club had so far issued only eight airship pilot certificates, with seven of these having been gained by soldiers. He argued that support from the air of military formations was not a question of either aeroplanes or airships, but that both could be developed. He examined the difficulties faced by airships which he listed as weather, transport and hostile aircraft. He regarded flying in strong winds as being quite safe; saw rain, snow, hail and mist as problems which could be overcome by carrying an adequate supply of ballast, which could be jettisoned if excess precipitation increased the weight of the airship; but recommended the avoidance of thunder and lightning. He discussed the development of a portable mooring mast, to which the airship *Beta* had been attached in successful trials earlier that month and which could be transported on a single lorry. (This was a tall pole fitted with a revolving cone, into which the nose of the airship was placed, allowing it to be moored into the wind, from whichever direction it blew.) Other stores, cylinders of compressed hydrogen, a portable ladder (to access the car when the airship was moored at its mast), repairing materials, wire, hemp cordage, leak detecting instruments, spares for the engine and tools; he estimated could be accommodated in a further two motor lorries, along with a ground crew of ten to twenty. As regards hostile aircraft, he suggested that the prudent airship captain should either run away or seek security at a greater height. As defensive armament he proposed a light gun capable of firing shrapnel shell (reminiscent of the swivel guns mounted on a wooden warship). He noted that an aeroplane could attack an airship by three methods: by getting above and dropping something on it, by firing from the same level, or by ramming it – which would be a fairly desperate last resort, one would hope. As regards artillery fire from the ground, he felt that at 1000 feet or below, the airship was vulnerable and that climbing to 4000 feet with the prevailing wind would promote reasonable safety. He emphasised that the proper role of the airship when confronted by a hostile aeroplane was defensive, and whilst it should have some means of defending

Beta attached to a portable mooring mast.

itself, running away was really the best option. The ideal crew should consist of a pilot, steersman, engineer, wireless operator, gunner and observer, while the optimum role was reconnaissance, with bomb dropping as an additional possibility.[161]

The Naval Airships Branch was reformed and a group of officers and men was attached to the Military Airship Branch. This for once, seems to have been a sensible decision, inter-service rivalry was set aside, the navy would learn from the army's airshipmen, becoming:

'Part of a small band of enthusiasts to whom disaster and disappointment were the salt of endeavour, and it was on the technical knowledge and experience of these pioneers that the country had to rely, when the need came, for the rapid building up under duress, of what was to prove an essential part of the defence against the submarine, one of the most subtle and powerful weapons that the country was called upon to meet.'[162]

The aim, according to the Aerial Sub-Committee of the CID was to:

'Train the Naval Wing of the Royal Flying Corps to handle the largest airships and to provide a sufficient number of these, together with the necessary sheds, hydrogen plant and accessories as soon as the personnel to take charge of them are ready. At the present time, however, the Military Wing has far more practical experience in handling airships than the Naval Wing. Therefore the function of the Military Wing in the new development of airships should be to train and assist the Naval Wing.'[163]

The same report noted that the airship was superior to the aeroplane for prolonged operations across the sea, as it could be steered accurately by compass and its position fixed by astronomical observation, for both of which it gave a much better platform. It also stated that the airship had a greater radius of action, was superior for the purpose of communication by wireless telegraphy, could carry a greater weight of explosives and could aim them with greater accuracy by hovering over the target, which quality would also allow for better photography and observation. Nor were airships believed to be especially vulnerable to artillery fire, as recent experiments made by the Ordnance Board had shown that no existing British gun could be relied upon to hit an airship. Moreover, great difficulty had been experienced in constructing a fuse which would cause a shell to burst on impact with an airship's gasbag, or in manufacturing an incendiary shell. The fairly small speed differential between airships and aeroplanes, and the greater ability of the airship to ascend rapidly, did not inspire great confidence in an aeroplane's capability to ensure an airship's destruction. It was considered that the answer might lie in the creation of a force of armed interceptor airships. Consideration was also give to the future provision of airships, it being decided that the best way ahead was to build gradually on the very limited number of small airships currently in military service by acquiring larger vessels over a period of time, as the personnel involved gained in experience. To this end the purchase of the Willows craft, an Astra-Torres type from France, a Parseval from Germany and the construction of an improved *Gamma* type was recommended, all of which were non-rigids; while the development of a rigid type should be kept, 'under close observation'.[164]

On 1 April 1912, Usborne was sent to Arnold House, Farnborough, as Squadron Commander, Naval Airship Section, Royal Flying Corps Airship Wing, with Commander Masterman also posted as the CO of the Naval Section, together with the future airship pilots, Lieutenants RN, F.L.M. Boothby and H.L. Woodcock, for the Airship Course, and a party of ratings.[165] (Sadly, only ten days before, his birthplace of Queenstown was the scene of the RMS *Titanic's* last landfall before proceeding across the North Atlantic on her doomed maiden voyage.) This was only a month after the first military use of airships, the Italian Army's small non-rigids P1 and P3 making reconnaissance flights over the Turkish lines near Tripoli taking still and motion pictures, dropping grenades and spotting for the artillery. *The Times* was; 'Profoundly impressed by the skill and coolness of their pilots, and firmly convinced of the practical value of aviation in war' and added; 'We are probably at the beginning of a long struggle between the advocates of the aeroplane and those of the airship. Both types of aircraft must be provided by a nation which has to consider the prospect of war.' Useful additional information included the fact that the Italians had three classes of airship – P for *piccolo*, M for *medio* and G for *grande*.[166]

Usborne was joining a group of experienced and capable army airshipmen. He would have to work hard and learn quickly in order to make his mark in their company. The knowledge that he would gain in flying the RFC's dirigibles would be of enormous benefit to him when it came to designing one of the most successful classes of dirigible ever built just a few short years in the future. Not long after he arrived at Farnborough he was given a task by the Admiralty, being directed to call on Messrs Barr and Stroud, the Glasgow-based firm of optical instrument manufacturers, to give them information concerning balloons and airships to assist in designing a rangefinder for use in anti-balloon firing.[167]

As has been described, *Beta* had been giving useful service since 1910 and had been the subject of a series of modifications, including being fitted with wireless. The portable mast experiment mentioned by Clive Waterlow had included leaving *Beta* out in a 33mph snowstorm (53kph) in which she had suffered no harm. It was reported by *Flight* Magazine on 1 June that Usborne had been taken up as a passenger in both the airships *Beta* and *Gamma*. In the same issue it noted that *Gamma* had undergone a programme of alterations which had improved its flying characteristics when taken out by Lieutenant Waterlow as pilot-in-charge, Captain Maitland steering, an NCO mechanic in charge of the engines and Captain Lefroy (the commander of the Wireless Experimental Section RE) handling the wireless apparatus. A flight of about twenty minutes was made, of which two minutes was occupied by the return journey with the wind. During the flight the steadiness and stability of the ship was most remarkable, an excellent straight course was maintained and a uniform elevation which appeared to be something under 500 feet.[168]

It was further noted that it was now becoming quite common to see the airships flying about in weather conditions when the aeroplane sheds remained firmly closed. *Gamma* had in fact been virtually rebuilt, with a new envelope of 101,000 cubic feet (2858 cubic metres), manufactured by Willows, a box elevator at the stern of the car replacing the previous fore and aft pair and two new 45 hp (33 kW) Iris engines, giving her a top speed of about 30mph (48kph). In April she had visited London:

'On the early morning of Monday, the reconstructed army airship *Gamma* paid another visit to the metropolis and circled round St. Paul's. Captain Maitland was in charge, assisted by Lieutenant Waterlow, while in the engine room were Mr Irving and Corporal Scovell, with Captain Allen and Lieutenant Carfrey as passengers. Farnborough was left at 6.15 and, pushing her way through a headwind, the airship reached St. Paul's about 8.30. Turning above the cathedral, she then started back on her return journey and, with the wind behind, was soon out of sight, Farnborough being reached again in fifty-seven minutes. On the 19th inst., with seven passengers on board, she was up to a height of a mile. *Beta* was also out with a full crew, while the three army aeroplanes made several tests. On Saturday morning *Gamma*, with Captain Broke Smith in command, was up to a height of 1,000 feet and flew to Haywards Heath and back'.[169]

An event of considerable note took place in May following the recommendations of the sub-committee of the Committee of Imperial Defence, now under the chairmanship of Colonel J.E.B. Seely. (Later Baron Mottistone, (1868–1947) he would succeed Haldane as the Secretary of State for War in June 1912 when Haldane became Lord Chancellor. During the First World War he commanded the Canadian Cavalry Brigade.) The Air Battalion RE was replaced on 13 May 1912 by the formation of the Royal Flying Corps (RFC), 'an aeronautical service for naval and military purposes'[170] which consisted initially of a Military Wing of one airship and man-carrying kite squadron, and two aeroplane squadrons, a Naval Wing, the Royal Aircraft Factory at Farnborough (which was directly descended from the old Balloon Factory, having been renamed the Army Aircraft Factory in April 1911) and the Central Flying School (CFS) at Upavon in Wiltshire. One of the first officers to take the CFS aeroplane course, Lieutenant Charles Longcroft, later wrote that he was surprised to find that the instruction began with a series of ascents in spherical balloons to learn the arts of aerial sketching and report writing, followed by a flight in *Gamma* and a number of free ballooning trips which continued for about six weeks, 'by which time we were all heartily sick of it'. It is possible that a lack of aeroplanes accounted for this seemingly retrograde step.[171]

It was also recommended that in view of the considerable cost involved it was not considered advisable to build rigid airships. Non-rigid airships were regarded as having military value as they could carry efficient wireless telegraphy apparatus, which the aeroplanes of that period could not. Kites were thought to be of use as they were the only means of aerial observation in really high winds. All were required by the War Office to work in close co-operation.

The King visited Farnborough on 23 May, and, as well as watching some evolutions performed by *Beta*, he visited the factory to see how work on the new airship, *Delta*, was progressing. It may well have been that some of Usborne's first flights with the army were in the dark, as it was reported in June:

'Army Airship in the Dark. Experiments were carried out last week at Farnborough with the army airships *Beta* and *Gamma* in the "wee small" hours. About 11 pm on the 29th, *Beta* went up and cruised until after midnight, and similar operations were carried out on the following day. On the 31st *Gamma* ascended, in charge of Captain Maitland, at 10.30 pm and carried out a cruise of an hour and a quarter, while *Beta* made a similar trip.'[172]

Following an inspection and air test on 10 June by Lieutenant Waterlow, on 18 July, the Willows No 4 airship and its shed were purchased by the Admiralty for £1050, being named as HMA No 2, despite Waterlow's positive but less than ringing endorsement:[173]

'The feature of the ship (Willows No 4) is its small size and remarkable handiness; everything can be packed up and taken to pieces with the utmost care. For pleasure purposes this ship seems to be ideal. It would also be useful to train NCOs and men on handling on the ground and in the air. While both ships (Willows No 3 and No 4) would afford valuable training to officers and men unacquainted with this class of work, they

Neville Usborne (in the white covered cap) in the reconstructed *Beta II* in 1912. (*Mays Aldershot via PS Leaman*)

The Willows No 4
was purchased by
the Admiralty and
renamed HMA No 2.

HMA No 2 in a natural
shelter near Odiham.

cannot seriously be considered for war purposes except, conceivably,
against a savage enemy.'[174]

Willows No 4 was a handy little ship with two or three seats, dual control and a
40 hp (30 kW) Renault engine driving a pair of wooden, four-bladed propellers.
It had a capacity for sufficient fuel and oil to give an endurance of seven
hours flying time. The envelope was made from oiled cotton, which was an
experimental material. It had a volume of 20,000 cubic feet (572 cubic metres),
was 110 feet (33.5 metres) in length and a diameter of 18 feet 6 inches (5.5
metres), which tapered towards the stern, giving a streamlined appearance. The
torpedo-shaped car was constructed of steel tube clad with sheet aluminium.
Usborne was appointed to command HMA No 2, 'and with a few naval ratings
was soon intriguing the soldiers with experiments on Cove Pond. The army
found him irrepressible.'[175] Willows himself had for several years been of the

mind that a small dirigible could be useful for naval scouting purposes, housed in the hold of a parent vessel, and being launched and recovered from the deck.

On the afternoon of 12 August 1912, at just after 2 pm, *Gamma* began a flight back to Farnborough from Larkhill with Usborne as pilot, Lieutenant Fletcher as course keeper, Sergeant McGrane as steersman and Sergeant Collins as mechanic. She also carried 200lbs (91kg) of ballast, and sufficient fuel and oil for six hours, 100lbs (45kg) of petrol being in tins and therefore available, in emergency, as ballast. Rising to 600 feet (182 metres) there was too much wind to make any progress, so they descended to 100 feet (30 metres) and were able to attain 8mph (5kph), against a wind of 22mph (35kph). They climbed to 900 feet to pass over the ridge of Ashdown Copse. The port engine had to be stopped due to a problem causing pre-ignition, with the result that *Gamma* could only just make headway and descended with great rapidity to only 50 feet (15 metres). Four bags of ballast were thrown out and an emergency landing was made behind the shelter of some trees. Having moored to the tallest tree, Sergeant Collins carried out repairs to the engine and within forty-five minutes they were ready to take to the air again, though Sergeant McGrane had to be left with the ground party to go home by motor tender in order to reduce the weight carried. The wind strengthened again and the depleted crew had a terrific struggle to negotiate a way around the village of Weyhill. Due to fierce upward air currents *Gamma*'s progress was somewhat erratic, varying in altitude from 150 to 750 feet (45 to 228 metres), and following a zigzagging route across the countryside. It was decided to land again and, with the ground party not having caught up, the grapnel was thrown out, catching in a hedge at the second attempt. However, mooring proved to be too difficult, with the grapnel dragging through the foliage and the airship once more ascended to 800 feet (243 metres). Further attempts were made to land near Longparish in a large field surrounded by trees, but were to little avail. Fortunately, a crowd of villagers had gathered to watch the spectacle, some of whom caught hold of the trail rope which had been thrown towards them, allowing *Gamma* to be brought to rest over a wooded hollow on the leeward side of the field, venting gas to descend. The grapnel rope had become tangled and had to be cut away by using borrowed ladders to climb up into the trees to effect this operation. By this time it was 6 pm, the wind had died away, but then it started to rain very heavily. The crew turned the airship broadside on in the hollow, pushed her nose hard into the trees, and picketed her down with sacks of earth and crowbars. It was not until 3.45 the next afternoon, after the rain eventually had ceased, that *Gamma* took off again for a final leg to Farnborough, taking only thirty-eight minutes at a speed of 50mph (80kph).

Illustration from Fletcher's
report. (*Via Nigel Caley*)

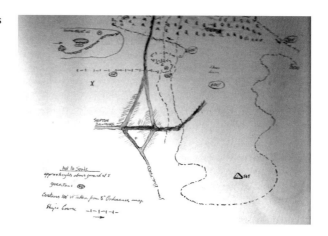

Another illustration from
Fletcher's report. (*Via Nigel
Caley*)

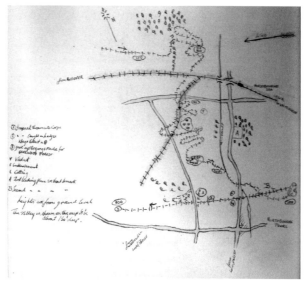

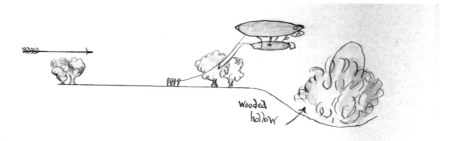

Third illustration from Fletcher's report. (*Via Nigel Caley*)

In September 1912 the Admiralty set up an Air Department to administer the Naval Wing. Captain Murray Sueter was tasked with overseeing all aspects of naval aviation. He had visited France, Germany and Austria three months earlier, while still on half pay, in the company of Mervyn O'Gorman, to inspect and report upon airship progress there. While in Austria they flew in a Parseval non-rigid airship from Aspern to Fischamend and inspected a kite-balloon and operating equipment (then regarded as on the secret list). The kite balloon, or drachen, was invented by Major von Parseval of airship fame in 1894. A spherical tethered balloon has the tendency to rotate about its vertical axis, thus making observation difficult and also possibly affecting the observers in the basket with nausea. The drachen overcame this effect by elongating and streamlining the hydrogen-filled balloon envelope, and adding a vertical lobe to the rear, containing air collected by a forward facing scoop. The nose was thereby kept head-on to the wind and the balloon was much more stable; in the same fashion as a weathercock. Despite repeated refusals from the German authorities, they made a voyage of some six hours duration in the Zeppelin airship *Viktoria Luise*, by the subterfuge of posing as Americans. On board were some twenty passengers, a civilian crew and a naval crew under training. The conditions were reasonably convivial, as apparently the German passengers spent most of the flight eating an enormous quantity of sausages and drinking champagne.[176] During the flight over Hamburg, Lubeck and Kiel, they made conversation with a German naval officer, who told them that he was to be the captain of the first German naval airship, then under construction. Sueter also noted the excellent visibility gained from the airship of the shoal water

LZ11 *Viktoria Luise* of DELAG.

when cruising over the Bay of Lubeck at a height of 3000 feet (910 metres) and overland, of deer running through corn from a height of 2000 feet (609 metres). In the course of their stay they uncovered the existence of thirty-three large airship sheds and half a dozen airship factories, and were particularly impressed by achievements in Germany, stating in their report, which was fully illustrated with photographs and sketches:

'We were struck with the popular reception given to the airship. On passing over villages, isolated farms, etc, everybody turned out and cheered and waved to us. In many hundreds of miles on our small English ships, including trips to London, Farnham, Guildford, Salisbury, and down south to near Portsmouth, no such interest is evoked.'[177]

The successful results of German endeavours were contrasted unfavourably with the attitude of the British authorities over the previous five years:

'German airships have, by repeated voyages, proved their ability to reconnoitre the whole of the German coastline on the North Sea. In any future war with Germany, except in foggy or stormy weather, it is possible that no British war vessel or torpedo craft will be able to approach within many miles of the German coast without their presence being discovered and reported. In short, every one of the tactical and strategic advantages which the Committee of Imperial Defence anticipated in 1909 when recommending the construction of a rigid airship for the Royal Navy, has been, or is in a fair way of being, realized by the German airships. These results have only been attained by perseverance under the most discouraging conditions of disaster and loss.'[178]

They also noted that they had been informed that for experimental purposes, loads of up to 1000lbs (453 kilograms) had been dropped from airships:

'While on the subject it may be remarked that for any nation to have a ton of explosives dropped above their admiralty, War Office or administrative buildings would, to say the least of it, be inconvenient, unless proper alternative underground offices have been foreseen.'[179]

The two authors may have resorted to irony and perhaps a certain amount of judicious exaggeration, but they made their case well and it was one of the contributory factors to the revival of the Naval Airships Section. It certainly encouraged Seely's technical sub-committee to action, as in its report of July 1912 it stated that the government's policy should move away from merely monitoring and keeping in touch with developments in aerial navigation, to hastening its progress. It was felt that the previous policy, which did not want to encourage a type of warfare which could directly threaten Britain's insular security, had been overtaken by events and was dangerously out of date. Sticking one's head in the sand and hoping that it would all turn out for the best would not suffice. The comparative merits of heavier-than-air and lighter-than-air craft had not yet been sufficiently proven to abandon one totally in favour of the other. Whilst it may have been thought that the fixed-wing aircraft had greater future potential, there was no effective anti-aircraft gun in existence which could guarantee the destruction of an enemy airship, nor were aeroplanes capable of so doing.

The army manoeuvres of September 1912 saw the debut of the new airship *Delta*, which was the largest British non-rigid so far, with a capacity of 175,000 cubic feet (4952 cubic metres). She had a pair of 110 hp White and Poppe engines, driving swivelling propellers, which allowed a top speed of 42mph (67kph). Her gestation period (since 1910) had been long because it had been the intention to construct *Delta* as a semi-rigid with an envelope made from waterproofed silk – both these ideas proved impractical and were abandoned. The manoeuvres were held in Cambridgeshire, with the opposing Red and Blue Armies commanded by Lieutenant General Sir Douglas Haig, KCVO, CB,

Beta II & *Delta* on manoeuvres.

KCIE and the 'portly but gifted'[180] Lieutenant General J.M. Grierson, CVO, CB, CMG respectively. The General Staff issued a preliminary memorandum which stated:

> 'There can no longer be any doubt as to the value of airships and aeroplanes in locating an enemy on land, and obtaining information which could only otherwise be obtained by force. In this year's army manoeuvres each force will be provided with a detachment of the Royal Flying Corps, consisting of one aeroplane squadron and one airship detachment. The detachment

A cache of hydrogen cylinders being stacked for the airships taking part in the Army manoeuvres of 1912. (*Via Nigel Caley*)

After the army manoeuvres in 1912, *Beta*, HMA No2 and *Delta*. (*via Nigel Caley*)

with each force will be under the immediate orders of the commander, who will employ it in co-operation with the other arms and more particularly with the cavalry, for obtaining information as to the movements of the hostile force. The work of cavalry will undoubtedly be aided greatly by a well-trained aeronautical service, but, except to a certain extent in long-distance reconnaissance, aircraft can in no way replace or revolutionize its action.'[181]

The Red Army was the theoretical invasion force marching on London, with the Blue Army intent upon halting its progress.

On Friday, 13 September, *Gamma* (Captain Maitland) and *Delta* (Captain Waterlow) departed from Farnborough en route for Kneesworth and Thetford. Unfortunately the newer airship, *Delta*, suffered engine trouble over Hampstead, but was able to use her wireless to send word of her non-arrival – this first aerial distress message was also received as far away as the Royal Navy's shore establishment in Portsmouth, HMS *Vernon*, giving further proof of its effectiveness. Accordingly, *Beta*, flown by Lieutenant Fletcher, was dispatched to take her place. The only difficulty was that *Beta* was not equipped with a wireless set, so depriving the Red Army of this facility – the fixed-wing aircraft did not have wireless sets. On Monday, the first day of action, the utility of *Gamma* and her wireless, which was driven by a generator powered by air from the engine's slipstream, rapidly became evident, with full details of the enemy's dispositions being supplied very early in the proceedings from a height of 4000 feet (1200 metres) to the ground station several miles away. It was shown during these early experiments that wireless messages could be received up to 35 miles (56 kilometres) away. The Blue Army was adjudged to have won the exercise, somewhat against the odds, as it was something of a scratch force in comparison to the Red Army, with *Gamma's* assistance being regarded as being more than helpful to the successful outcome. One night flight was made with the object of gaining experience in reconnaissance and bomb-dropping. The exercise was judged a success and the inherent flexibility of airships was shown when *Gamma*, being unable to recover to her field base, rather than risk landing at an unknown spot in the dark, simply remained in the air until after dawn. Grierson out manoeuvred Haig and also concealed his troops from aerial observation much more efficiently. Both airships departed back to base at the conclusion of the manoeuvres a few days later. The chief umpire for the manoeuvres was no less a person than the Chief of the Imperial General Staff, General Sir J.D.P. French, GCB, GCVO, KCMG, ADC. It is to be hoped that Douglas Haig was moved to amend his views as previously expressed: 'Tell Sykes [Major Frederick Sykes, the CO of the Military Wing RFC] he is wasting his time; flying can never be of any use to the Army.'[182]

Haig was not instinctively opposed to change; it was more a question of being convinced of its practicality and utility. He regarded the reforming Secretary of State for War, R.B. Haldane with some favour, writing in his diary that he was: 'A big fat man, but with a kind, genial face. One seemed to like the man at once – a most clear-headed and practical man – very ready to listen and weigh carefully all that is said to him.'[183]

In fairness, it must be noted that Haig did indeed in time take heed of the lessons of one of the most embarrassing episodes of his professional career and in due course came to appreciate the efforts of the RFC in France.

It was not only British generals who doubted the value of military aviation; the future Allied Commander-in-Chief of 1918, Généralissimo Ferdinand Foch, apparently stated in 1913, 'aviation is fine as sport. I even wish officers would practise the sport, as it accustoms them to risk. But, as an instrument of war, it is worthless (c'est zéro).'[184] He changed his mind just two years later:

> *Groupe des Armées du Nord*
> *PC le 21 Juin, 1915*
> *Etat-Major*
> *Le Général Foch*
> *Commandant le Groupe des Armées du Nord*
> *À Son Excellence le Premier Lord de l'Amirauté,*
> *Whitehall,*
> *London, SW*

Depuis les débuts de la campagne, une escadrille d'aviation maritime Anglaise est stationnée a St Pol-sur-Mer. Commandée successivement par le Commandant Samson, puis par le Commandant Longmore, elle a toujours prêté son concours aux aviateurs francais pour l'accomplissement de la tâche commune, sollicitant même les missions les plus périlleuses.

Le General Foch est très heureux d'adresser à tout le personnel de L'escadrille ses remerciements pour cette collaboration; il le félicite chaudement des exploits qu'il a mis à son actif, dûs autant à son initiative qu'à son audace.

Le Général Foch serait très reconnaissant à Son Excellence le Premier Lord de l'Amirauté de bien vouloir transmettre ses félicitations aux intéressés.

(Signed) F. Foch[185]

There is also the possibly apocryphal story that one of the generals complained that the aircraft had completely spoiled the war, which was rather missing the point. Certainly General Grierson was in no doubt as to *Gamma's* contribution to the successful outcome:

'The impression left on my mind is that their use has revolutionized the art of war. So long as hostile aircraft are hovering over one's troops, all movements are liable to be seen and reported, and therefore the first step in war will be to get rid of the hostile aircraft. He who does this first, or who keeps the last aeroplane afloat will win, other things being approximately equal. The airship, as long as she remained afloat, was of more use to me for strategical reconnaissance than the aeroplanes, as, being fitted with wireless telegraphy, I received her messages in a continuous stream and immediately after the observations had been made. It is a pity that the airship cannot receive messages by wireless, but doubtless modern science will soon remedy this defect.'[186]

Gamma had a few adventures on the way back to Farnborough with five officers on board, passing over Cambridge, to which it subjected a fusillade of celebratory Very lights, refuelling in Wiltshire, making a night stop at Chirton Manor and then colliding with a hayrick at Devizes, causing the envelope to heel over. In order to prevent any further damage, Major Maitland, who was in command, decided to deflate the envelope. The airship was then packed up and returned on a lorry to Farnborough for minor repairs.

In a report from the War Office by the Director of Military Operations the following points were made:

'65. The airships *Beta* and *Gamma*, both renovated and considerably improved, were also employed, one on each side, continually cruising over the battle area on Monday and Tuesday, a proportion of the naval crews under training being used. It should be noted that the airships employed have been constructed with a view to the training of personnel, and not for war.

'69. The following points brought out during the manoeuvres are of interest:-

Night work – No night work was carried out by aeroplanes. The airship *Gamma* made one night flight with the object of gaining experience in reconnaissance and bomb dropping. After carrying out the exercise successfully she failed to land at her field base on her return, and rather than risk a landing at an unknown spot, she remained in the air until after dawn. Method of Communication – the great advantage of fitting a wireless telegraphy apparatus in aircraft was shown by the work accomplished by the airship *Gamma*.'[187]

Another great lesson was the necessity for concealment; 'No body of troops could be moved under observation from the air without being detected and reported.'[188] The airships were active again in October:

'Several trials have been made with both *Beta* and *Delta* at Farnborough during the past few days. On Wednesday week the latter was out and made one or two lengthy voyages with five passengers on board. She was also out on the following day, and on Sunday and Monday. *Beta* was tested on Saturday, and on Monday she took a crew of naval men from Sheerness for an instructional voyage.'[189]

And also Usborne's own command:

'The baby dirigible built by Messrs E.T. Willows, of Cardiff, for the British Navy, has made a very favourable impression at Farnborough. The little torpedo-shaped car, for the pilot and his assistant, which is slung beneath the main beam running fore and aft, gives the aircraft a very smart and businesslike appearance, and the 35 hp Anzani engine, driving two four-

Beta II in September 1912, with Lieutenant J.N. Fletcher, RFC, and Lieutenant Neville Usborne, RN, in the car.

Delta on the ground.

bladed Rapid propellers, has shown itself capable of giving the airship a speed of over 50 miles an hour.'[190]

Certainly the airship as designed offered less air resistance, but to reach such a speed it is likely that there was a fairly strong following wind. In November there were a couple of minor mishaps. Firstly, with Willows himself at the helm and, in all probability, Usborne as his passenger, the motor stopped dead as the airship was circling to land at Farnborough. They drifted a little while and, managing to cast the trail rope and grapnel, descended near the Basingstoke Canal, but somewhat too close to a sewage farm for absolute comfort. The watertight nacelle proved its use. It was discovered that they had run out of petrol. A fresh supply was brought by car and a successful ascent was made; no doubt both the crew were glad to be aloft and away from noxious odours. As darkness had fallen, the landing at base was made with the aid of a searchlight. All in all it was thought that this was a pretty good effort for a new ship.[191] Then two weeks later; 'The Willows airship was out on Friday. Unfortunately she came down at Cove, buckling the main boom of the nacelle, but she was safely towed back by bluejackets without further damage.'[192]

In December, the First Lord of the Admiralty, Winston Churchill, answered questions in the House of Commons on the subject of naval aeronautics. He announced that he was pleased with the progress of the Willows airship and quoted a much more realistic figure for its top speed of 30mph (48kph). He also mentioned the scales of pay applicable at that time:

'The extra rates of pay for naval and marine officers of the Royal Flying Corps are as follows: Ordinary pay of squadron commander, 25 shillings a day; flight commander, 17 shillings; flying officer, 12 shillings. The flying pay is 8 shillings a day. The commanding officer of the Naval Wing receives £800 a year. Flying pay is paid continuously to aeroplane flyers, but only on days of ascent in the case of airships.'[193]

A contemporary observer thought that leaving the pay and conditions of airmen who had come to the RFC from the Royal Navy to their Lordships of the Admiralty was not a good idea, and later wrote:

'This was a snag which was to upset the boat. It seems almost incredible that anyone, even a politician, could have been so obtuse as to fail to realise that a scheme which involved the joint command and administration of a force by the War Office and the Admiralty was doomed to failure. No intelligent person could anticipate for one moment that the arrogant bureaucrats at the Admiralty would be content to take the inferior position demanded of them by this project and to submit to accepting orders from their fellow civil servants at the War Office.'[194]

Churchill also made reference to the non-rigid Astra-Torres and Parseval airships which had been ordered by the Admiralty in 1912. In 1910–11, the Spaniard, Torres Quevedo, had designed a small non-rigid airship with an innovative, trefoil-shape gasbag (three lobes interconnected internally with porous fabric curtains). It increased the stiffness of the envelope so it retained its shape better and also reduced the external rigging, which decreased air resistance. In 1911 he flew in it to France and subsequently made a deal with the Astra Airship Company to develop the Astra-Torres type airship. As previously mentioned, Major August von Parseval was a German military officer who, as well as inventing kite balloons (which would be used extensively by both sides for

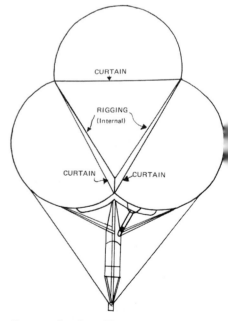

Cross section Astra Torres type.

observation purposes in the First World War), also developed a flexible non-rigid airship type that was sold to several countries. The pace of events had forced the Committee of Imperial Defence, and the Admiralty, to move away from the Haldane policy and buy off the shelf, hoping that the results would be better than the embarrassing Lebaudy and *Clément-Bayard* episodes. Churchill commented that the country's leaders could no longer afford to wait until the relative value of airships and aeroplanes was settled, airships required serious study as soon as possible, and if there were no British types to study, then vessels had to be purchased from abroad with a view to establishing a fleet of dirigibles as soon as possible. Matters requiring urgent attention included the best means of anti-airship countermeasures – aeroplanes, gun defences, or armed airships?[195] Churchill's views were supported by the Second Sea Lord, Vice Admiral Sir John Jellicoe, KCB, KCVO, who favoured airships over aeroplanes because their greater range would make them of more use for scouting purposes.[196]

Meanwhile, Usborne was also flying some of the other airships, including, in December:

> 'Some little excitement was reported in Portsmouth on Tuesday last by the appearance overhead of an airship, until it was noticed that the vessel was flying the White Ensign and it was recognised as one of the British craft – in fact it was *Beta* with Lieutenant Usborne in charge. The dirigible carried a crew of four naval officers and sailed from Aldershot to Portsmouth at a height of 500 feet. Over the harbour the dirigible elevated to 2000 feet, then returned to her station at Aldershot.'[197]

Beta II at Aldershot in 1912.

Then in January 1913:

'Manned by a naval crew with Commander E.A. Masterman in command and Lieutenant N.F. Usborne as pilot, the army airship *Gamma* cruised on Wednesday morning from Farnborough to London. The airship turned above the Chelsea football ground and arrived back at Farnborough just in time to avoid a heavy storm of sleet and snow.'[198]

Another incident which was reported must have been very frightening for the mechanic concerned:

'One of the mechanics holding down *Gamma* after her trip to Portsmouth and back on Monday, failed to hear the officer's order to release when another ascent was made and was carried up to a height of 100 feet. Fortunately, he held on to the rope while the airship descended as quickly as possible, so that he escaped with nothing worse than a shaking.'[199]

There was also some praise for the small airships generally:

'Last week in misty weather *Gamma* was out on Wednesday manoeuvring round the district. She was handled in a skilful manner and gives one the impression of being more useful than the exponents of heavier-than-air-machines care to admit. Some of the disadvantages peculiar to this type of aircraft appear to be, on second thoughts, overweighed by their better qualities, and the construction and equipment of small, handy dirigibles would by no means be a step in the wrong direction.'[200]

Public and Parliamentary Concern

During the winter months of 1912–13 there was once more a certain degree of agitation in the Press and Parliament concerning aerial defence. The first incident was at Sheerness in October 1912, when it was claimed that, under cover of darkness, an airship had probed the defences of this strategically important location. Much of the concern was due to the alleged sightings of the navigation lights of mystery airships around the south coast of England. It was in fact a mixture of fact and fiction, as well as the release of fire-balloons by practical jokers. It apparently became known to the Admiralty that the German civil Zeppelin *Hansa*, flown by a naval crew, did make a number of incursions, though this was vigorously denied by German newspapers.[201] The First Lord of the Admiralty informed his fellow members of the Committee of Imperial

Defence that there was very little doubt that the airship reported to have passed over Sheerness was a German vessel.[202] Whatever the truth of the matter the main point at issue was that if an airship or airships had flown over, either on a spying mission or one with more hostile intent, there were no effective means of preventing this. Questions were asked in the House of Commons to which the government was able to give no satisfactory answer.

Commander Masterman nailed his colours to the mast in a trenchant letter to his superiors of January 1913:

> 'I consider that, on account of the position that I now hold, I might be held to have been guilty of a grave neglect of duty if I do not officially place, on paper, my firm conviction that the construction of a rigid naval airship should once more be undertaken and that as soon as possible. This is not only my view, but is the firmly expressed view of my officers, experts in the Royal Aircraft Factory, Army Airship Officers, and, in fact, all who have studied the matter.'[203]

In the House of Lords, Lord Montagu of Beaulieu drew unfavourable comparison on the amounts being spent by other powers and Great Britain on aviation:

> 'If we are likely to be in danger of invasion by dirigibles, or aeroplanes, we must have an adequate number of both to meet that danger. Comparison of the aircraft strength of different countries showed that Germany had twenty-four airships, 420 aeroplanes and twenty-five hydro-aeroplanes. France had twenty dirigibles and 585 aeroplanes – the largest of any foreign power; Russia was a difficult country from which to obtain information, but it was believed she had twelve airships and upwards of 200 aeroplanes. Italy had six dirigibles and 135 aeroplanes. Germany proposed to spend, in the coming year, seven millions on dirigibles and aeroplanes; France £1,500,000; Great Britain £501,000; Italy £450,000 and Japan £250,000. In view of these figures it was to be hoped the government would realise what was being done and remember that we were only at the beginning of huge development in this direction.'[204]

In early 1913 it is doubtful if the RFC could have fielded as many as fifty aircraft, and no more than four airships.[205] The Committee of Imperial Defence, chaired by the Prime Minister, Mr Asquith, discussed the question of airships at considerable length on 6 February 1913. It was concluded that steps should be taken to hasten their development in response to the increasing use of airships, with success, by France, Germany and Italy.[206]

Neville Usborne Gains More Aerial Experience

On 27 February 1913, Usborne was reported in *The Times* as having flown the army airship *Gamma* over Aldershot in the course of a two hour instructional flight. He was not content with flying lighter-than-air craft only, as *Flight* Magazine noted concerning the events at Hendon aerodrome on 1 March 1913:

> 'Sunday morning was again fine and the pupils were out at 7.10., Lieutenant Usborne, RN, a new pupil doing straights on the 35 hp Caudron at his first attempt.'

Two weeks later it was noted that he was making good progress in the hands of his instructor, M Baumann, making nice straight flights in the 35 hp Caudron on both the Saturday and the Sunday. By the beginning of April he was flying circuits in 'an excellent manner' and progressing to figures of eight on the following day. In order to qualify for the issue of the Royal Aero Club 'ticket', a pilot had to satisfy two experienced observers that he could fly two groups of five figures-of-eight, land within 50 yards of a given spot and attain a set height. By the end of that week it could be reported:

> 'The event of the day – passing all his tests after only six days practice by Lieutenant Usborne in the 35 hp Caudron. Flying at an altitude of fully 250 feet, he handled the machine in brilliant style and both his landings were almost dead on the mark.'[207]

Lieutenant C.J. L'Estrange Malone, RN, who in a year's time would be the best man at Usborne's wedding, was also aloft that day; 'Putting up some fine flying in the 80 hp Gnome-Caudron, being in the air some forty-five minutes.'[208]

A Caudron G.3. (*JM Bruce JS Leslie Collection*)

Following distinguished service in the First World War, rising to Commander/ Lieutenant Colonel, Malone became a left-wing Member of Parliament; at different times supporting the Liberal, Labour and Communist interests. He died in 1965 at the age of seventy-five.

On another page it was reported that Aviator's Certificate No 449 had been awarded to Lieutenant Neville Usborne, RFC, flying a Caudron Biplane at the Ewen School, Hendon. His fellow airship pilots, Masterman, Maitland, Boothby, Hicks and Woodcock, also gained Aviator's Certificates during the course of 1913. Usborne was not alone in impressing the press with his skills:

'The Naval members of the Royal Flying Corps are to be congratulated on their skilful handling of the airship *Gamma*. A party who are at present undergoing courses of instruction in the handling of aircraft at the Balloon Sheds, South Farnborough, made a splendid cruise during the middle of the day as far as London and back. After some manoeuvring over the district during the morning, *Gamma* was headed for London, the voyage occupying about four hours there and back. Commander Masterman, RN, Chief of the Naval Wing, was in command; Lieutenant Husband acted in the capacity of pilot, while Lieutenant Woodcock had charge of the engines. Ascending in a very hazy atmosphere from Farnborough Common she disappeared from sight in a north-easterly direction. Somewhere about 3.15 pm she was again sighted returning from the north and, after being cleverly handled above Farnborough Common, was safely housed in the big dirigible shed, being taken in under cover of the huge sailcloth wind screen which protects the entrance of the shed from the wind. Although the journey to London was made at no great altitude, it was most interesting and successful, and, owing to the hazy atmosphere and low-lying clouds, the courses were set and steered by compass. Crossing the Thames at Hampton Court, on arriving over Fulham and Chelsea, the *Gamma* was headed back home, as the weather was by this time beginning to look somewhat threatening, and about four o'clock it commenced to snow, by which time, however, *Gamma* had been successfully grounded and docked. Some fine manoeuvring also took place round the district on Monday and Tuesday this week, particularly on Tuesday, as it was foggy up above, and *Gamma* could be more often heard than seen, which gave a somewhat weird effect. At times during the morning one could see her slipping along at a low altitude like a grey shadow, only to vanish away quickly in the mist. The conditions up above were such that steering could only be done by map and compass.'[209]

Delta.

The airship *Delta* also created a favourable impression early in 1913 when she was taken to the Aero Exhibition at Olympia in London and exhibited over the central aisle for all to see. Those visitors of a technical bent would have been impressed by the colour coding used for the pipework in the car: water – blue, petrol – red, oil – yellow, compressed air – white.[210]

More Parliamentary Activity

In March, the Secretary of State for War, Colonel Seely, answered questions in the House of Commons regarding the current policy in respect of dirigibles. He stated that the army did not have any large rigid dirigible:

'Not because it is feared to face the expense in the least degree, but because it was deliberately laid down from the start that the British Army at the present time does not require Zeppelins. Our army is an expeditionary army. To use a Zeppelin for the purpose of, let us say, the reinforcement of Egypt, or the sending of a large body of men to the frontier to India, operations that are not very likely, but against which we are obliged to guard – to use a Zeppelin in these instances is obviously impossible. This gigantic engine could not be taken there, or if it could be it would be with the utmost difficulty, and the provision of hydrogen for it would be an almost impossible problem.'[211]

He contended that the small, portable, non-rigid airships used by the army were much more practical for its specific needs:

'We therefore decided that the army should have small dirigibles, which could be packed up in a box, put on motor lorries, or on ships, and sent wherever they are required.'[212]

[Author's note: This, of course, never happened in that way, though some of the RN's small airships were delivered to their war stations by rail.]

He went on to boast in the normal political and unsubstantiated fashion:

> 'These dirigibles, I say without hesitation – and all who understand the matter will agree – are superior to any other kind of portable airship. They have various mechanical advantages which I do not wish to dwell upon, because those concerned believe the secret is our own, enabling them to rise more rapidly in the air, and enabling them, above all, to avoid having to part with hydrogen when they rise, and therefore, there is no necessity for re-enforcing that hydrogen when they fall. They have these advantages, which we believe are superior to those of any other nation; but whether that be so or not, the fact remains that the particular balloon which some members of the House saw the other day is an advance upon anything which is known to be in the possession of any foreign power. It goes at a great speed. The speed is 45 miles an hour, and for a small airship that is a remarkable thing.'[213]

The aviation press did not totally agree with the Secretary of State:

> 'The small airships that have been built there are truly quite inadequate from the standpoint of national requirements, but the measure of their size is also the measure of the financial support the government has, at any rate hitherto, been willing to devote to this aspect of aeronautics, and, in consequence, there has been nothing for it but to try and make the best of the funds available. Many of the lessons learned from the construction of these small airships are at any rate likely to be extremely useful in many ways.'[214]

Colonel Seely then made some very interesting points about the division of responsibilities between the Army and the Royal Navy:

> 'The main division between the army and the navy, I think, should be, in this matter of aerial warfare – if warfare there must be – that the navy should take all lighter-than-air and the army should take all heavier-than-air; that is to say, the navy should have the airships and the army the aeroplanes. That is a natural division, because those who know most about it will tell you that the navigation and management of an airship are

more like the management of a ship, and the management of an aeroplane is more like the management of a horse. There are exceptions in the case of our small dirigibles that we pack in boxes, and in the case of the hydro-aeroplanes in possession of the Royal Navy, which are, of course, heavier-than-air.'[215]

More Flying

The Parseval airship PL.18, which became HMA No 4, took to the air for the first time on 23 April 1913. She was 312 feet (98 metres) in length, with a diameter of 51 feet (15 metres) and a capacity of 364,000 cubic feet (10,301 cubic metres). Two 180 hp (133 kW) engines gave a top speed of 43mph (69kph). She could carry two officers and a crew of seven men:

'The Navy's Parseval over London. The Metropolis has had an early opportunity of seeing the Parseval airship purchased by the British Government for the navy. On Monday afternoon, at about half past four, the airship was brought out, and after circling round Farnborough Common, and getting up to a height of 2000 feet, she was headed for London. Steering a direct course, the airship passed over Brooklands and then across South London, past the Houses of Parliament to St. Paul's Cathedral, where the airship was turned. With the wind behind, the Parseval made a fast run back to Farnborough, which was reached at a quarter past six. The wind had veered round a little, and so the vessel was moored in the open for some time until the weather conditions were more suitable for getting her into the shed, Nine passengers were on board, including Lieutenant Stelling, of the Parseval Company, in charge;

Parseval Airship No 4 at Farnborough. (*Via PS Leaman*)

Herr Schaak, in charge of the motors, and a German mechanic; Captain Sueter, RN, Commander Masterman, RN, Commandant of the Naval Wing, Royal Flying Corps; Lieutenants F.L. Boothby and Wilson, RN; Engine Room Artificers Marchant and Cahill; and Mr Ryan, representing Messrs. Vickers.'[216]

Sueter enjoyed the flight and was able to look in through his office window at the Admiralty.[217]

Three weeks later *Flight* noted:

'2½ – Hour Trip by Naval Parseval. With Lieutenant Boothby in command and a crew of nine on board, the new Parseval airship of the Naval Wing of the Royal Flying Corps made a trip from Farnborough to Cowes, Isle of Wight, and back, a distance of about 100 miles in 2 ½ hours on Monday.'[218]

The airship had a very narrow escape in July when a fire broke out inside its shed at Farnborough, which, not surprisingly, was reported as having created 'considerable excitement' before the blaze was brought under control by the airmen with their own fire appliances. It had apparently been started accidentally within a heap of waste on the floor of the shed.[219]

In Usborne's opinion:

'The Parseval made some good flights, but difficulty was found in preventing the envelope stretching during inflation; also the fabric was badly stressed in the wake of the patches that the rigging was secured to. All these stresses made the envelope bad for retaining hydrogen.'[220]

While the Parseval was carrying out its early flights, the First Annual Report was issued by the Air Committee on the Progress of the Royal Flying Corps. With regard to airships it recommended that a policy of active development should be adopted, but not necessarily of large rigid types – to, 'allow the progressive education of the members of the Royal Flying Corps in this class of work with the ultimate end in view of being able to evolve an airship in no way inferior to those in the hands of foreign powers.'[221] The existing position was summarised thus:

Beta, *Gamma*, *Delta*, *Eta* – Military Wing
Epsilon – Military Wing (not yet constructed)
Willows (HMA No2), Astra-Torres, Parseval – Naval Wing

No. A/22

Dated 26 January 1912

THIS IS TO CERTIFY, that Mr. Neville F. Usborne

has served as Lieutenant on board H.M.S. Hermione
(additional for service with Naval airship No 1)
under my command, from the twenty-sixth day of September 1910
R.N.

to the twenty-fifth day of January 1912, during which period

he has conducted himself * with Sobriety and to my entire satisfaction.
Lieutenant Usborne is a very zealous and capable officer.
He has worked hard in making himself an expert in aeronautical
work and has considerable knowledge in this line.
I have strongly recommended Lieutenant Usborne for promotion.
He was selected as captain of naval airship N°1

Murray F. Sueter

{ Captain,
{ H.M.S. Hermione
Inspecting Captain of airships

* Here the Captain is to insert in his own handwriting the conduct of the Officer,
including the fact of his Sobriety, if deserving of it.

No. A.20

Dated 22nd December 1913

THIS IS TO CERTIFY, that Mr. Neville F. Usborne

has served as Lieutenant on board H.M.S. "Hermes" (Farnborough)
Squadron Commander
under my command, from the 9th day of May 1913

to the 23rd day of December 19 13, during which period

he has conducted himself * with sobriety, zeal, and entirely to
my satisfaction. He is a most capable Airship Pilot,
with an excellent knowledge of all branches of
Aeronautical work.

Gerald Vernon
Commd. R.N.

{ Captain,
{ H.M.S. Hermes

* Here the Captain is to insert in his own handwriting the conduct of the Officer,
including the fact of his Sobriety, if deserving of it.

Two of Neville's pre First World War Certificates of Service. (*Via Sue Killbracken*)

It was noted that none of these craft were as large as the big German airships and that it was likely that larger airships would be needed for naval purposes, to which end negotiations had been entered into by the Admiralty with regard to the purchase or construction of these. It was added that no airship in military service had been involved in a major accident leading to loss of life, that both mooring masts and sheds were required, and that the question of the manufacture and storage of hydrogen was in an unsatisfactory state.

On a more personal level, to cover the period May 1913 to December 1913 at Farnborough as Lieutenant and Squadron Commander, Usborne was formally reported on by Commander Masterman (the location is given as HMS *Hermes*, as this temporarily and rudimentarily converted cruiser was at this time carrying the HQ of the Naval Wing on its books). 'He is a most capable airship pilot with an excellent knowledge of all aspects of aeronautical work.'[222] While awaiting arrival of the Astra-Torres and as a, 'naval cuckoo in the Farnborough nest',[223] Usborne trained the additional naval officers gradually appointed there in free ballooning, and in flying and handling the smaller military airships. He made a return visit to Portsmouth in *Beta* in mid-1913, with a mixed naval and military crew. This time signals were made 'from a considerable height' asking for permission to land at Whale Island Gunnery School. While the necessary preparations were made to assemble a ground handling party, the airship circled Portsmouth Harbour and Spithead as she gradually descended to land on a lawn in front of the officers' quarters.[224]

The King and Queen, along with Princesses Mary and Victoria, visited Aldershot in May and were treated to some aerial displays:

'On his arrival at Aldershot the King witnessed a cavalry display, and then saw some manoeuvres by *Beta*. From the airship a photograph was taken of the King and the plate sent down on a parachute, and developed in one of the field dark rooms. They then inspected *Gamma* and *Delta* in the shed, and also the car of the new Astra-Torres airship, and subsequently *Gamma* made an ascent.'[225]

That evening:

'Some night flying was indulged in, the airship *Beta* being up and cruising over the Royal Pavilion. Several aeroplanes were flying in the moonlight, and one machine, owing to a failing engine, brought down some telegraph wires. The King sent a message to his troops, luckily not by telegraph, "I was glad to find a marked development in the work and administration of the Royal Flying Corps, and what courage and *esprit de corps* animate all ranks of this newly-formed arm.'"[226]

Early the following month, at the King's Birthday Parade, *Gamma* and *Beta* performed some attractive evolutions during a mass fly-past (including four BE-type biplanes, six Maurice Farmans, two Henri Farmans, and a Blériot) over Laffan's Plain at Farnborough:

> 'The machines flew at an altitude of about 150 feet, and each (including the airships), on passing the saluting point, dipped almost to the ground, the graceful way in which the manoeuvre was carried out being very impressive. The airships in particular showed the ease with which they can be handled, descending as they did, to within a few feet of the earth, and then up again in a gentle sweeping movement.'[227]

The magazine featured a very attractive photograph of the two airships in flight with the Blériot circling around them. Not long afterwards *Gamma* was despatched on a six-day reconnaissance tour, making camp at Bracknell in Berkshire with the Irish Guards.

The first flight of the Astra-Torres XIV, HMA No 3, was made at Farnborough on 12 June 1913 with the French pilot, M Rousell in charge and a French crew, but with Usborne and others on board; it was not very successful. Masterman later wrote:

HMA No 3 at Farnborough in 1913.

'During the trial the blower broke down and the ship lost pressure, Usborne displayed great coolness and assisted to avoid disaster in the free balloon landing subsequently carried out.'[228]

Onlookers saw the envelope begin to sag in the middle, being almost doubled up before the car touched the ground. It was later reported that the problem had been caused by slippage of the belt that drove the fan to maintain the air pressure inside the envelope.[229]

It was a much larger craft than the other British non-rigids, having a capacity of 280,000 cubic feet (7924 cubic metres) and was driven by twin Chenu engines of 210 hp (155 kW) each. She carried a crew of six, was equipped with wireless and could be armed with machine guns. The car could be moved fore and aft for trimming purposes, either by power or by hand; this proved unsatisfactory and was abandoned. During the same week as HMA No 3 made her debut, *Delta* undertook a successful flight of nearly 200 miles (321 kilometres) in a time of some four hours, which indicated a ground speed in the region of 50mph (80kph).[230]

The most interesting events in July were a visit by the Prince of Wales on the twentieth, when he was taken up for a half-hour cruise in *Beta* by Major Maitland,[231] and a little later in the month some experiments in dropping bombs, *Beta* having been fitted with a, 'special mechanism attached to a sighting apparatus.'[232]

On 19 August 1913, Usborne was in command of HMA No 2 (Willows No 4) when it experienced engine failure due to a broken crankshaft, near Odiham in Hampshire. He managed to return it as a free balloon to its shelter at Odiham

A view from the ground showing No 2 being towed by *Eta*. (*Via Nigel Caley*)

The start of the tow,
Eta above and HMA
No 2 below.

and was able to assess his options: (a) Leave her broken down at Odiham, which was undesirable as a large social gathering was due be held there. (b) Deflate the envelope and return to Farnborough by road, which would mean terminating observations of the airship's new-type fabric. (c) Repair the engine

Airship No 2 being towed, as seen from *Eta*. (*Via Nigel Caley*)

on site, which would take two weeks. (d) To walk her home; which would be both conspicuous and laborious. (e) Seek a tow, an operation which had never before been attempted.[233]

He opted for this latter course. The airship would be towed back to Farnborough by Captain Waterlow in command of the latest army airship *Eta*, which was still in the hands of the Royal Aircraft Factory. Therefore, Usborne sought the permission of the assistant superintendent, S. Heckstall-Smith, and also the Officer Commanding No 1 Squadron, Major E.M. Maitland, which was readily granted. Lieutenant Woodcock prepared the ship, while Usborne took charge of laying out the towing cable. Waterlow arrived at 6am on 20 August, by which time Usborne had laid out 600 feet (183 metres) of 1½ inch (4 cms) hemp rope to the leeward of his craft. The front end was secured behind the ballonet tube of *Eta* and run aft. To prevent the rope fouling the rudder a 15lb (6.81 kg) bag of sand was hung from a cable at that point, while the line was attached to the centre of No 2's car. No 2 was trimmed with negative buoyancy to avoid fouling *Eta*, the coxswain doing this with the hand pump. The slack was taken up and the tow began gently on one engine. When No 2 was clear of the trees, Waterlow started his second engine. The 8 mile (12.8 km) trip was made at a ground speed of 25mph (40kph) against a 5mph (8kph) headwind and at a height of 200 feet (60.96 m). Also taken on board as a passenger was Denys Corbett Wilson, who was the first man to complete the crossing from Great Britain to Ireland by aeroplane (on 22 April 1912 he flew in a Blériot monoplane from Fishguard to Enniscorthy in one hour and forty minutes).

Over Farnborough the height was increased to 400 feet (121.92 m), the tow line was slipped and the sandbag dropped away. The landing party caught the mooring rope and No 2 came to rest exactly on its alighting mark. So unusual was the incident that it even received the attention of the *New York Times*:

'The novel sight of an airship towing her disabled companion was witnessed at Aldershot this afternoon. The British Army airship *Eta* and a naval airship were manoeuvring when the machinery of the latter became disabled. The *Eta* attached a hawser to the other dirigible and towed her to the factory for repairs.'[234]

Waterlow later received a letter of thanks and commendation from the Admiralty. Commander Masterman's report on the incident stated; 'This evolution demonstrates once more the great value of swivelling propellers; it confirms views previously held that towing of airships would be practicable and useful and is, I believe, the first experiment of the kind to be carried out anywhere.'[235]

Captain Sueter noted that; 'It opens out considerable new possibilities in the employment of airships.'[236]

Usborne himself summarised the incident and lessons learned as follows:

'From these experiments I consider: (1) Towing is a safe and useful manoeuvre. (2) That with practice and certain preparations, airships may in due course be relied upon to take in tow <u>in the air</u>. (3) That material use can be made in war, for the execution of a very long voyage, or for the carriage of a very large amount of explosives, of the idea of towing a suitable old envelope (of which there are always a number available) which could carry only additional petrol, or say, five tons of explosives. (4) A great deal of experience is still necessary as regards length of tow line, relative buoyancies of the two ships, etc, before the operation can be regarded as the same straightforward affair it is at sea.'[237]

Eta had just that month been accepted into service for trials, making her first flight on the evening of 18 August. Her design was the culmination of all the experience gained in the previous six years. Her suspension system was innovative in that it did away with much of the normal bridle and netting by replacing it with six rigging cables. These sub-divided several times until thirty-six attachments were affixed to the envelope by means of adhesive patches, which were also stitched on, thus the load was spread much more evenly.

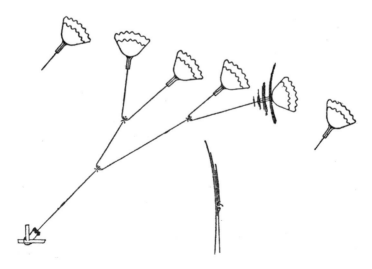

Rigging with *Eta* patches and bridles.

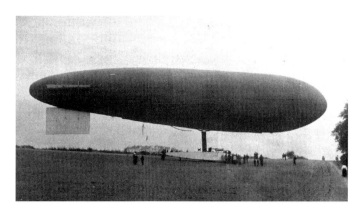

Eta, which had just entered service, before giving HMA No 2 a tow.

Eta's capacity was 118,000 cubic feet (3339 cubic metres) with two 80 hp (58 kW) Canton-Ume engines, each chain-driving a swivelling propeller mounted on an outrigger. Their function was described as follows:

'As the airship ascends, these propellers are swivelled round, so that ultimately their axes are horizontal for full speed ahead. In order to stop the airship they can be turned completely round so as to thrust backwards, and they can similarly be used for lowering the airship for the purposes of descent.'[238]

Eta successfully completed the trials in September with an eight and a quarter hour cruise from Farnborough to Portsmouth and back, in the very capable hands of Clive Waterlow. Cruising with and against a 14mph (22kph) wind, she maintained a mean speed of 42mph (67kph) at a height of 4200 feet (1280 metres). This was hailed as a duration record for a British airship. Three airships, *Beta*, *Delta* and *Eta*, and three squadrons of fixed-wing aircraft, took part in the army manoeuvres in the area of Daventry and Aylesbury, with the two armies being commanded by Generals Haig and Rawlinson. *The Times* commented:

'Failing defeat in the air, or fire from below, modern aircraft will, at all times, except in continuous bad weather, enable a commander to learn with very fair accuracy the position and direction of hostile columns while they are several days' march away from him.'[239]

Delta and *Eta* were both equipped with wireless sets for the manoeuvres and were based at Dunchurch, near Rugby in Warwickshire. In total, *Delta* sent sixty-six messages in the course of seven flights and, on 24 September, carried out a successful night reconnaissance. *Eta*, due to engine trouble, played no effective part in the manoeuvres, but during her journey from Farnborough to Dunchurch, she maintained wireless contact with Aldershot until reaching Woodstock in Oxfordshire, then she called up Dunchurch and kept in communication for the remainder of the flight. Captain Lefroy, RE, who was the RFC's wireless expert, stated in his report:

'It seems probable that HM Airships *Delta* and *Eta* can exchange messages with each other when 100 miles (160 kilometres) apart in the air, which may prove useful for organization purposes, etc. I received clear signals from the North Foreland station (and a ship to which she was talking) when 130 miles (208 kilometres) NW of it, and whilst HMA *Eta* was cruising northwards at touring speed.'[240]

The Times noting the good work of the airships, and *Delta* in particular, sagely and judiciously commented:

'So far as airships and aeroplanes are concerned, the honours for obtaining information were fairly divided and do not appear to justify the threatened elimination of the airship from our war material. The *Delta* was usually out first and home last. She brought early, accurate and valuable information. The airship alone can work in the mists and fogs so prevalent in our islands, and she alone can at present travel safely by night and report bivouacs and railway movements. It would not be a good reply to the policy of other great powers were we to put all our money into aeroplanes and to neglect the dirigible, even if we all agree that the aeroplane has the greater future in front of her.'[241]

During the course of the manoeuvres, Major Maitland expressed his concern about the lack of provision of measures to permit aircrew to escape safely from damaged airships or aeroplanes. Given his successful experiments with parachute descents, he should have been listened to much more carefully, but at this stage he was at odds with the views of senior officers – who were not the ones risking their necks. Murray Sueter had a very high regard for Maitland, whom he described as, 'a most courageous pioneer airman; his parachute descents were famous. He would drop from an airship perfectly unconcerned. Just before he made one of his perilous descents with a parachute of no great efficiency I asked him in a casual way what he thought of death? He gave me a characteristic reply, '"Oh, nobody should mind death. Why should anybody mind it? They should look upon death as a great adventure.'" Sueter noted that Maitland regularly used a Guardian Angel static-type parachute, invented by a Mr E.R. Calthrop and which saved the lives of many kite balloon crews during the First World War.[242]

Delta experienced both misfortune and success. On a test flight, she broke down near Faversham in Kent and was forced to land. Wireless messages of distress were sent out, the aerials being fixed to a neighbouring tree, and in response Commander C.R. Samson, RN, and Captain G.V. Wildman-Lushington, RMA, flew over in Short biplanes from the Naval Flying School at Eastchurch to render assistance. Having been repaired and now piloted by Clive Waterlow, *Delta* next left Farnborough early in the morning and travelled to the Isle of Sheppey before the wind rose. There, several naval pilots turned up and flew round her 'joyously'. Leaving Sheerness about 11 am, she reached London about midday, assisted by a strong breeze from the south-east, and passed over St Paul's and St James's Park. She crossed the Royal Aero Club building with about 50 feet (15 metres) to spare and went up Bond Street, the pilot showing her to be under excellent control. Finally, she reached Farnborough safely, having beaten the *Eta's* record as she had been in the air about eight and a half hours.[243]

The Astra-Torres, HMA No 3, emerged again on 8 September, after some months out of commission for necessary alterations. Its first half hour flight was again in the hands of M Hugon, M Rousell and a French crew, with Usborne, Commander Oliver Schwann and Commander Masterman as passengers. It performed satisfactorily, was formally accepted by the RN and soon began a successful trials programme. This included a six hour flight around Portsmouth, the Isle of Wight, Bournemouth and Portland. She also established a record speed for a British airship of 51mph (82kph) during the course of a one hour

HMA No 3, Astra-Torres, is secured at a portable mooring mast at Farnborough in the spring of 1914. (*Ces Mowthorpe Collection*)

flight, with Captain Sueter and Lieutenant L'Estrange Malone as passengers. Usborne was appointed to command in October, with Lieutenant W.C. Hicks as his flying officer,[244] and later wrote:

'The Astra-Torres was of a tri-lobe form, and allowed an internal system of rigging that distributed the load fore and aft the length of the envelope. This Astra-Torres patent for suspension was a good system and the envelopes on the whole kept their shape well.'[245]

A newspaper report a few days later stated:

'The naval airship Astra-Torres, navigated by Lieutenant N.F. Usborne, RN, and a crew of seamen, made an evening flight yesterday. A heavy fog obscured her from view almost from the first moment of her ascent. The aircraft returned after dark and was lighted to her landing by a row of lamps, while a semi-circle of electric lights indicated the door of her shed. Earlier in the day the naval craft was flying with the *Eta* and displayed a faster turn of speed than the army dirigible balloon.'[246]

On the twenty-fourth of the month he took Winston Churchill for a flight, of which *The Times* wrote:

'In the meantime the Astra-Torres naval airship had arrived at the Isle of Grain from Farnborough, descending on the marshes near the air station at half past twelve. While at the aeroplane station, the ship took Mr Churchill and Sir Ian Hamilton on board, and, under the command of Lieutenant Usborne, RN, made a circuitous flight lasting an hour and a half. After landing her passengers the airship, leaving at 4.20, returned to Farnborough Common, where she arrived at 5.45. On the homeward and outward journey the ship carried, besides Lieutenant Usborne and his crew of sailors, Commander Masterman, RN, Engineer Lieutenant Cave-Browne-Cave, RN, and Lieutenant Hicks, RN.'[247]

The distinguished passenger enjoyed the flight and availed himself of the opportunity, not long afterwards, to fly in both *Beta* and *Delta*. He later wrote of the Astra-Torres:

'I went in her for a beautiful cruise at about 1000 feet around Chatham and the Medway. She is a very satisfactory vessel and I was allowed to steer her for an hour. She was very easy to steer.'[248]

Mr Churchill had arrived at the Isle of Grain from Eastchurch for his flight with Usborne in the Short Biplane No 3, flown by Commander C.R. Samson, RN, having been conveyed there in the morning by the Admiralty yacht *Enchantress*.[249] By the end of the year the airship was reported as having made a number of successful flights visiting Portsmouth, Sheerness and Chatham. On 18 October, the intrepid Major Maitland made the world's first parachute descent from an airship, namely *Delta*, which was being piloted by Captain Waterlow. He jumped from 1800 feet (548 metres), swaying to and fro in an arc of some 50 feet (15 metres) as he descended under the canopy. The parachute fell into deep water at Cove Reservoir, but Maitland, being just at the end of one of the oscillations, came down in a shallower part. When the jump took place *Delta* rose sharply with the reduction in payload, but this was swiftly arrested by Waterlow.[250]

On another flight in the Astra-Torres, Captain Sueter, who was flying as a passenger, made an unusual request. He asked Usborne to bring along three dozen eggs. As the airship circled over Farnborough, the eggs were dropped at regular intervals from a height of 800 feet (243 metres). It was a perfectly still day and the eggs dropped and penetrated the earth like bullets, without smashing. By this means Sueter was able to ascertain the turning circle of the airship and to judge how responsive it was to the action of the rudder.[251]

Also in October 1913, airships became the sole responsibility of Naval Wing. *Beta*, *Gamma*, *Delta* and *Eta* were handed over by the army to the navy – apparently as the result of an informal discussion between Winston Churchill, the First Lord of the Admiralty and Colonel Seely, the Secretary of State for War. Major Sefton Brancker, 'the monocled, deceptively foppish Indian Army officer, whose approachability, drive and enthusiasm belied his image and who

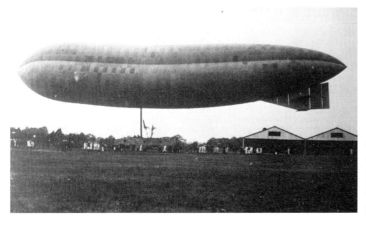

Another view of the Astra-Torres, HMA No 3, at Farnborough. (*via PS Leaman*)

was one of the principal motive forces in British aviation for twenty years,'[252] who was serving with the Military Wing as the Assistant Director of Military Aeronautics later wrote:

> 'This was a bombshell! The General Staff were furious, and the Military Aeronautics Directorate threw up their hands to heaven and called down curses on the heads of all politicians. We soldiers loved our little airships and fought hard to retain them; they were small but they led the world in efficient handling and we felt they were the germ of a great future.'[253]

He added:

> 'But Seely was absolutely right. In practice at their then state of development, our airships would have been perfectly useless to the army, whereas they proved invaluable to the Admiralty in the Great War.'[254]

This division of responsibility had in fact been considered by Seely's technical sub-committee in 1912, which had recommended the attachment of naval officers to the military wing of the RFC for airship duties (the first of whom was Neville Usborne) to learn the ropes with a view to the naval wing taking the lead in due course.[255] The airships, along with their equipment and plant, were valued at £65,000, with the Admiralty agreeing that such an amount should be placed by the Treasury to the credit of the War Office. The officers and men of the former airship squadron of the RFC would henceforth be attached to the naval wing and placed under the command of Commander E.A.D. Masterman, RN, with Neville Usborne as his deputy. He later wrote:

> 'These small airships were good for training, but they could only make short flights and their engines were none too reliable.'[256]

Masterman commented:

> 'This period was one of the happiest of his life, he was continually active and quite willing to start again at the beginning in the hope of gradually building up a naval airship service.'[257]

In the same year, works commenced at Kingsnorth, on the Hoo Peninsula at Medway, not far from Sheerness and Chatham. Two large airship sheds were planned, one made of metal and the other of wood, as well as all the necessary accommodation and services, including hydrogen generating plant, gas tanks, fuel tanks, workshops, wireless station and a light railway, for what would become an important Royal Naval Air Station – the principal airship dockyard, centre of research and development, and major training establishment.[258]

On 3 December 1913, Captain Clive Waterlow, AFAeS, RE, read a paper before the Aeronautical Society of Great Britain titled: 'The Coming Airship'. This was followed by a lantern show with slides showing the construction, method of working and the control of the airships *Gamma*, *Beta*, *Eta*, Willows, Parseval and Astra-Torres. In his talk he argued that, until relatively recently, there had been a prejudice in the press against airships and that journalists seemed to regard airships in wartime as being at the mercy of any aeroplane. He countered this by saying:

> 'I don't think it is generally realised that the airship has by no means reached such an advanced stage of development as the aeroplane; the possibilities and probabilities of the future are very rosy and very wonderful.'[259]

He went on to discuss the differences between the lines of airship development in England and on the Continent. In England the focus had been on producing smaller craft with greater handiness and control, in Europe the aim had been to build the largest ships possible with the longest range. Waterlow then described how, on manoeuvres with the army in September 1913, *Delta* and *Eta* had coped well in the field with rain and bad weather, needing only a small handling party. He looked forward to a day soon when airships would go as fast as 55 or 60mph (88 to 95kph). He added:

> 'If ever airships achieve 70mph (112kph) it is difficult to see where the aeroplane, as we know it today, will come in at all for war purposes; and this, of course, applies equally to seaplanes.'[260]

Waterlow was underestimating the potential of the aeroplane in this respect, as the world absolute speed record for a fixed-wing aircraft stood at 111mph (179kph) in 1913 – though it should be noted that the aircraft was unencumbered by any warlike stores or other useful load.

On the question of safety he saw fire as the greatest hazard – from the engines, the wireless apparatus, or other sources, 'such as defective wiring in the electric lighting circuit, matches and so on'.[261] The combustible material which could be set alight he identified as, 'the gas within the envelope, the petrol for the motors, and such portions of the car and framework as are not made of metal'. He believed that the risk of fire from the engine could be rendered small by guards on the carburettor and the exhaust pipes, as well as silencers which also acted to cool down exhaust gases; rogue sparks from the wireless could be eliminated by careful design, and risk from other sources could be dealt with by good safety procedures. As regards the combustible materials, hydrogen was the only suitable gas available and it was essential to allow some means for it to be vented when required. He looked to the development of a satisfactory automatic valve placed on the top of the envelope, and encouraged chemists to seek a light non-inflammable gas which could be mixed with hydrogen and make it inert, but not materially impair its lift. In 1903, large reserves of the light and inert gas – helium – were found in the natural gas fields of the USA. The world's first helium-filled airship, the US Navy's C-7, first flew on 1 December 1921.

Petrol was also necessary, though he hoped that it could eventually be replaced by heavy oils. In the meantime it should be carried on board aft of the engine and as far away from it as possible. As regards non-metal items, they should be fireproofed. He regarded the greatest danger to a non-rigid airship being a propeller blade breaking off and slicing into the envelope. To counteract this he recommended that the envelope should be divided internally with partitions to minimise the damage caused by a foreign body of any sort making a hole in the envelope. He then moved on to examine design; firstly the envelope, which was usually made of a fabric of cotton and rubber, dyed yellow. Other possibilities were goldbeater's skin or silk. The main aim was to produce an outer skin which could be easily manufactured, would hold gas well, would not deteriorate and would absorb no moisture. Next, he emphasised the desirability of internal partitions and noted that the latest Zeppelin had seventeen separate gas containers. As regards armament, he recommended a gun should be mounted on top of the envelope. Concerning the powerplant, he thought a six cylinder engine (or engines depending upon the size of the airship) driving a four-bladed propeller would be sufficient. Swivelling propellers were very useful in assisting smooth landings at all weights. The control system should be easily within the reach and view of the pilot, or in a larger airship there should be a telegraph instrument. Finally, he considered the use of the airship in military and commercial roles. He recommended for military use a non-rigid type slightly bigger than the Astra-Torres airship HMA No 3, with a speed of 55mph (88kph), a crew of eight or nine, nine hours endurance and two guns mounted in the car and on the top of the envelope, 'both designed to shoot all around the compass.'[262] He saw a great future ahead for the civil airship and wondered why a service from London to Paris was not already in being. Newspaper and mail delivery from the air to rural areas, dropped by parachute to village shops, was also seen as a promising way ahead. Aerial yachts for the rich were also predicted. In conclusion, he described an imaginary voyage from London to Paris in the airship *Albatross*. The first of the audience to rise and discuss Waterlow's paper was Neville Usborne. His main point was that he considered the speaker to have been overly pessimistic with regard to the future potential top speed of airships. He thought that the prospects for an airship attaining a speed of 70mph (112kph) in the near future were excellent and went on to say:

> 'High speed would enable an airship to face any gale and be largely independent of weather conditions, which are always a factor in aerial navigation.'[263]

[Author's note: On 27 October 2004, the American adventurer, the late Steve Fossett, and his co-pilot Hans-Paul Stroehle, in the Zeppelin NT, set an officially verified speed world record for airships over a 1000 metre course of 115kph (71mph). This is below the maximum performances of Zeppelin LZ 129 *Hindenburg* and LZ130 *Graf Zeppelin II*, which attained more than 130kph (80.5mph), and the American airship ZRS-5 *Macon*, which reached 140.3kph (87mph). However, these speeds were never verified by the official body responsible for keeping these records, the *Fédération Aéronautique Internationale*. [www.records.fai.org]

Others who spoke after Neville Usborne included the man-lifting kite pioneer, Major B.F.S. Baden-Powell, E.T. Willows, the airship manufacturer, Mervyn O'Gorman, the superintendent of His Majesty's Aircraft Factory at Farnborough and F.M. Green, the factory's design engineer, who were all generally in agreement with the points made by Waterlow. It was noted that the meeting concluded with a vote of thanks to Captain Waterlow for his excellent paper.[264]

   In January 1914, as had been agreed, the Admiralty took over the airships, work plans and aerodrome at Farnborough from the Military Wing. The airship branch at this time consisted of six officers, thirty-eight men and civilian repair staff under the command of Commander Masterman, RN. Naval and military seniorities were adjusted to a common list, which was a very delicate matter. It is appropriate at this point to consider the rank structure in the RN air branch at this time:

Wing Captain = Captain RN
Wing Commander = Commander RN

Squadron Commander (in command) = Lieutenant Commander RN
Squadron Commander (not in command) = Lieutenant RN of over four years seniority (but senior to all Flight Commanders)
Flight Commander = Lieutenant RN of over four years seniority
Flight Lieutenant = Lieutenant RN
Flight Sub-Lieutenant = Sub-Lieutenant
Warrant Officer 1st Grade = Commissioned Warrant Officer RN
Warrant Officer 2nd Grade = Warrant Officer RN[265]

The flying rank was not necessarily the career officer's substantive rank. As an example, a Lieutenant RN could be appointed to flying duties as a Flight Lieutenant, Flight Commander, Squadron Commander, or even Wing Commander. If and when an officer reverted to general service, he could find himself back as a Lieutenant. Ranks in the RNAS were denoted by stars over the sleeve lace (for Flight Lieutenants and Squadron Commanders) and three stripes in the sleeve lacing for Wing Commanders. All pilots wore the RNAS eagle badge above the loop of their left sleeve lace. For an officer transferring in the airship service as it moved from the Royal Engineers to the RFC, RNAS and finally the RAF, the position could become even more complicated, particularly when rapid wartime promotion, temporary and brevet ranks were factored in. For example, E.M. Maitland was a Lieutenant in the Essex Regiment when he was attached to the Balloon School in 1910; by the following year he was a captain in the Air Battalion, Royal Engineers. Within a few months he was a major in the Royal Flying Corps and, at the commencement of the First World War, he was promoted not only to lieutenant colonel, but also wing commander in the RNAS, rising to colonel in the RFC and wing captain in the RNAS. In 1918 he became a brigadier general in the RAF and, when the rank structure for the new service was agreed in 1919, he was firstly a permanent commission as a group captain and then promoted to air commodore. Maitland therefore served as an officer in the infantry, RFC, RNAS and RAF.
    Masterman wrote:

'Usborne's position in the airship world rose through this move. From being almost a guest of the RFC at Farnborough, he was now a person of importance in the combined service, and his capabilities and knowledge were fully recognised by his former hosts.'[266]

Usborne was promoted to commander RN – a substantive, not an 'air duties' rank – on 1 January 1914[267] and the following notice appeared in *Flight* Magazine of 28 February 1914:

'Wedding Bells: CONGRATULATIONS to Commander Neville Usborne, RN, of the Naval Wing of the Royal Flying Corps, who was married on Monday at St. Margaret's Church, Westminster, to Miss Betty Hamilton.'

The Times noted:

'The bridegroom and the best man, Lieutenant C.J. L'Estrange Malone, RN, Assistant to the Director at the Air Department of the Admiralty, were in full uniform, and there was a guard of honour at the church from the Naval Airship Section and from the bridegroom's ship, Naval Airship III.'[268]

Betty Usborne.

Helen Monteith 'Betty' Hamilton, who was 21-years-old, was the daughter of the artist and tea-planter Vereker Hamilton, and was also the niece of General Sir Ian Hamilton, who would command the ill-fated Mediterranean Expeditionary Force during the Battle of Gallipoli.

Almost a Taste of Action

The airship branch almost got a taste of action in the spring of 1914 when two Squadron Commanders, F.L. Boothby and R. Bell Davies, were sent to the British Protectorate, Somaliland, to survey the possibility of airships being used there. The intent was that they should assist the Camel Constabulary in suppressing Sayyīd Muhammad `Abd Allāh al-Hasan, 'the Mad Mullah', and his dervishes, who were raiding the country from Ethiopia and Italian Somaliland. Airships had been decided upon by the Admiralty because aero engines were at that time so unreliable the inevitable result of mechanical failure for an aeroplane would be a forced landing, which the Mullah could claim as being due to his magical powers.

A paper was circulated by the First Lord of the Admiralty considering the proposal of the Colonial Office to use aircraft, which noted that the whole wealth of the Mullah was in camels and livestock and that very considerable damage could be inflicted upon him, apart from actual offensive operations, by stampeding his stock and keeping them from their wells.

It was considered that three airships would suffice, two of the Parseval type with modified cars for operations, accompanied by *Eta*, also modified to enable her to carry stores to the advanced base, to assist with a photographic survey of the trade routes and to be available as a spare ship in case of necessity. One portable and two canvas sheds would be needed, a hydrogen plant, armament from the Ordnance Department, spares (including envelopes), petrol, oil and photographic equipment. It was envisaged that eight officers and forty-nine other ranks would be required, supplemented by Indian troops from Berbera should further manpower be required for handling parties. The experience of the Italian airships at Tripoli was cited as proof that airships could operate satisfactorily in the climatic conditions prevailing in the Somalian winter. The total cost was estimated at £75,000.[269]

In the event the onset of hostilities in Europe concentrated minds elsewhere; the Mad Mullah had to wait until 1919–20, when aircraft of the RAF did the job – one of the first examples of air control beloved by Air Chief Marshal Sir Hugh Trenchard.

A Parting of the Ways

June 1914 brought the final breach between the two wings of the RFC when the Admiralty issued a series of regulations governing the organisation of the Royal Naval Air Service, which thereby became a distinct branch of the Royal Navy in much the same fashion as the Royal Marines. Remarkably, the Admiralty was able to make this move without either being questioned or contradicted by either Parliament or in the Press. It was very much a unilateral declaration of independence. The second (and final) annual report on the RFC to include notes on airships was issued at about this time, and reported that in the previous

Gamma over Portsmouth in June 1914.

HMA No 3 at Kingsnorth in 1914 by Vereker Hamilton.

year a distance of 5,275 miles (9,160 kilometres) had been flown by airships without casualties, with an additional 12,848 miles (20,557 kilometres) by free balloons, much used for training purposes.[270]

In mid-1914, Kingsnorth was commissioned as a constructional, experimental, and class G station, with the stated purpose of protecting Chatham and Sheerness. It was decided that Astra-Torres and Parseval airships would be stationed there. Remarkably, the First Lord of the Admiralty found the time to write to the Director of Air Services about the security arrangements on 7 June:

'The wooden shed at Kingsnorth would be a fine quarry for the suffragettes and it appears to me that it should be watched. The existing watchman informs me that he watches all night long and on Sundays from 12 noon till 7 o'clock next morning. This means that he probably walks round once or twice and goes to sleep for the rest of the time. The matter should have your attention and a regular watch established pending the time when the men enter.'[271]

Kingsnorth

On 1 July 1914, Usborne was appointed as wing commander and confirmed in command of Kingsnorth. He had been there since mid-June and had to deal with a potentially dangerous fire in the metal airship shed on 28 June.

Masterman wrote of this period:

> 'The Airship Branch was unprepared for hostilities, but Usborne was full of schemes for the use of such material as was available and specialised in the mooring out of non-rigid airships in the open so that they could be available for patrol work over the sea. Godmersham Park was the scene of some of his activities.'[272]

Napoleon believed that an army marched on its stomach; from correspondence between Usborne and an applicant for the post of messman at Kingsnorth it would appear that Usborne believed that a well-fed wardroom was a happy and efficient one. It also shows that he paid considerable attention to detail and gives a very good indication of the style of life enjoyed by RN officers of that period.

W.H. Gunner sought a position as messman in a series of letters to Usborne commencing in August 1913. The agreement was written in Usborne's own hand:

> Victualling agreement with W.H. Gunner – messman.
>
> Each Officer, 2/- (10p) per day or £3 per month, guest 3/6d (17½p) per day.
>
> Breakfast – porridge, fish, bacon & eggs or sausages, omelettes or kidneys, boiled eggs, tongue, two jams, and marmalade.
>
> Luncheon – soup, two hot dishes (fish, steak chops or joint), three cold joints, potatoes, second vegetable (in season), sweet (twice weekly), cheese, pickles, celery or salad (in season).
>
> Sunday Supper (in lieu of dinner) – soup, fish, roast meats, galantine or pie, ham, tongue, potatoes, sweet cheese, pickles, celery or salad (in season).
>
> Tea – pot of tea, plate of bread and butter or buttered toast. Extras in rotation: Fullers bake, crumpets, biscuits, rock cakes.
>
> Dinner – soup, fish or entrée, one joint, sweet, savoury and coffee.
>
> Only the best articles of food are to be purchased by the messman and another brand of tea or coffee shall be supplied by him if that provided

does not give satisfaction. Best Parisian coffee will be served after lunch at 2d (1p) per cup and gratis after dinner. Special attention should be given to the variety of meals avoiding any monotony. All beers, minerals (including a good brand of ginger beer), cigars, cigarettes and tobaccos to be supplied by messman at lowest current prices.[273]

He was also concerned about the suitability of neighbouring Hoo and Rochester as places of resort for the men when off duty. He regarded Hoo as, 'a particularly undesirable village, full of public houses of the low agricultural type.'[274] He therefore proposed that a wet canteen, ie, serving alcoholic beverages should be constructed on site, so that social drinking could be monitored and, hopefully, controlled. Further suggestions included the provision of games, indoor pastimes and garden allotments, 'so there is no reason why the place should not become a happy, self-contained colony.'[275]

Both airships, No 3, which was a particularly comfortable ship, with an enclosed car and a radio set, and No 4, made a good number of successful flights from Kingsnorth during 1914, including, in April, another circuit of London landmarks, this time by No 4.

In July 1914 the Naval Wing was renamed the Royal Naval Air Service. It comprised the Air Department at the Admiralty; the Central Air Office at Sheerness; the Royal Naval Flying School at Eastchurch; the Royal Naval Air Stations, and all seaplanes, aeroplanes, airships, seaplane ships, balloons and kites employed for naval purposes. The first Director of the Air Department of the Admiralty was Captain Murray Sueter, CB. There were six wing commanders, who were, in order of seniority: O. Schwann, E.A.D. Masterman, F.R. Scarlett,

A Zeppelin flies over the visiting warships of the Royal Navy at Kiel in June 1914.

E.M. Maitland, N.F. Usborne and C.R. Samson. Personnel already serving in the RN, RM, RNR and RNVR could apply for transfer. This was shortly before the Royal Fleet Review at Spithead, which was held from 18–22 July 1914. The Astra-Torres HMA No 3 flew over the fleet in July 1914 under the command of Wing Commander Usborne, with Flight Lieutenant W. Hicks as 2nd Officer. It was joined from Farnborough by HMA No 4 (Parseval), Squadron Commander H.L. Woodcock and Flight Commander J.N. Fletcher; HMA No 18, *Gamma*, Flight Commander J. Boyle and Flight Lieutenant A. Cunningham, and HMA No 19, *Delta*, Squadron Commander C.M. Waterlow and Flight Commander J.D. Mackworth. No 3 and No 4 escorted the Royal Yacht out of Portsmouth harbour. Seventeen fixed-wing seaplanes from Isle of Grain, Dundee, Yarmouth, Felixstowe and Calshot, as well as twelve fixed-wing, land-based aircraft from Eastchurch also participated. When manoeuvring directly over the assembled fleet, one of the airships took the first ever vertical photograph of a battleship taken from the air.

(b) *Airships.*
Station.—KINGSNORTH.
Commanding Officer.—Wing Commander N. F. Usborne.

Airship No.	Type.	—
3	Astra Torres - - - -	Captain.—Wing Commander N. F. Usborne. 2nd Officer.—Flight Lieutenant W. Hicks.

Station.—FARNBOROUGH.
Commanding Officer.—Squadron Commander H. L. Woodcock.

Airship No.	Type.	—
4	Parseval - - - - -	Captain.—Squadron Commander H. L. Woodcock. 2nd Officer.—Flight Commander J. N. Fletcher.
18	Gamma - - - - -	Captain.—Flight Commander J. Boyle. 2nd Officer.—Flight Lieutenant A. Cunningham.
19	Delta - - - - -	Captain.—Squadron Commander C. M. Waterlow. 2nd Officer.—Flight Commander J. D. Mackworth.

Officers for duty at stations :—
Kingsnorth.—Flight Lieutenant J. W. Dalgleish (to join up temporarily from July 13th).
Farnborough.—Flight Lieutenant R. G. Lock.
Fort Grange.—Wing Commander E. M. Maitland.
Gosport.—Flight Lieutenant A. C. Wilson.
These numbers, both for seaplanes and airships, are subject to slight modification as found necessary before the assembly.

The General Orders for the assembly of aircraft at Spithead, on 18–22 July 1914, included instructions specifically for the airships. General orders covered some more specific stipulations: 'Uniform for all officers will be monkey jacket, breeches and putties, optional flying kit to be worn over it when actually flying. Officers may also wear any form of headgear when flying, but must carry a uniform cap to wear at all other times.' (*via Sue Kilbracken*)

Chapter Four

From August 1914 to February 1916

The First War Patrols

O n 4 August 1914 Usborne reported to the Admiralty that he had, under his command, four RNAS flying officers, a meteorological officer, seventy-seven ratings, an airship handling party of two petty officers and forty-eight boys, a military guard of sixty-two NCOs and men, commanded by two RE officers, and one further RE officer and twenty-nine men, whose concern was the completion of a blockhouse.[1] Building work was continuing and accommodation was chiefly under canvas. After the declaration of war, the Kingsnorth airships carried out very valuable, long duration patrols over the Straits of Dover, escorting the troopships taking the British Expeditionary Force to France between 9 and 22 August. No 3 had a greater range than No 4 and could fly further to the north-east over the Channel approaches. Indeed, the initial British aerial missions of the war were carried out by these two airships. On the very first night of the war, No 4 came under the fire of territorial detachments at the mouth of the Thames on her return to her station. The enthusiastic, but trigger-happy soldiers, presumably imagined that she was a German airship on a spying mission over the naval dockyard at Chatham.

Log of No. 3 Airship, 13 August 1914.

7.10 a.m. Rose.

7.37 Passed Sittingbourne.

7.45 Passed Teynham Station.

7.50 Passed Faversham.

8.20 Passed Canterbury.

9.00 Passed Coastguard Station.

9.49 Sighted No. 4 Airship.

10.41 Sighted seaplane on starboard quarter.

5.50 p.m. Altered course for Coastguard Station.

6.25 Coastguard Station.

6.54 Faversham.

7.40 Sittingbourne.

7.34 Landed.

A chart of a patrol by
Airship No 3 on 14
August 1914.

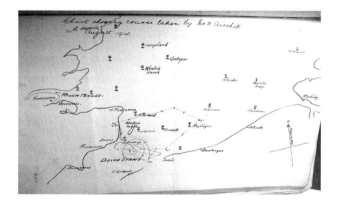

Chart of patrol of Airship
No 3 on 11 August 1914.

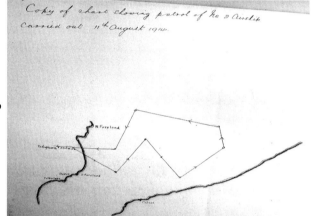

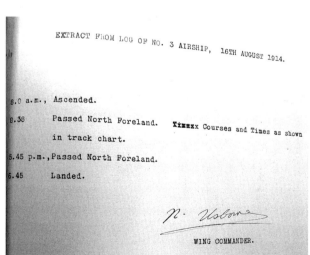

Neville's account of a
patrol on 16 August 1914.

Log of No. 4 Airship, 13 August 1914.

7.40 a.m. Left Kingsnorth.

9.28 Passed Coastguard Station, shaped course for Calais.

10.35 Shaped course for Dover.

11.25 Shaped course for Calais.

11.35 Broke one blade of port propeller, rendering it necessary to change two for new blades. Off Dover one blade of the port propeller burst and flew off, narrowly missing damaging the rigging near the envelope. We were able to fit two new blades while under way and continue the patrol. This took one hour and twenty minutes.

12.55 pm Proceeded to Calais.

1.40 Shaped course for Dover.

2.12 Course as requisite to arrive at Calais.

2.52 Dover.

3.20 Calais.

4.00 Dover.

4.45 Calais.

5.45 Deal.

7.30 Arrived at Kingsnorth.

7.53 Landed.

It will be seen that the Parseval, which could not fly for a whole day without landing for the replenishment of fuel, plied continually between Dover and Calais, while the Astra-Torres, which was the stronger ship, laid her course far to the east and north-east to search the Channel for the approach of hostile craft. Once the expeditionary force was safely across the Channel, these routine patrols were discontinued, though both airships and seaplanes continued to make special scouting flights over the North Sea and Channel.[2]

Murray Sueter related a story which he believed spoke volumes for the average naval officer's appreciation of the RN's aerial assets at that early stage of the war:

'During one of the patrols an amusing incident occurred, which I relate to show how little the navy bothered to study airships before the war. One of our coast patrol cruisers, with the admiral on board, suddenly sighted one of our airships. They at once cleared lower deck, and placed below all surplus ammunition not required to fire at the airship, which they thought was a Zeppelin. A few days after this incident, the Chief of Staff sent for me, and wanted to know what I meant by letting one of my airships go

EXTRACT FROM LOG OF NO. 3 AIRSHIP,   14TH AUGUST 1914.

7.30 A.M.,	Ascended.	
8.20	Passed Whitstable.	
8.31	Passed Herne Bay Pier.	
9.17	Passed Coast Guard Station.	
9.30	Altered course for Ixxx Calais.	
6.0 P.M.,	Passed Coast Guard Station.	
6.57	Landed.	

Courses and times as shown on track chart.

N. Usborne

WING COMMANDER.

Account of a patrol of eleven and a half hours.

COPY OF LOG OF NO. 3 AIRSHIP,   13TH AUGUST 1914.

7.10 A.M.	Rose.
7.37	Passed Sittingbourne.
7.45	Passed Teynham Station.
8.50	Passed Faversham.
8.20	Passed Canterbury.
9.0	Passed Coast Guard Station.
9.49	Sighted No. 4 Airship.
10.41	Sighted seaplane on starboard quarter.
5.50 P.M.	Altered course for Coast Guard Station.
6.25	Coast Guard Station.
6.54	Faversham.
7.4	Sittingbourne.
7.34	Landed.

Courses as shown on track sheet.

N. Usborne

WING COMMANDER.

Log of No 3 Airship for 13 August 1914.

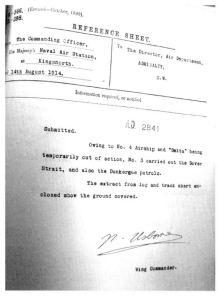

546. (Revised—October, 1899).
398.

REFERENCE SHEET.

The Commanding Officer,	To The Director, Air Department,
His Majesty's Naval Air Station,	ADMIRALTY,
at Kingsnorth.	S.W.
14th August 1914.	

Information required, or notified

Submitted.   A.D. 2841

Owing to No. 4 Airship and "Delta" being temporarily out of action, No. 3 carried out the Dover Strait, and also the Dunkergue patrols.

The extract from log and track chart enclosed show the ground covered.

N. Usborne

Wing Commander.

Report for 14 August.

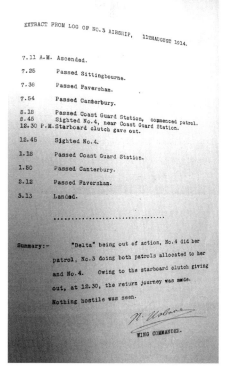

EXTRACT FROM LOG OF NO.3 AIRSHIP,   11TH AUGUST 1914.

7.11 A.M.	Ascended.
7.25	Passed Sittingbourne.
7.38	Passed Faversham.
7.54	Passed Canterbury.
8.18	Passed Coast Guard Station, commenced patrol.
8.45	Sighted No.4, near Coast Guard Station.
12.30 P.M.	Starboard clutch gave out.
12.45	Sighted No.4.
1.18	Passed Coast Guard Station.
1.50	Passed Canterbury.
2.12	Passed Faversham.
3.13	Landed.

. . . .

Summary:-   "Delta" being out of action, No.4 did her patrol, No.3 doing both patrols allocated to her and No.4.   Owing to the starboard clutch giving out, at 12.30, the return journey was made. Nothing hostile was seen.

N. Usborne

WING COMMANDER.

Extract from Log of Airship No 3 on 11 August 1914.

near this patrol cruiser, as the admiral thought it was a German Zeppelin.
I said, "He couldn't possibly have thought that, sir, as it was the tri-lobe
Astra-Torres, commanded by Wing Commander Usborne (one of our
ablest naval torpedo officers and expert airman) and not in the least like
a Zeppelin, and the admiral, who had been Director of Operations at the
Admiralty for two years, ought really to know the difference."

"'Do not be absurd, DAD [Director of Air Department]," was the
answer, "how could you expect the Director of Operations to find time to
go and look at one of your airships? What nonsense, indeed!" Of course,
the naval airmen were always wrong. After this I had a book of silhouettes
of every aircraft – our own, allied, and enemy – specially prepared and
circulated for guidance of those who had been too busy to spare a second
to look at our airships.'[3]

Further remedial measures included supplying naval control centres with the
start and finish times of patrols, the issue of 'dozens of photographs and line
drawings showing the difference between our ships and German Zeppelins' and
large White Ensigns with jacks being supplied to the airships, 'it is not seen that
much more can be done at present'.[4]

On the other hand, Sueter himself was not the easiest of subordinates, being
enthusiastic, unorthodox and somewhat impatient of minds unable, or unwilling,
to grasp matters which he perceived to be of fundamental importance. In
return, salt-horse senior officers regarded the RNAS in general, and Sueter in
particular, as insolent upstarts who needed the beneficial lash of old style naval
discipline at regular intervals.

On 23 August 1914, a letter was sent to Usborne from Commander Edward
Masterman, now at the Air Department in the Admiralty. It noted that he was:

'Disappointed by the failure to get No 4 (Parseval) back to Farnborough at
the required time. The sooner she gets back the better, as her propellers
are practically ready for her. She will have to do without reversing gear
for a bit as that is not yet designed, but I don't think it highly essential. I
do not think, nor do others, that she ought to continue flying with metal
propellers after the accident in the air the other day.'[5]

On an early war patrol, No 4 had shed a propeller blade, but as she carried a spare,
this was changed in mid-air. However, the airship drifted towards the Belgian
coast where the flashes of gunfire illuminated the gathering dusk. Masterman
went on to remind Usborne that Maitland was in charge at Farnborough and

anything wanted from him should be by request and not framed as an order. (As will have been noted, Wing Commander E.M. Maitland had a considerable background in lighter-than-air aviation – he took up ballooning in 1908 and, on 18 November 1908, together with Major Charles C. Turner and Professor Auguste Gaudron, he flew in the *Mammoth* from Crystal Palace to Mateki Derevni in Russia, a distance of 1,117 miles (1,787 kilometres) in 36½ hours – a new British long-distance balloon record. In 1909 and 1910 he was attached to the Balloon School and whilst there he also undertook experiments with powered aircraft, but, following a bad crash, decided to concentrate on airships. On one occasion, he took a couple of young ladies aloft in a balloon, only to come down on the rooftops of Kensington, necessitating rescue by the fire brigade. He had been serving in positions of authority since 1911.) Usborne was urged to be 'more tactful'. Masterman went on to make some recommendations as to future commands:

'Fletcher, No 6 (Parseval Vickers) with No 5's (Parseval Vickers) crew, Woodcock, No 7 (Parseval Vickers) with Cook as coxswain, No 4, Hicks or Cunningham. Can you straighten this out now as you think?'[6]

And concluded by warning:

'Look out you don't get an incendiary bomb dropped on the wooden shed by an aeroplane from Ostend.'[7]

In the event, HMAs 5, 6 and 7 suffered delays and were not completed until later in the war. On 28 August, HMA No 3 (Astra-Torres), which carried – as offensive weapons – a Hotchkiss machine gun and four Hales grenades, left Kingsnorth at 06.30 under the command of Neville Usborne and landed at Ostend at 09.45, joining a detachment of RNAS aircraft and armoured cars. Other officers on board included Flight Lieutenants W.C. Hicks, Flight Lieutenant E.H. Sparling and Flight Sub-Lieutenant Hartford. Moored out under the ingenious principle of what Usborne termed virtual mooring, involving only the use of wires and screw pickets, it was used for scouting along the Belgian coast to the Schouwen Bank lightship. It returned to Ostend each evening before nightfall. After Ostend was occupied by the Germans, it moved to Dunkirk, where a photograph showed No 3 moored to a portable mast alongside Commander Samson's Dunkirk Squadron. It carried out a daring reconnaissance flight over the town in broad daylight – no hostile action taken, as the enemy must have been too astonished to react. Usborne and

HMA No 3, Short Biplane No 42 and BE2a No 50, near Dunkirk in September 1914. (*J.M. Bruce; G.S. Leslie Collection*)

No 3 returned to England after a week. He reported to the Admiralty that the, 'following services could be rendered:'

1. By day, scouting for the fleet, which was short-handed in the matter of small craft.
2. By night, standing over the fleet and assisting the destroyers in detecting any attacks.
3. By night, watching the movements of any large body of troops in the vicinity, whose positions might have been ascertained by day.
4. For spotting the fall of shot fired by light cruisers and mortar boats against hostile troops advancing to the attack on land.[8]

Night flights over London were made from Kingsnorth to evaluate possible Zeppelin attacks, and give the searchlight crews and night fighting aircraft some practice. One of these was the future Air Chief Marshal Sir Arthur Harris, who, as a newly qualified lieutenant, flew anti-Zeppelin patrols from Northolt:

'I was told to see if I could find an airship which was going to fly around pretending it was a Zeppelin. Well, by the most astonishing bit of good fortune, both for the airship and myself, I found it by nearly running into it. It had put its lights on when it saw me coming and I suppose that was regarded as a bit of skilful scouting navigation on my part, whereas, as a matter of fact, all I had done was to fly blindly into the night and hope for the best.'[9]

Beta was detached from Farnborough, firstly to Roehampton and then to Wormwood Scrubs, making a number of flights over London, apparently in defence of the capital:

'On Tuesday, Wednesday and Thursday, the airship *Beta* carried out a number of evolutions over the Metropolis. After circling above St. Paul's, Buckingham Palace, and other prominent places, the airship came down very low when in the neighbourhood of Trafalgar Square, and then rose to a great height before disappearing in the haze. The King and Queen watched the movements of the airship with great interest from Buckingham Palace.'[10]

On 22 September, on a calm but foggy night, *Beta* ascended from Wormwood Scrubs, but lost her bearings and was unable to return to base. Cruising at 500 feet (152 metres) *Beta's* crew found it impossible to determine whether she was over the metropolis or open countryside. A navigational fix was eventually made by spotting the sign at Golders Green Underground station in North London, which was picked out in electric light. A circuitous and careful return to base was made at a height of 300 feet (91 metres) or lower, landing safely after a stressful two and a half hours in the air.[11] Sueter wrote that these evolutions had a useful practical purpose:

'Orders were promulgated for controlling the lighting of London, and I sent Wing Commander Maitland across London in the airship *Beta,* commanded by a very able airman, Flight Lieutenant K.J. Locke, to inspect and report on the restricted lighting arrangements, also Commander Groves was sent over in a free balloon for the same purpose. Other balloons were sent over from time to time, and I also sent Wing Commander Neville Usborne, the gallant Commander of No 3 Airship, to inspect the lighting of the Strand, Regent Street, Oxford Street, and Trafalgar Square from the air.'[12]

Good practice was also obtained by the crews of guns and searchlights in picking up and training on the airship. *Beta* inspected the lighting at Woolwich Arsenal a few days later.[13]

In the summer of 1914, two further Astra-Torres had been ordered by the Admiralty, HMA No 8 (very similar to HMA No 3) and the smaller HMA No 10. Usborne was directed to travel to France in October 1914. His passport, signed by the Foreign Secretary, Sir Edward Grey, noted his age as thirty-one and his rank as commander RN. The purpose of travel was given as, 'to assist with delivery of an Astra-type airship.'[14] A further letter of endorsement, dated 13 October 1914, was written by Wing Commander Oliver Schwann, RN, from the Admiralty Air Department:

'Wing Commander Usborne is proceeding to Paris to assist in taking delivery of an Astra-type airship built for the Admiralty. If circumstances permit and the French Government allow of this, he should visit Epinel to examine the airship facilities at that place. It is requested that he may be rendered any assistance possible in carrying out his duties.'[15]

On 2 November 1914, No 3 took part in successful trials with the steamship SS *Princess Victoria*, when the airship dropped a tow rope onto the quarter deck of the ship from a height of 300 feet (91 metres). The rope was made fast and the airship was towed into and against a 15mph (24kph) wind, whilst the steamer worked up to her full speed of 21 knots (39kph). The crew of the *Princess Victoria* experienced no difficulty and the airship's helmsman was able to maintain complete control at all times. The purpose of the experiment was to ascertain if it would be a practical proposition to tow airships in this way, thereby increasing their range and utility as fleet scouts, and improve the radius of action in the anti-submarine role. It was also judged to be reasonable to assume that the airship could have been hauled down close enough to the ship to permit the changeover of crew or refuelling. An observation car capable of being lowered from an airship was also designed, built and tested. A proposal to tow HMAs No 3 and No 8 across the North Sea on a cloudy night, lower the observation cars and then drop bombs on a chosen target from low-level, progressed no further than as a demonstration of Usborne's fertile imagination and desire to get to grips with the enemy.[16] Another trial at this time involved the use of a motorised mooring trolley running on rails laid along the length of the airship shed, using the old airship *Delta*.[17] On 17 December, No 3 was deflated for overhaul and on 22 December, under Usborne's command, Astra-Torres HMA No 8 was flown at Kingsnorth. Some defects were found so it had to be deflated again for alterations.

An event of considerable interest took place at Kingsnorth on 17 December. C.G. Spencer & Sons Ltd, 'Makers of Balloons, Airships, Parachutes, Gas containers and Aeronautical Apparatus of Every Description,' in the form of Mr Spencer himself, demonstrated a parachute which the firm had designed and manufactured. Spencer jumped from HMA No 3 from a height of 1000 feet (305 metres), the parachute opening within 100 feet (30.5 metres) and landed almost precisely on the intended spot below. The C.G. Spencer Static-Line (Automatic) Parachute was adopted for use by the crews of stationary observation kite balloons, but not at this stage for airship personnel, or – until after the war – for pilots, observers and gunners of fixed-wing aircraft. Shamefully, the Air Board did not approve of parachutes for pilots, in case it encouraged them to abandon damaged aircraft rather than trying to recover them to base for repair. While this experiment was taking place, Clive Waterlow was engaged on a series of trials at Kingsnorth testing the suitability of the smaller airships for carrying weapons such as a Lewis gun mounted on top of the envelope, or the heavier calibre Davis recoilless rifle.

As the year drew to a close, Stanley Spooner, the editor of *Flight* Magazine, in his final editorial of the year, gave his views on lighter-than-air craft in general and Zeppelins in particular:

'As regards airships, or dirigibles, Germany has continued to be the greatest supporter of this variety of aircraft. While we have always held the view that dirigibles have certain well-defined uses, it would appear as if the war has demonstrated them to be outclassed by the heavier-than-air type of aircraft. Certain it is, that so far, despite all the efforts of the enemy to instil into the mind of the British public a fear and dread of their Zeppelins, the practical capabilities of these much vaunted airships have yet to be proved. That we are not sitting still to await the attack of these dirigibles may be accepted in advance, and it may be that if we are to be surprised by the Zeppelins, they on their part may find some even more startling surprises awaiting their coming than ever they can conceive. The Germans again have not been alone in their development of anti-aircraft guns, both France and this country being now well equipped in this direction, and ready to cope promptly with any attempt of invasion by air.'[18]

The First Lord of the Admiralty wrote a memorandum to the War Council on 1 January 1915, setting out his views on the level of threat posed by the Zeppelins:

'Information from a trustworthy source has been received that the Germans intend to make an attack on London by airships on a great scale at an early opportunity. The Director of the Air Department reports that there are approximately twenty German airships which can reach London now from the Rhine, carrying each a ton of high explosives. They could traverse the English part of the journey, coming and going, in the dark hours. The weather hazards are considerable, but there is no known means of preventing the airships coming and not much chance of punishing them on their return. The unavenged destruction of non-combatant life may therefore be very considerable. Having given most careful consideration to this subject and taken every measure in their power, the Air Department of the Admiralty must make it plain that they are quite powerless to prevent such an attack if it is launched with good fortune and in favourable weather conditions.'[19]

A letter from Usborne dated 9 January 1915 has survived. It is addressed:

'From Kingsnorth Air Station. To my dearest old chum. I just love marriage. I think Betty will have a baby in six months' time. [Their daughter Ann was born in August 1915.] I have had a dull time recently, but this is nearly over, in another six weeks I hope to have newspaper cuttings for you. The Zeppelin effort is still to come. It may prove a fiasco, or it may prove fatal to us as a nation. Aeroplanes will do a lot more this summer.'[20]

Just over two weeks later, on 26 January, Usborne's old airship, HMA No 2, was the last airship to fly out of Farnborough when all operations were finally moved from there to Kingsnorth. She never flew again, but her envelope would be put to good use in the development of one of the most numerous and successful of British airship types.

Kingsnorth was described by a young airship officer as:

'Where intensive training was being given to the small band of budding airship officers, in both theory and practice, including gunnery and much drill. The long days were filled with lectures on aeronautics, navigation, engineering and meteorology, interspersed with the practical work of flying, rigging and engine overhaul.'[21]

The influence of the commanding officer is evident here; the training is focused on what is necessary to produce capable officers for the airship service and

HMA No 8 Astra-Torres at Kingsnorth in the spring of 1915. (*Ces Mowthorpe Collection*)

requires dedication and enthusiasm to shine. On 25 February, HMA No 8 resumed flying at Kingsnorth and entered service under the command of Flight Commander W.C. Hicks on 10 March, making a patrol of nine hours along the Sussex coast. Routine Channel patrols continued until 11 May, when it was replaced by HMA No 3. In April, Usborne would have no doubt witnessed a very tragic accident:

'One of the air-mechanics – William J. Standford – attached to the airship station at Kingsnorth, Hoo, near Rochester, was killed on 23 April 1915 while assisting in mooring one of the naval airships. From the evidence at the inquest it appears that while being hauled down by a landing party, the airship was carried away by the wind, which was blowing at thirty miles an hour. All the men let go except Standford, who apparently thought the party would regain control. He was carried to a height of about 500 feet, and, after hanging on for nearly ten minutes, dropped to the ground and was instantly killed. Flight Lieutenant James William Ogilvy Dalgleish, RN, the commander of the airship, said that the man was about fifty feet from the ground when he first saw that he was on the rope. He immediately let out gas to get down, but the airship continued to rise until the rope was off the ground. The airship was rolling, which made it more difficult for Standford to keep on. She started to come down, and the witness hoped it would land in time, but Standford dropped off. A verdict of accidental death was returned.'[22]

As for the airships *Beta*, *Gamma*, *Delta* and *Eta* – *Eta* was the first to go. On her way to Dunkirk on 19 November 1914, she flew into a snowstorm near Redhill, and, having made a forced landing, broke away from her moorings and was so badly damaged as to be incapable of repair. *Gamma* and *Delta* were both lying deflated at Farnborough at the outbreak of the war, and in *Delta's* case the car was found to be beyond repair, so she was deleted. *Gamma* was inflated in January 1915 and was used for mooring experiments. *Beta* saw active service, as she was based for a short period, early in 1915, at Dunkirk on spotting duties, under the command of Wing Commander Maitland, with the Belgian artillery near Ostend. By May 1916 all had been deleted from the active list and scrapped.

The SS Class Airship

Usborne's next important contribution was assisting with the design of the SS Class airship. After the repulse of the initial German advance and the establishment of a system of trenches running from Belgium to the Swiss

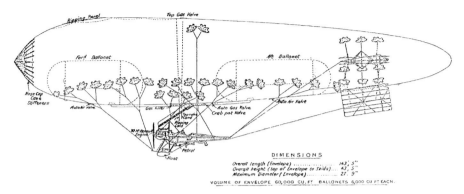

A plan of the SS-Class non-rigid airship.. (*Via Patrick Abbott*)

border, the war in France had come to something of a stalemate. A decision was made to try and break the deadlock by the application of a change of tactics at sea. On 4 February 1915, a communiqué had been issued by the Imperial German Admiralty which declared:

'All the waters surrounding Great Britain and Ireland, including the whole of the English Channel, are hereby declared to be a war zone. From 18 February onwards, every enemy merchant vessel found within this war zone will be destroyed without it always being possible to avoid danger to the crews and passengers. Neutral ships will also be exposed to danger in the war zone, as, in view of the misuse of neutral flags ordered on 31 January by the British Government, and owing to unforeseen incidents to which naval warfare is liable, it is impossible to avoid attacks being made on neutral ships in mistake for those of the enemy.'[23]

This declaration opened the first phase of what was to become known as unrestricted submarine warfare. Restricted submarine warfare had meant the U-boat would surface, warn its intended victim, give the crew time to abandon ship and then sink it. Neutral cargo ships and all passenger liners, probably even Allied ones, would be spared.

In order not only to prosecute the war and to supply its troops with food and munitions, but also to survive on the home front, Britain relied heavily on seaborne trade. If Germany could break, or even seriously disrupt, the flow of merchant vessels, then Britain's ability to have waged war, or indeed feed its population, would have been rendered either difficult or impossible. This was the nature of the problem facing the Admiralty under the political

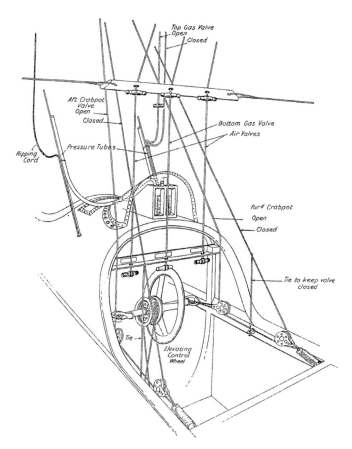

The pilot's controls in a typical SS Class blimp. (*Via Patrick Abbott*)

direction of the First Lord, Winston Churchill. However, he recorded in his book, *The Great War*, the Admiralty was not too concerned at that stage. The Germans had moved too soon, there were simply not enough U–boats available in 1915 to make unrestricted submarine warfare any more than a considerable nuisance rather than a major threat. They compounded this error with a major miscalculation. On 7 May 1915, off the Irish coast, the British liner RMS *Lusitania* was sunk by a single torpedo fired at a range of 700 yards (640m) by U–20, commanded by Kapitanleutnant Walther Schweiger. The great ship was destroyed in a sudden violent detonation (it was carrying a secret cargo of shells, ammunition and explosives) which resulted in the deaths of nearly 1,200 of the 1,959 souls on board. Over 100 of the dead were American citizens and such was the outcry that the Germans prudently scaled down the unrestricted nature of the submarine campaign in order to avoid incurring greater wrath from the USA.

[Author's note: The distress signals sent from the *Lusitania* reached Queenstown; Vice Admiral Sir Charles Coke instructed the captains of all available vessels – all relatively small – to sail to the scene of the tragedy. They arrived two hours after the sinking. When they got there, they rescued any people still alive in the water and from only six lifeboats, which were all from the starboard side; 764 passengers and crew were picked up by boats from Queenstown. Many bodies were washed ashore along the coast and brought to the town for identification. The bodies of many of the victims were buried at either Queenstown, where 148 bodies were interred in the Old Church Cemetery, or the Church of St Multose in Kinsale, but the bodies of the remaining 885 victims were never recovered.]

To return to naval aeronautical matters, the Admiralty was not, however, unmindful of the potential threat posed by a greater submarine force. The professional head of the Royal Navy, the First Sea Lord, Admiral Lord Fisher, called a meeting at the Admiralty on 28 February 1915. He requested proposals to enhance the capability of the navy to provide surveillance and deterrence from the air. He had in mind a small airship type to the following specification:

(a) The airship was to search for submarines in enclosed or relatively enclosed waters.

(b) She was to be capable of remaining up in all ordinary weather, and should therefore have an airspeed of 40 to 50mph (25 to 31kph).

(c) She should have an endurance at full speed of about eight hours, carrying a crew of two.

(d) She should carry a wireless telegraphy outfit with a range of 30 to 40 miles (19 to 25km).

(e) She should take up about 160lbs (72kg) weight of explosives in the form of bombs.

(f) She should normally fly at about 750 feet (238m) altitude, but be capable of flying up to 5,000 feet (1524m).

(g) The design was to be as simple as possible in order that large numbers of these ships should be produced without undue delay.

(h) An ample allowance of lift to be made for gas deterioration, so that each ship should remain in commission on one charge of gas as long as possible.[24]

The unsuccessful SS-1.
(*Via Patrick Abbott*)

In the words of the by then, Rear Admiral Murray Sueter, CB, MP, RN (Ret'd), in a deposition written in 1925 to the Post War Royal Commission of Awards to Inventors in respect of a claim made jointly with the Executors of the late Commander Neville Usborne, RN:

'Lord Fisher summoned an important conference to consider the proposal of Mr Holt Thomas to build a large number of small airships for anti-submarine patrols. Until then the Admiralty Airship Officers could get practically no support. But with Lord Fisher's powerful interest, airship work was given a new lease of life. Holt Thomas was given an order for a small airship of Willows design, and to compete with this, Commander Usborne was given instructions to develop a small envelope of 60,000 cubic feet (1,703 cubic metres) capacity. Captain Sueter consulted Commander Usborne and Commander Masterman, and suggested that as he had some BE2c aeroplanes that the pilots did not like because Commander Samson had sent in an adverse report about these machines, that the chassis of one of them should be tried with one of the old envelopes of the army

SS-2 at RNAS Capel in 1915. (*Ces Mowthorpe Collection*)

airships. This was done with No 2 envelope I believe. The result of tests with this machine promised well and a two-ply envelope of 60,000 cubic feet (1,703 cubic metres) capacity was ordered from Messrs Shorts. As Shorts had expertise in balloons, Commander Usborne had to develop the whole of this envelope work. At first we had considerable trouble with the dope, because of very small holes in it, but Commander Usborne had developed Ioco dope for the first rigid and brought his great experience into play, and gradually the dope became so good that he managed in later airships to save much weight by using single ply fabrics, which were lighter than rubber proofed fabrics.

'When the new Shorts envelope was fitted to a BE2c chassis it was christened SS-3 – Submarine Searcher No 3. The first experiment was SS-1, which was a failure due to the fact that the envelope was a poor holder of hydrogen. The Holt Thomas airship was SS-2 and comparative trials were carried out between SS-2 and SS-3. SS-3 – after some difficulty in determining the best position for slinging the car and the best position for fins and rudder – was an undoubted success. The government supplied airships of this type to France, Italy and the United States.'[25]

The Royal Commission of Awards to Inventors had been set up in 1919 and would sit for the next fifteen years reviewing 1,834 claims from those who considered that their ingenuity had contributed to the war effort in such a way as to be worthy of monetary recompense. A brief report in *The Times*[26] notes that Sueter's claim in this case was not successful. It is interesting to note that Vivian Usborne had been paid £6000 from the commission in 1920 for his work on mine defence equipment for ships, additional to £4800 from Messrs Vickers Ltd in respect of patent rights.

SS-3 on trials.. (*Ces Mowthorpe Collection*)

It is possible that Sueter may have been in error as regards some of the details. The airship authority, the late Ces Mowthorpe, stated in a conversation with the author that the competition was between the RN's SS-1, which was indeed a BE2c fuselage attached to the envelope of HMA No 2, and the Holt Thomas SS-2. He adds that SS-3 was a production model which came later and served in the Dardanelles campaign. Be that as it may, the general points made by Sueter are not in doubt and are supported in an article written in 1934 by Air Commodore Masterman. He wrote:

'The Airship Branch was threatened with disintegration, but revived when Fisher became First Sea Lord – Usborne came into his own. He devised, in conjunction with others, the SS Class. Kingsnorth became a factory or assembly place for small non-rigids under Usborne's direction. In all, his influence was apparent, difficulties were overcome in a Napoleonic way, nothing was allowed to delay progress and many ingenious devices were adopted. Here, his driving force had full sway and an ideal outlet.'[27]

The official historian is succinct and to the point:

'The idea seems to have been struck out during a conversation in the mess at Farnborough at which there were present the late Wing Commander N.F. Usborne, Flight Lieutenant T.R. Cave-Browne-Cave, and Mr F.M. Green of the Royal Aircraft Factory.'[28]

This statement is corroborated by one of Usborne's contemporaries, who wrote that he went straight down to Farnborough after leaving the Admiralty to talk over the requirement with Cave-Brown-Cave and Green.[29] According to another renowned airship historian it was a, 'splendid improvisation.'[30] Certainly Usborne had a very major role to play in sorting out what could have become a very serious problem. There was considerable difficulty in obtaining a sufficient supply of envelopes, as all the regular manufacturers were much too busy with aeroplane orders to accept any new orders. He made personal visits to six manufacturers specialising in waterproof clothing or rubber goods, described the exact requirement, placed the orders directly and arranged for experts from each of the companies to come to Kingsnorth for intensive tuition on the correct preparation of the material. There is no doubt that his efforts were appreciated by Murray Sueter, who wrote that he was placed in charge of all the envelope work, as he had done such good service with the *Mayfly's* gasbags and outer cover.[31]

The peril in which the Airship Branch then stood is highlighted by a minute from the First Lord of the Admiralty dated 18 January 1915:

AIRSHIPS AND AEROPLANES.
Secretary.
First Sea Lord.
Fourth Sea Lord.
Director of the Air Division.
18 January 1915.

The general condition of our airship service, and the fact that so little progress has been made by Vickers in the construction of the rigid airship now due, makes it necessary to suspend the purely experimental work in connection with airships during the war, and to concentrate our attention on the more practical aeroplane, in which we have been so successful.

1. The Director of Contracts should, in conjunction with the Director of the Air Division, make proposals for suspending altogether the construction of the Vickers rigid airship. The material which has been accumulated should be stored, and the shed in which it is being constructed should be thus set free.
2. The repairing staff of the airships, which is now at Farnborough, should be moved with the utmost despatch to Barrow, and should be accommodated in the neighbourhood of the new rigid airship shed and make the shed their repairing shop. Arrangements should be made to this effect with Vickers, so that we take over this shed completely from them during the war.
3. The Farnborough sheds are to be handed back to the army as soon as possible, thus meeting their urgent demands.
4. Messrs Vickers are to be urged to expedite as much as possible the two non-rigid airships they are building in the old Admiralty shed at Barrow. These, when completed, will give us five airships – three Parsevals and two Astra-Torres, besides the small military ones. These five airships will be accommodated, three in the wooden shed at Kingsnorth and two in the old Admiralty shed at Barrow. The iron shed at Kingsnorth will thus become available for the large numbers of aeroplanes which are now being delivered. All necessary steps must be taken to enable aeroplanes, in skilful hands, to alight or ascend from the neighbourhood of Kingsnorth.

5. Temporary housing accommodation for the aeroplane staff is to be at once provided near Kingsnorth, which is to become an aeroplane as well as an airship base.

6. The personnel of the Royal Naval Airship Service are to be reduced to the minimum required to man and handle the five airships. The balance, including especially the younger naval officers, is to be transferred to the aeroplane section. The military officers are to remain with the airships. I am not at all convinced of the utility of keeping this detachment at Dunkirk, and unless they are able to show some good reason for their existence they should be withdrawn.

W.S.C.[32]

The success of the RNAS blimps later caused him to change his mind when he wrote his four volume history of the war:

'Had I had my way, no airships would have been built by Great Britain during the war (except the little blimps for teasing submarines).'[33]

The SS Class was a fairly simple and basic design, but it had several merits. The production model met the specification as regards speed, 40–50mph, and endurance, 8–12 hours. It could climb with its crew of two to a height of more than 5000 feet. It was also cheap – with a unit cost of £2500. The shape was reasonably streamlined, being blunt at the nose but tapering towards the tail. The gasbag had a capacity of 60,000 cubic feet and was 143 feet 6 inches in length, with a maximum diameter of 27 feet 9 inches. [As a comparison this is about twice the length of a Short 360.] The two internal ballonets mounted fore and aft not only ensured that the envelope kept its shape, but could also be used by the pilot to adjust the airship's trim. They were inflated by means of a metal scoop mounted to catch the slipstream of the propeller. Two non–return valves made from fabric, the 'crab-pots', controlled the flow of air into and out of the ballonets. The gross weight which the airship could lift – including its own structure – was 4180lb, which gave a net lift available for crew, fuel, ballast and armament of 1434lb. The disposable lift with a crew of two on board and full fuel tanks was 659lb. The envelope was made of rubber-proofed fabric, reminiscent of an old-fashioned mackintosh. It consisted of four layers, two of fabric, with a layer of rubber in-between and on the inner surface. At the tail of the gasbag a single vertical fin and rudder were fitted ventrally, while horizontal fins and elevators were affixed to port and starboard.

To make them completely gastight and protected from the ravages of weather, saltwater and sun, four coats of dope were applied to the outer surface, with a top coat being of aluminium varnish. The BE2c fuselage was retained, stripped of its wings, rudders, elevators and eventually wheels, axles and suspension.

Propulsion was by means of a 75 hp air-cooled Renault engine driving a large four-bladed propeller. The observer, who also operated the wireless set, sat in the front seat, with the pilot behind him. It was powered by two four-volt accumulator batteries rather than by fitting a generator driven by the engine. This had two advantages; it was lighter and would still operate in the event of an engine failure. Communication was by means of Morse code. The wireless telegraphy receiver and Type 52 transmitter had a range of between 50 and 60 miles, when flying at not less than 800 feet. A long trailing aerial, some 200 feet in length, with a lead weight on the end to keep it from fouling any part of the airship, was wound down from a reel fitted to the side of the car. Small bombs, eight 16lb or two 65lb and a Lewis machine gun, could be carried by way of armament. A lever bombsight was fitted and the release was operated by Bowden wire control. It was considered to be capable of being flown by a young midshipman with small-boat training. To this end, junior officers were brought in from the Grand Fleet by means of ships' captains being asked to select one of his midshipmen who was willing to volunteer for special temporary and hazardous service. One of these was Thomas Elmhirst, from the battlecruiser HMS *Indomitable*, whom we shall meet shortly. Enthusiastic, young, direct entry civilians were also induced to join up – specifically for this purpose. An intensive training course at Wormwood Scrubs, lasting about a month, was given in the theory of aerostatics (aeronautics, navigation, meteorology, engineering, rigging and engine overhaul), practical balloon flying and mastering the controls of a small airship. The training balloons all had girls' names such as *Joan*, *Alice*, *May* and *Hazel*. Normally their baskets could carry up to five trainees and an instructor. The young officers greatly enjoyed the balloon flying, eight qualifying flights – six under instruction (including a night flight), one trip as second in command and finally, a solo. Elmhirst's solo was in Suffolk, when the only difficulty encountered was after landing in a thorn hedge and an inquisitive local with a smoking pipe in his mouth began to closely examine the gas valve aperture. He was dissuaded from this dangerous practice very quickly.

Admiral Fisher demanded that forty more of these small airships should be produced as expeditiously as possible. Neither the First Sea Lord nor the First Lord were to remain at the Admiralty long enough to see the SS Class into operation. In May, following the tragedy of the Dardanelles Campaign, Winston Churchill resigned and Jackie Fisher also departed. They were succeeded by the former Prime Minister, Arthur Balfour and Admiral Sir Henry Jackson, respectively.

It is hard to imagine now just what it would have been like for the crews of the Submarine Scout airships, suspended in an open cockpit, between a few hundred and a few thousand feet above the cold, grey sea, making slow headway against the wind. Luckily two such pilots recorded their impressions. Air Marshal Sir Thomas Elmhirst recalled his experiences as a young pilot of only nineteen years of age:

'I controlled height by means of a wheel in my right hand linked by wires to elevator planes stuck on the after end of the gasbag, and direction by foot pedals, again connected by wires to a rudder at the after end of the gasbag. My other controls, to be operated by the left hand, were the engine, the gas valve, two ballonet air valves and an air pressure control cable. I had a red cord to rip the top off the gasbag in case of a forced landing and a handpump to top up the main fuel tank under my seat from the gravity feed tank for the engine. I had made a wooden bombsight – quite simply two nails as foresight and backsight, the foresight being moveable to a scale marked with the speed of approach, 20 to 50 knots. My other instruments were mounted on a board to the front of the cockpit – a watch, airspeed and height indicators, an engine revolution counter, an inclinometer, gas, oil and petrol pressure gauges, and a glass petrol level indicator. These all had to be monitored closely. Provision was made for illuminating the instruments by four small bulbs. Navigation was by means of chart and floor-mounted compass. A map case with a celluloid front formed the door to a small cupboard.'[34]

Whilst doing all of this, he also had to pass messages back and forth to his wireless operator, read his maps, take compass bearings, plot his course, and at the same time keep a constant watch on the sea below. It should be noted that conditions were cramped and confined on board, exposed to the cold and at the mercy of the elements – the speed through the air of these craft could be reduced to only a few knots when flying into a headwind. This would not be a pleasant experience when returning from a long patrol – tired, hungry and cold. Another airship pilot of the period, T.B. Williams, wrote:

'As the pilot could not leave his little bucket seat during a flight of often many hours duration, he just didn't get a meal. It was also difficult to answer the call of nature. I evolved an arrangement made up from a petrol funnel to which was attached a piece of rubber hose passing to a watertight junction in the hull under my seat. The petrol funnel was hung on a brass cup hook near my elbow. I had some difficulty in inventing a purpose for this gadget when explaining the instruments and controls to the wife of a VIP on one occasion.'[35]

There is no doubt that Neville Usborne's drive, imagination and technical knowledge were of considerable importance in the rapid design and production of this exceptionally useful weapon which helped to win the first U-boat war. His estate later made two specific claims regarding the design of the SS Class – the rigid umbrella nose frame, which helped maintain the shape of the gasbag, and the 'crab pot' system, which diverted air from the propeller's slipstream through a non-return valve to keep the internal ballonets charged, and so retain the shape and trim of the airship.[36]

The intent with the SS Class airships was to guard the eastern entrance to the English Channel with stations at Capel, near Folkestone, and Polegate, near Eastbourne, and the Irish Sea to the north and the south from bases at Luce Bay in Wigtownshire and the Isle of Anglesey. Bases were then added at Mullion in Cornwall and Pembroke in Wales. They operated from four locations in Ireland; Ballyliffin, Co Donegal; Bentra, Co Antrim; Johnstown Castle, Co Wexford and

SS-23 approaching to make a landing at Luce Bay. (*Via Donnie Nelson*)

Malahide Castle, Co Dublin. Bentra and Ballyliffin were sub-stations of Luce Bay; an airship shed and supporting huts were erected at Bentra. Johnstown and Malahide were sub-stations of Pembroke and Anglesey respectively, neither had a hangar.

The SS Class were simple to fly and easy to produce in the numbers required at short notice. They were fairly crude designs and the engines were somewhat unreliable, but they provided the air cover needed when no other type of aircraft could have done so within the necessary timescale. An experienced airshipman of the period wrote:

'At that time no aeroplane could carry out flights of eight, ten or more hours, as we did regularly – nor did we need a prepared aerodrome. Flights were possible in all but the very worst weather conditions. Fog did not stop us flying. In favourable weather we could land gently into the hands of a few men comprising a landing party. In unfavourable weather we could land by trail rope. Night flying was a little more difficult than by day and no elaborate landing lights were needed. I once landed in a flat calm, by the light of matches, and at best we only had a few oil flares to guide us.'[37]

They also gave a new generation of naval airshipmen a wealth of practical experience, so preparing them for the command of the larger and more capable non-rigid airships which were to follow.

The Coastal Class Airship

As the activities of the U-boats grew, more extended cruises were required, and according to Murray Sueter, Usborne suggested using the Astra-Torres patents and building 180,000 cubic feet (5109 cubic metre) airships which would have greater range than the SS Class and moreover would benefit from twin-engine reliability. Sueter agreed and indeed claimed to have invented the double-ended car as used in these larger airships – named Coastals. He also wrote that he developed the 150 hp (111 kW) Sunbeam for seaplane work and recommended placing a Sunbeam engine at the end of each car. Later, further improved airships resulting from the Coastal design were the Coastal Star and North Sea types. In 1925 he wrote:

'Admiral Sueter desires to place on record his high appreciation of the hard work and devotion to the airship cause displayed by Commander Usborne. Far into the night and the early hours of the morning, this

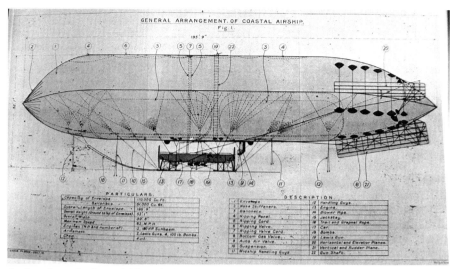

A plan view of a Coastal Class airship.

scientific officer worked to make these airships a success and due to him in large part their wonderful success was due.'[38]

The Coastal design was indeed based on the Astra-Torres tri-lobe envelope, all connected by porous internal curtains, with four ballonets fitted in the lower lobes, and was developed by the design team at Kingsnorth. The envelope used was that of HMA No 10 and the control car was produced by adapting the fuselages of two Avro 510 seaplanes to produce a push-pull, twin-engine layout.

A Coastal Class airship on patrol.

The prototype was named the *Yellow Peril* because of the chrome yellow dope used on the envelope. There was a problem with the dope and air bubbles as it was applied to the fabric, which was sorted out by Usborne's ingenuity.[39] C1 flew for the first time on 26 May 1915. The production of thirty was agreed on 19 June 1915. The first production airship flew at Kingsnorth in September 1915 and was ready for service in the spring of 1916. It proved to be a very valuable workhorse for the RNAS lighter-than-air division, with its capacity to carry a crew of four or five, a wireless set, two Lewis guns, nearly half a ton (500kg) of bombs or depth bombs, an endurance of up to 22 hours and a maximum speed of 52mph (83kph).

Later in the war Tom Elmhirst was the captain of C19 and described his service at Howden in Yorkshire as follows:

'Weather and serviceability permitting, C19 was seldom off patrol. Dispatched at dawn and told to stay on patrol for at least twelve hours was hard going. Hard on the eyes, watching the gasbag pressure, watching the course the coxswain was steering and one eye all the time looking for the enemy – whom I never saw. He could see me from twenty miles distant and submerge. I could only hope to catch sight of a periscope 400 yards away. It was hard on the hands and I came home with blisters from the elevator control wheel after a "bumpy" day, also hard on the backside sitting concentrated for long hours. Food was a pleasant relief and a problem. It did not always taste well in the slipstream of an open-exhaust engine using castor oil! I eventually settled for a large packet of marmalade sandwiches and a bottle of Malvern water. My crew and I did not smoke or "drink" in the air, but just looked forward to a cigarette and a beer on landing.'[40]

Before leaving Kingsnorth, Usborne made significant input to an 80-page report which would be issued by the Director Air Services in December 1915, which would give a highly detailed account of: 'The Experimental Work in connection with Airships, Balloons and Kite Balloons from November 1914 to November 1915', firstly at Farnborough and then, from March 1915, at Kingsnorth.

The Zeppelin Menace

Meanwhile, on 13 August 1915, Usborne was appointed Inspecting Commander of Airships (Building) at the Admiralty. His restless mind was continually occupied by the aeronautical requirements of the war and looking beyond his own immediate task, focussing on the problem of how to increase the range of British aeroplanes and how they would be best used after the end of the war.

Usborne's most pressing task, later in 1915, was to draw up schemes to combat the Zeppelin menace. As the RFC was fully stretched in providing support to the BEF in France, it had been agreed in September 1914 that the air defence of Great Britain should be the responsibility of the Admiralty rather than the War Office.

'On 3 September, Lord Kitchener asked me in cabinet whether I would accept, on behalf of the Admiralty, the responsibility for the aerial defence of Great Britain, as the War Office had no means of discharging it. I thereupon undertook to do what was possible with the wholly inadequate resources which were available.'[41]

Since the early experimental days in the first decade of the twentieth century, Zeppelins had been developed considerably in reliability and carrying capacity. Between 1910 and 1914, the Zeppelin Company had established the first scheduled commercial airline, DELAG, (*Deutsche Luftschiffahrt Aktien Gessellschaft*) with passenger airships including LZ6, LZ7 *Deutschland*, LZ8 *Deutschland II*, LZ10 *Schwaben*, LZ11 *Viktoria Luise*, LZ13 *Hansa* and LZ17 *Sachsen*, offering short haul air tours in Germany. At first it was a modest success at best, but with Dr Eckener as Flight Director it was established on a much sounder basis by greater emphasis being placed on crew training, ground handling, engine performance and reliability, and weather forecasting. He summed up the achievement as follows:

'More and more we learned to overcome our difficulties by making proper arrangements and developing a sure skill. The DELAG fulfilled its main purpose, which was to train a nucleus of qualified commanders and steersmen, and above all to develop a familiarity with the elements in which the craft had to fly in the ocean of the air, with all its dangerous tricks. The DELAG became the university of airship flight.'[42]

A total of 34,028 passengers were carried in more than 2000 flights, with a total distance covered of more than 100,000 miles (160,900 km) and an excellent safety record. One airship alone, the *Viktoria Luise* made a total of 1000 trips between Hamburg, Heligoland and Copenhagen in the years 1912–14. As has been noted, the War Office in London was slow to appreciate the potential of aerial warfare, noting in 1910 that it was; 'Not convinced that either aeroplanes or airships will be of any utility in war' and that it seemed unlikely that it would be possible to, 'arrest or retard the perhaps unwelcome progress of aerial navigation.'[43] It is of interest to note that the Admiralty's attitude to the introduction of steamships some 100 years before was similarly unwelcoming; 'Their Lordships felt it their bounden duty to discourage to the utmost of their ability the employment of steam vessels, as they consider that the introduction of steam is calculated to strike a fatal blow at the naval supremacy of the Empire.'[44]

The Imperial German Navy's Airship Division was formed in 1912 with the plan to take the war to the enemy by means of a bombing campaign. The first naval Zeppelin was the LZ14, which was commissioned into service as the L 1. It was lost at sea the following year; among those killed was the senior officer of the Naval Airship Division, Korvettenkapitän Metzing. His replacement as commanding officer was Korvettenkapitän Peter Strasser, who was convinced that the Zeppelin was a strategically important weapon which could make a real difference to winning the war, saying that Britain could be defeated: 'Overcome by means of airships, through increasingly intensive destruction of cities, factory complexes, dockyards... .'[45]

Field Marshal Helmuth von Moltke, the Chief of the German General Staff from 1906 to 1914, believed that Zeppelins possessed potent possibilities, as also did the German aviation press. On 24 December 1912 he advised the War Ministry that:

'In the newest Zeppelins we possess a weapon that is far superior to all similar ones of our opponents and that cannot be imitated in the foreseeable future if we work energetically to perfect it. Its speediest development as a weapon is required to enable us at the beginning of a war to strike a first and telling blow, whose practical and moral effect could be quite extraordinary.'[46]

In 1914, the Zeppelin represented a threat, with a payload of 500lbs (227kg) of bombs, at a time when fixed-wing aircraft were deemed suitable for unarmed reconnaissance only. It was also an unknown quantity with all the fear that such a novelty would bring. The First Lord of the Admiralty, Winston Churchill, was more sanguine, stating in his speech following a banquet at the Mansion House on 5 May 1913:

'Any hostile aircraft or airships which reached our coast during the coming year (1914) would be promptly attacked in superior force by a swarm of very formidable hornets.'[47]

Hornets would indeed have had to do the job, as there was a distinct lack of suitable aircraft. Indeed, when Flight Sub-Lieutenant Eric Beauman reported for duty with the RNAS Air Defence Flight at Hendon in September 1914, he was somewhat disquieted to discover that there was one aircraft and one pilot (himself) allocated for the aerial protection of London.[48]

However, at this early stage of the war, neither the German Army nor the Imperial Navy had an abundance of airships available for service. The army had six Zeppelins and one wooden-framed Schütte-Lanz type. Three of these were lost in ill-advised missions in support of the invading troops in the initial war of the frontiers. The navy had only one operational airship, which was fully tasked with reconnaissance for the High Seas Fleet.

The Schütte-Lanz Airship Company had been founded in 1909 by Dr Johann Schütte and Dr Karl Lanz with the backing of a group of industrialists. Its growth had been encouraged by the army, perhaps to provide a counterweight to the Zeppelin monopoly. Some twenty of these had been constructed in equal number for the army and navy before the end of the war. The laminated plywood used was successful only up to a point. It was undoubtedly lighter than metal, but beyond a certain size lacked sufficient strength. Moreover, a nautical environment was particularly unforgiving. In the words of Peter Strasser: 'Most of the Schütte-Lanz ships are not usable under combat conditions, especially those operated by the navy, because their wooden construction cannot cope with the damp conditions inseparable from maritime service.'

The first city to be bombed by a Zeppelin was Antwerp on 24–25 August 1914, where twenty-six citizens were killed. Shortly afterwards, three Zeppelins were in action on the Eastern Front, bombing the town of Mława on the Russo-Prussian frontier. That autumn, the citizens of London were subject to air raid precautions for the first time, with street lamps being extinguished and a blackout being imposed. It was defended by a handful of guns that had been modified to fire at a higher angle, searchlights were ordered and training in night flying was recommended – though the few available aircraft had neither the speed, climb rate, nor weapons, to be a credible counter to any marauders. A Zeppelin could climb at 850–1000 feet (260–300m) a minute, whereas a BE2c took an hour to reach the Zeppelins' cruising height of 10,000 feet (3004m). One of the finest of Zeppelin commanders, Kapitan-Leutnant Heinrich Mathy of the Imperial German Navy commented:

'As to an aeroplane corps for the defence of London, it must be remembered that it takes some time for an aeroplane to screw itself up as high as a Zeppelin and by the time it gets there the airship would be gone.'[49]

The raiders did not come in late 1914 and a false sense of security developed. Aggressive countermeasures were taken, however, by the RNAS, bombing Zeppelin sheds at Düsseldorf and Friedrichshafen. The Kaiser hesitated to attack, for he was fearful of the effect that such an unprecedented form of warfare would have on neutral opinion.

In early 1915, with nine newly constructed Zeppelins ready for action, he gave qualified approval for attacks on military targets only – a somewhat futile gesture, as bombs could not be dropped with such a degree of accuracy. Accurate navigation by night was very difficult, compounded by the fact that the airships' commanders were reluctant to use the radio navigation aids available in case they revealed their position to the enemy. They were also highly subject to the weather conditions – heavy cloud, strong winds or storms, made missions impossible and they were not usually able to find out what weather they would encounter over England until they got there. The initial Zeppelin raids across the North Sea were made in January 1915 to King's Lynn and Yarmouth, and were followed by an attack on Tyneside, the Humber area and East Anglia in April. In May, the German High Command ordered that Zeppelin raids should aim to bomb Britain into submission. London and Southend were attacked in May, Hull and Jarrow in June, London again in September and October. A total of over 200 civilians were killed and more than 450 injured in twenty-three successful, or attempted raids, during 1915. There was also considerable damage to property, but of even more value were the psychological effects and the defensive efforts which had to be diverted from other theatres (eventually some 17,000 officers and men were employed on AA defence in the UK). The public demanded a visible response, and a degree of hysteria and xenophobia was whipped up by the press, with headlines such as; 'The Coming of the Aerial Baby-killers.'[50] Reaction in German newspapers was understandably different:

> 'The most modern air weapon, a triumph of German inventiveness and the sole possession of the German forces, has shown itself capable of carrying the war to the soil of old England.'[51]

Indeed, a naval air service contemporary of Usborne's did not believe that the Germans were deliberately aiming to kill civilians:

> 'Most of us believed that the Zeppelins set out to bomb military targets, only bombing open towns and villages as a result of losing themselves in the dark.'[52]

It is certainly true to say that they did not want to believe that the German naval officers, with whom they had been on excellent terms at far flung stations all around the world in the long years of peace, could be capable of wilful atrocities. Whatever the case, there had to be a concentrated effort to find an effective solution and it was this problem that Usborne attempted to resolve. In October 1915, he wrote a paper on Anti-Zeppelin Defence, which he submitted to his superiors in the Admiralty, reviewing current proposals for defensive measures.[53] The first involved stationing balloons all over London, each fitted with a car containing two men and a Davis, 6-pounder, recoilless gun. These would be capable of ascending to 12,000 feet (3657 metres) inside six minutes. When a Zeppelin was spotted all the balloons would be released and the nearest one would engage the intruder. His recommendation was to carry out a trial of the installation. The second idea was to use a balloon to lift an aeroplane to patrol height. The aircraft would only be slipped from the balloon if a Zeppelin was spotted, otherwise it would simply descend by gently deflating the envelope. The third was to moor an armed kite balloon at a similar altitude to the ceiling of the massed balloons. He regarded this as being the most technically challenging and costly plan. A fourth notion was to suspend nets over London by means of balloons, which was dismissed as totally impracticable. The fifth was a design which would become known as the Airship Plane and which will be discussed in more detail below. The final scheme was an aerial torpedo carried by a model airship, released from the ground and directed, 'by W/T or other suitable means.' To this end experiments with sound detection and radio control were in progress. A few months later, in January 1916, just as the Germans were resuming raiding following a suspension forced on them by the winter weather, Usborne received a letter from Vickers comparing the weight, horsepower, maximum rate of climb and maximum/minimum speed of a range of aircraft:

Scout – 1000lbs, 110 hp, 7000 ft/8 ½ min, 118–50mph,
Fighter old – 2200lbs, 110 hp, 300 ft/7 ½ min, 72–42mph,
Fighter new – 2200lbs, 110 hp, n/k, 85–45mph,
2 engine fighter – 2800lbs, 2x110 hp, n/k, 105–40mph,
New big – 20,000lbs, 1000 hp, 3500 ft/9 min, 95–45mph[54]

None provided the perfect answer to getting explosive material quickly enough and closely enough to the Zeppelin's gasbag to detonate the highly volatile hydrogen it contained, as Flight Sub-Lieutenant Rex Warneford had proved on 7 June 1915 when he destroyed LZ37 over Ghent by bombing it from his Morane Parasol. Captain Sueter's satisfaction with Warneford's success was

LZ37, which was destroyed by Flight Sub-Lieutenant Rex Warneford.

tempered by a summons to a meeting with three Sea Lords. Instead of receiving congratulations on behalf of the work of one of his young officers, he was taken to task for permitting sub-lieutenants to go to music halls at night while under training to become SS Class airship pilots.[55]

How was the problem to be solved of an aircraft attaining height rapidly enough to be able to attack a Zeppelin successfully on a regular basis? Moreover, could an aircraft be given the longer endurance required to patrol at height and so intercept an enemy airship? Usborne's fertile brain devised a solution which has been described by the airship author and expert Ces Mowthorpe as a brilliant concept – suspending a complete BE2c from an envelope similar to that used by the SS type airship. The idea of the Airship Plane was that it could patrol as an airship and then, on spotting the Zeppelin, the aircraft section could be slipped to intercept, while the gently deflating envelope made its way slowly to earth. In a letter to Admiral Fisher, Usborne wrote:

'It is recognised that an aeroplane, once it gets above a Zeppelin, can destroy the latter without great difficulty. On the other hand, it is recognised that for an aeroplane, flying at night is almost too dangerous to be practical as a routine, also, that the rate of climb of an aeroplane is so slow that it cannot reach the altitude of a Zeppelin in the time available. The idea is to substitute a complete aeroplane for the car normally carried by a small airship. This aeroplane will be attached in such a way as it can slip itself from the envelope once it has established itself above the Zeppelin.'[56]

And in his report, written in October, he had remarked:

'This is obviously the most completely satisfactory proposal of all. The problem has been worked at, on various lines, for some three months. A successful result is confidently anticipated in the course of a few weeks more.'[57]

He also believed that the idea could have offensive possibilities, increasing the range of bombing aircraft which could be detached from the mother airships over the target.

The Airship Plane was flown without separation by Flight Commander W.C. Hicks in August 1915 and the first release, without a crew, was also successful. On 19 February 1916, permission was given for a manned slipping trial, with the pilots being given a completely free hand to choose their day and time, with an unknown staff officer adding in his advice to the Director of the Air Service, Rear Admiral Charles Vaughan-Lee:

'I regard it as most inadvisable to allow the trial to take place in front of important visitors, as their presence necessarily exercises a certain compulsion on the pilots, and, in case of accident, the impression created is very undesirable. On this subject of experimental work I have some knowledge and never allowed any submarine trials to be undertaken other than in secret. It is difficult to carry out aircraft trials in secret, but as much secrecy as possible is most desirable.'[58]

Therefore, on 21 February, Usborne and Squadron Commander Wyndor Plunkett de Courcy Ireland (the CO of the Great Yarmouth Air Station, who had been born in Co Tipperary in 1885[59]) ascended from Kingsnorth on the manned trial of the AP-1. The craft climbed in a series of circles to about 4000 feet (1219m), watched by an anxious group of officers below. The AP-1 exceeded its equilibrium height, causing a drop in gas pressure, and the instability thereby created resulted in the premature detachment of the forward suspension cables. The nose of the aircraft plunged downwards, overstressing the remaining two wires, which failed. Apparently, Ireland had tried to climb along the fuselage to release the remaining cables, but to no avail. The controls of the BE (Serial No 989) were in all probability damaged as it parted company from the envelope, so making a safe descent impossible. The BE section was seen to sideslip and turn over, throwing out Ireland, who fell into the River Medway and was drowned. Usborne remained with the BE, which crashed

The AP-1 at Kingsnorth. (*J.M. Bruce; G.S. Leslie Collection*)

in Strood Railway Station goods yard. It is poignant to think that their lives could possibly have been saved had the parachute demonstrated at Kingsnorth some eighteen months before been adopted, particularly for test crews and other high-risk ventures. The Admiralty immediately banned any further experiments of this nature until one of the new rigid airships should become available, and the planned AP-2 never flew. To the modern mind the Airship Plane seems something of an outlandish conception. But yet, was it any odder at

The AP-1 in flight at Kingsnorth in 1915.

that stage in its development than another idea which had, in its early days, been given considerable support by figures such as Winston Churchill and Murray Sueter? It was a large, ungainly steel box which lumbered across the ground on cumbersome treads at a speed far less than that of a walking man. Its crew were subject to deafening by the noise of the unenclosed engine with which they shared a cramped compartment, par-boiled by the intense heat which it gave off, and semi-asphyxiated by the pungent fumes of its exhaust, with guns firing from its barbettes like a turn-of-the-century armoured cruiser. It was, of course, the tank, which in the end would prove a most useful battlefield asset.

A Court of Inquiry was held, but the record of its deliberations and verdict does not appear to have survived, apart from some fragments of commentary upon it, made in March 1916.[60] It is addressed 'Admiral' and is unsigned, but concludes:

'I cannot speak too highly of Commander Usborne's and Lt Commander Ireland's sacrifices. They were trying to evolve a machine that could compete with Zeppelins and they gave their lives in this endeavour. Regarding paragraph 8 of the finding, it is submitted that these two gallant officers be given some post-mortem honour.'

Air Commodore Masterman wrote in 1934:

'Thus fell two gallant men, giving their lives for an experiment which since, under different conditions, had proved to be practicable, mourned by all who had the privilege of knowing them. As far as Usborne is concerned no one can talk of early British airship days without mention of his name and work, and no one can say what the subsequent history of this service would have been, had he been spared to assist in its development. A personality was lost on that February day which was irreplaceable.'[61]

Masterman, who knew Usborne so well, and would later be instrumental in founding the Royal Observer Corps, lived to the age of seventy-seven, passing away in 1957.

Betty Usborne had a dream three nights beforehand – a black car from the Admiralty had drawn up at the door of their house in South Kensington to tell her of Neville's death. On waking she asked him to postpone the test. He wouldn't. When the day came she determined to stop the dream coming true by leaving with him first thing and not returning till after midnight. But at midnight the black car was waiting. A fellow airshipman at Kingsnorth, Commander Harold Woodcock, wrote to Mrs Usborne:

'He was a man of vast ability, energy, initiative and fearlessness, his death is a great blow to the service; we shall all miss his personality and genius more than I can say.'[62]

Another contemporary described him as; 'The brilliant experimental non-rigid pilot.'[63]

The Official Historian wrote of him:

'Commander N.F. Usborne, whose tenacious ability had done much to sweep aside the difficulties and prejudices that dogged the early development of the small airship, typifies the vision and courage which the personnel brought to their work. The science of aeronautics was young. Ideas which seemed to work out in theory had always to stand the ultimate practical test in the air. The risk in this, the supreme test of the inventor's faith in his machine, had to be accepted, not in the excitement of battle, but in cold blood.'[64]

Betty, who married Hugh Godley, later the second Lord Kilbracken, died in 1958, and Ann, who never married, passed away in 1985. Betty's son, John Godley, later the third Lord Kilbracken, and a distinguished Fleet Air Arm pilot in the Second World War, wrote:

'As her second marriage disintegrated, she increasingly idealised her first husband, Neville. Their years together (at least in recollection) had been so perfect, the gentle lover, the wise father, the brilliant man of invention. He was more than an outstanding naval officer, a visionary with an eager mind, as well as great charm and magnetism.'[65]

Her father, the artist Vereker Hamilton, died in 1931 and his obituary in *The Times* noted that his painting, *The Airship Flown by Captain Neville Usborne, RN*, was held in the collection of the Imperial War Museum.[66]

The Zeppelins were eventually defeated by interceptor aircraft armed with a machine gun firing a mixture of explosive ammunition to punch holes in the fabric covering the outer skin and the gas cells within, and incendiary bullets to ignite the escaping gas, anti-aircraft fire from the ground and their own inherent unsuitability for the role of strategic bombing. Almost 100 Zeppelins and Schütte-Lanz airships served with the German Army and Navy during the war. Nearly three-quarters of these were lost due to being shot down, bombed in their sheds, catching fire accidentally, being wrecked by heavy landings, or succumbing to adverse weather conditions. They made 4720 operational flights covering over 1,250,000 miles (2,000,000 kilometres), dropping just 202 tons (203 metric tonnes) of bombs, which resulted in the deaths of 556 and injuries to 1358 more.[67] Of the navy's seventy-three ships, no less than fifty-three were destroyed and forty per cent of the crews were killed – a loss rate comparable to those sustained by the German U-boat Service and the RAF's Bomber Command in the Second World War.[68] Murray Sueter calculated that the RNAS, RFC and RAF were directly responsible for the destruction of twenty-one enemy airships, with the BE2c taking part in nine of these.[69] The German airships totally failed to live up to either the expectations of their operators, or the fears of the countries against which they were directed. It is arguable that they could have been put to better use on long-range reconnaissance missions, scouting for convoys and passing information by wireless to shore bases or U-boats. Undoubtedly they were of considerable assistance when used by the High Seas Fleet for scouting, carrying out more than 200 such missions over the North Sea and may well have saved it from destruction at Jutland. Indeed, Admiral Jellicoe later wrote that:

'Our position must have been known to the enemy, as at 2.50am, the fleet engaged a Zeppelin for quite five minutes, during which time she had ample opportunity to note, and subsequently report the position and course of the British Fleet.'[70]

Taken as a whole, however, the Kaiser's rigid airships were a costly flop in comparison to the much simpler and cheaper Royal Navy non-rigids, which carried out a valuable but unheralded service throughout the war.

In 1921, the Royal Aeronautical Society founded the Usborne Memorial Prize for a lecture on an airship subject, in memory of Wing Commander Neville F. Usborne. Indeed, the Secretary of the RAeS, Lieutenant Colonel W. Lockwood Marsh, wrote to *The Times* suggesting that Usborne's name be coupled with that of Air Commodore E.M. Maitland, who had recently lost his life in the R.38 airship disaster.[71] The terms of the award were subsequently changed to:

'Awarded annually – at the discretion of the council – for the best contribution to the society's publications written by a graduate or student on some subject of a technical nature in connection with aeronautics.'

The revised terms were similar to another of the Royal Aeronautical Society's awards, the Pilcher Memorial Prize. The two were subsequently amalgamated to become the Pilcher-Usborne Award, which was awarded through to the late 1980s.

In the papers which have survived are some unfinished report forms on the fifteen officers at RNAS Kingsnorth, which Usborne was probably working on before his final, fatal flight. His concise, no-nonsense summaries are a mark of the man and may serve as an epitaph:

W.C. Hicks – 'A good common-sense officer. Not much ingenuity or initiative.'

J.N. Fletcher – 'A very intelligent, keen officer. Has a somewhat unfortunately brusque manner.'

A.D. Cunningham – 'An excellent messmate.'

J.W.O. Dalgleish – 'This officer has a tendency to become depressed and grumpy.'

E. Sparling – 'An indefatigable and reliable officer. Has the gift of instantly establishing cordial relations with strangers.'

A.C. Wilson – 'Hard working but not clever. An excellent odd job officer, but will never be brilliant at anything.'

G.C. Colmore – 'An unusually fine officer with a very strong personality. Has been all over the world and had every sort of adventure. Specially recommended for promotion.'

Unfinished: T.H.B. Hartford, Blundell, Hunter, Merchant, Brice, Hibbard and Park.[72]

Chapter Five

Usborne's Achievements and his Legacy

Neville Usborne made important contributions to the early development of four strands of naval aviation: the rigid airship, the SS Class non-rigid, the Coastal Class non-rigid and the airship-launched aeroplane. How did these progress in the years following his unfortunate demise?

British Rigid Airships

The Royal Navy's rigid airship programme was suspended in 1911 after HMA No 1's less than happy debut. HMA No 9r was originally ordered from Vickers in 1913, but, due to frequent changes of ministerial and naval policy, was not delivered from Barrow to the Rigid Trials Flight at Howden until April 1917, having become the first British rigid to fly on 16 November 1916, commanded by Wing Captain Masterman. Murray Sueter wrote; 'When hostilities broke out No 9 Rigid was in her design stages. Then it was brought to the notice of the Admiralty that munitions were of greater importance than airships, so the work on No 9 was stopped, against the advice of the Director of the Admiralty Air Department (myself).'[1] Her design was by then somewhat outmoded, being largely derived from a pre-war Zeppelin which had force-landed in France in 1913. She was slow and heavy, deliberately being strongly built to withstand ham-fisted handling by inexperienced crews. Her dimensions were: length

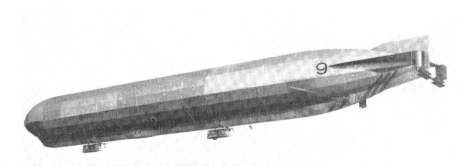

HMA No 9r in 1916.

526 feet (160 metres), a diameter of 53 feet (16 metres) and a capacity of 846,000 cubic feet (23,942 cubic metres). The lack of a British rigid airship for reconnaissance at the Battle of Jutland in 1916 was regretted by the Director of the Naval Air Department:

'I have always been convinced that if the naval airmen had been allowed to develop proper aerial reconnaissance of the North Sea, we could have done so much better on the naval side throughout the whole war period. The lack of British Zeppelins at Jutland was no fault of Lord Jellicoe.'[2]

No 9r was used mostly for training and experimental work, but did carry out one operational patrol over the North Sea in July 1917. She was scrapped in June 1918 after a flying life of only 198 hours; 20 feet (6 metres) of her bow was salvaged by the commanding officer of Pulham Airship Station in Norfolk, for use as a bandstand and rose trellis.

The next British rigids were the four airships of the 23 Class, 23r, 24r, 25r and R26, which were delivered in 1917–18. In essence they were more advanced versions of 9r. For self-defence purposes, 23r was fitted experimentally with a two-pounder gun mounted on top of the envelope. They were used mostly for training, patrols and convoy work, though on 25 October 1918, R26, which was the best ship of the four, flew over London as part of the Lord Mayor's Show, a unique appearance by an airship at this event. They were all deleted in 1919.

Airship R24 at East Fortune in 1917.

R29 at East Fortune in 1919.

The 23X Class, R27 and R29, followed; R27 was soon destroyed in an accidental fire in the hangar at Howden. R29 was more successful and was the only wartime rigid to see action, bombing a suspicious oil patch on 29 September 1918 off the coast near Sunderland, while on convoy duty. Signals made by Aldis lamp called in the destroyer escorts and subsequently the sinking of UB-115 was confirmed.

The next two airships, R31 and R32, were unusual in that their hull frameworks were based on the German Schütte-Lanz practice and were made of wood. During trials, R31 reached a speed of 70 mph (112 kph), but was scrapped after a career of only four hours and fifty-five minutes. R32 was seconded to the National Physical Laboratory for experimental work in manoeuvring and parachuting. One oddity of both ships was that their wooden frames flexed so much in flight that, 'anyone standing in the control room doorway and watching a friend at the tail-end of the keel gangway would see him "disappear" and then "reappear" during turns.'[3]

Airship Service personnel had become members of the Royal Air Force on 1 April 1918, but ownership of the airships was not passed from the Admiralty to the Air Ministry until October 1919, by which time the number of rigid and non-rigid airships on charge had been greatly reduced.

Some idea of the comparative utility between the rigid and non-rigid RN airships during the war may be gained from the fact that – in total – the eight rigids flew 1500 hours of wartime patrols, whereas one non-rigid alone, the SSZ11, flew no less than 1610 hours. In one month in 1918 the SSZ11 was aloft for 259 hours – given the fact that the airships flew in daylight; this was more than half the actual hours available in the month. Another, SSZ20, flew 28,299 miles (45,278 kilometres) in 1918 in 1263 hours – a round-the-world journey at an average speed of 20 knots (23mph/37kph). One airship historian goes as far as to say:

R33 was registered as a civilian airship G-FAAG in 1920. Note the pair of Gloster Grebe fighters suspended below the envelope.

'Although they never received the same public acclaim that was so often bestowed upon the undeserving rigid airships, the SS Zero blimps were truly the unsung heroines of the war against the U-boats.'[4]

Two of the most successful British airships were the R33 and her sister ship, R34, of 1919. Both were almost identical copies of the Zeppelin L33. Among the highlights of the R33's career was the time that a brass band played on her top platform in flight and the early example 'eye in the sky' duty, when assistance was given to the police monitoring car traffic at the Epsom races in 1921. R33 continued to give valuable service until 1926. The R34 was built by the firm of William Beardmore, in Glasgow, and achieved considerable fame on 2–6 and 9–13 July 1919, when she made the first double crossing, including the first east-west crossing, of the Atlantic, from East Fortune in Scotland to Long Island, New York. The outward trip took 108 hours and 12 minutes, and the return trip to Pulham, assisted by the prevailing winds, took 75 hours and three minutes. This was only a few weeks after Alcock and Brown's first west-east crossing from Newfoundland to Clifden, Co Galway, in their Vickers Vimy. The first east-to-west crossing by a heavier-than-air machine was not until 12–13 April 1928, in the Junkers W33 D1167, *Bremen*, flown from Baldonnel to Greenly Island, Labrador, by Captain Hermann Kohl, Baron von Hunefeld and Commandant James Fitzmaurice – the commanding officer of the Irish Air Corps. (In October 1910, Walter Wellman and his crew of five (plus dog) made an unsuccessful attempt to cross the North Atlantic from west-to-east in the small non-rigid airship *America*. Following engine problems and other difficulties, they were rescued by the SS *Trent*.)

Sadly, a minor accident, which was followed by severe weather damage while the R34 was moored out of doors on the ground, brought a premature end to this fine airship in January 1921.

R36 flew only 80 hours before being deleted and broken up for scrap in 1926.

The R36 was registered as a civil aircraft, G-FAAF, and used for passenger transport experiments. She was 673 feet (205 metres) in length, with a diameter of 79 feet (24 metres) and a capacity of 2,101,000 cubic feet (59,458 cubic metres). Her passenger cabin was luxuriously appointed with accommodation for fifty. On 27 June 1921, forty-nine MPs were taken for an hour's flight, returning to the mooring mast at Cardington in Bedfordshire, which had recently been fitted with a lift. Her navigating officer was Flight Lieutenant Tom Elmhirst, who was one of Lord Fisher's original young midshipmen drafted from the Grand Fleet in 1916 to fly the SS Class.

The first entirely post-war rigid was the ill-starred R38, which at the time of its construction was the largest airship in the world, being 699 feet long (213 metres), with a diameter of 86 feet (26 metres) and a capacity of 2,750,000 cubic feet (77,825 cubic metres). She was built by the Royal Airship Works at Cardington in response to an order from the US Navy and made her maiden

R38 leaving her shed at Cardington for the first time on 23 June 1921. (*Ces Mowthorpe Collection*)

flight on 23/24 June 1921, being re-registered in American markings as the ZR-2 in August. On 23 August she broke up in mid-air over the Humber; among the forty-four British and Americans on board was Air Commodore E.M. Maitland, CMG, DSO, AFC, whom it will be remembered, Usborne had rubbed up the wrong way slightly some seven years before. The R38 was badly designed and poorly stressed, so was unable to cope with the forces experienced during low-level manoeuvring. Much had been riding on the project; if it had been a success and had pleased the Americans, it was hoped that this would lead to an airship industry in Britain exporting its products around the world.

Barnes Wallis, who had worked on airships for Vickers since 1913, designed the beautifully streamlined R80, which had considerably reduced drag compared to any of her predecessors; 'There is little doubt that she would have proved the finest British airship.'[5] Her maiden flight was on 19 July 1920, but before being scrapped in 1924, the R80 accumulated only seventy-five hours flying time:

> 'This was a decision taken by a Labour Government to avoid a challenge from private enterprise, as R80 was costing less to maintain than the bigger ships designed by the official constructors' team. Politically, the evidence was inconvenient.'[6]

The final two British rigids could not have had more contrasting stories. The Cardington-built R101, G-FAAW, had a length of 777 feet (237 metres), a

The 'government ship', R101, approached the mooring mast at Cardington.

diameter of 131 feet (40 metres) and a capacity of 5,500,00 cubic feet (160,000 cubic metres), regaining for Britain the title of world's largest aircraft. She was too heavy, lacking in engine power, and had leaking gasbags. The design was at the very edge of the technology then available. It was an experimental craft rushed – for reasons of political expediency – into a major and challenging flight before she was either ready or fully tested. The R101 was wrecked at Beauvais on her way to India on 5 October 1930 with a large loss of life, forty-eight of the fifty-four on board. The victims included the Secretary of State for Air, Lord Thomson, the Director of Civil Aviation, Sir Sefton Brancker and Major G.H. Scott, one of the most renowned airshipmen of the period.

Air Vice-Marshal Sir W.S. Brancker, KCB, FRAeS, (1877–1930) a regular army officer, made his first flight in India in 1910 and from that time devoted the whole of his considerable talents to the furtherance of British aviation. During the First World War he held a succession of staff appointments in the RFC and then the RAF. In 1919 he left the service to become one of the great advocates of civil air transport, becoming Director of Civil Aviation in 1922. He was a very well known and popular figure of boundless energy and enthusiasm. His death in the R101 disaster of 5 October 1930 was a severe blow to the cause of aviation in the United Kingdom and beyond.

The R100, G-FAAV, was another creation of Barnes Wallis and was built at Howden, which was reactivated for the purpose in 1925–26. The chief calculator

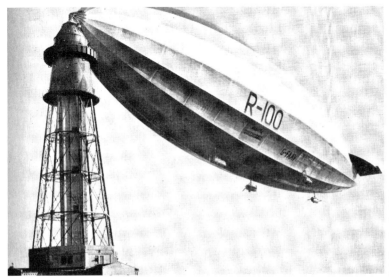

Also, seen here at Cardington, the 'private' contract, R100.

assisting Wallis was N.S. Norway, who later gained fame as the novelist Neville Shute, and whose autobiographical book, *Slide Rule*, includes the story of the two competing designs.

The R100 was 719 feet in length (219 metres), with a diameter of 133 feet (41 metres) and a capacity of 5,156,000 cubic feet (146,000 cubic metres). She is a strong contender with the R80 for the title of Britain's finest airship; she was certainly the fastest, with a top speed in excess of 80mph (128kph). Her maiden flight was on 16 December 1929. In 1930, commanded by Squadron Leader R. Booth, she flew successfully to Canada and back. In the aftermath of the R101 disaster, there was a complete collapse of confidence in official circles in Britain as regards airships and, through no fault of its own, the R100 was grounded and scrapped, with less than £600 being raised by the sale of this. No British rigid has been built since then.

Squadron Leader R.S. Booth, AFC, (born 1895) was originally in the Royal Navy, transferring to the RNAS in 1915 to become an airship pilot, firstly of the SS and Coastal classes. He was appointed first officer of the rigid airship R24 in 1917; from 1924–26 he was the first officer and then captain of the R33, and in 1929–30 he captained R100, during which time the airship made its successful double crossing of the Atlantic.

Rigid Airships in the USA

The American experience post-war was different in that it was the only country to have sufficient supplies of helium to make using this much safer gas a viable proposition. Their only large post-war airship using hydrogen was the semi-rigid *Roma*, purchased from Italy in 1921. It crashed at Langley Field, Virginia, in 1922 with the loss of thirty-four lives. The first of three rigid, helium-filled, airships was the USS *Shenandoah*, ZR-1, which was 680 feet (207 metres) long, 78 feet (24 metres) in diameter and had a capacity of 2,235,000 cubic feet (63,295 cubic metres). On 3 September 1925 she broke in two during a violent storm over Ohio; there were twenty-nine survivors from the crew of forty-three, who were saved by riding buoyant sections of the airship which fell to the ground like free balloons. On 4 April 1933, the USS *Akron*, ZRS-4, was forced down into the sea off the coast of New Jersey with the loss of seventy-four crew members out of seventy-seven, the world's worst airship accident. Her sister ship, the USS *Macon*, ZRS-5, encountered a storm off Point Sur, California, on 12 February 1935 and suffered a similar fate, fortunately with a very much lower loss of life. These last two airships were among the largest ever built, being 785 feet (239 metres) in length, with a diameter of 132 feet (40 metres) and a capacity of 6,497,960 cubic feet (184,000 cubic metres). It is an odd fact that

USS *Shenandoah.*

The USS *Akron* moored inside the Goodyear air dock.

all three succumbed to adverse weather conditions. The USA joined Britain in abandoning the rigid airship. This left the field to Germany.

Zeppelins

In the aftermath of the First World War, Germany had been greatly restricted by the terms of the Treaty of Versailles with regard to the further development of airships.

Article 198
The armed forces of Germany must not include any military or naval air forces. No dirigible shall be kept.

Article 202
On the coming into force of the present treaty, all military and naval aeronautical material must be delivered to the governments of the Principal Allied and Associated Powers. In particular, this material will include all items under the following heads which are, or have been, in use, or were designed for warlike purposes:

Dirigibles able to take to the air, being manufactured, repaired or assembled.
Plant for the manufacture of hydrogen.
Dirigible sheds and shelters of every kind for aircraft.
Pending their delivery, dirigibles will, at the expense of Germany, be maintained inflated with hydrogen; the plant for the manufacture of hydrogen, as well as the sheds for dirigibles, may, at the discretion of the said powers, be left to Germany until the time when the dirigibles are handed over.

A brief resumption of commercial services in 1919, during which 103 flights were made and 2450 passengers carried, terminated when the Zeppelins LZ121 *Nordstern* and LZ120 *Bodensee* had to be handed over to France and Italy respectively as reparations. The Zeppelin works was saved by the order of an airship from the USA; this was the LZ126/ZR-3 USS *Los Angeles*, which was completed in 1924. While the Zeppelin workforce was happy, the *Berlin Morning Post* was not, commenting unfavourably on a ship, 'built in Germany by German workers and engineers, paid for with German money, but which belongs to America.'[7] Her delivery flight on 13–15 October 1924, commanded by Dr Hugo Eckener, was the third airship crossing of the Atlantic, after R34's double run in 1919. In US service the hydrogen originally used was replaced with helium. She was the most successful rigid airship ever operated by the US Navy and had an unblemished eight year flying career of nearly 5000 hours.

The greatest rigid airship of all time first took to the skies on 18 September 1928. This was LZ127, the *Graf Zeppelin*. She was 775 feet long (236 metres), 100 feet in diameter (30 metres) and with a capacity of 3,700,000 cubic feet (104,784 cubic metres). Her five Maybach engines of 550 hp (410kW) each, gave her a top speed of 80mph (129kph) and a cruising speed of 68mph (109kph). For the next decade she was one of the most famous aircraft in the world, regularly making the headlines and newsreels with spectaculars, including a round-the-world flight in August 1929, with a research trip to the Arctic in 1931, and multiple crossings of the North and South Atlantic. The *Graf Zeppelin's* engines ran on 'Blau Gas', which had several advantages over liquid fuels such as petrol. It was non-explosive, and because it was only slightly heavier than air, burning it and replacing its volume with air did not lighten the airship – eliminating the need to adjust buoyancy or ballast in flight.[8] She was followed by the largest flying machine ever built, the LZ129, *Hindenburg*, which measured 800 feet (245 metres) in length, had a diameter of 135 feet (41 metres) and a capacity of 7,000,000 cubic feet (198,240 cubic metres). The *Hindenburg* was destroyed by fire as she arrived at Lakehurst, New Jersey, on her first commercial flight to the USA on 6 May 1937. A sister ship, the LZ130, *Graf Zeppelin II*, flew briefly in 1939 and carried out some electronic intelligence gathering missions probing British radar defences, but in 1940, both LZ127 and LZ130 were broken up for scrap. So ended the rigid airship era which had lasted for some forty years.

LZ129 *Hindenburg.*

Proof of concept with regard to intercontinental flights had been established by the exploits of LZ104, the *Afrikaschiff*, in November 1917. She took off from Yambol in Bulgaria to fly to German East Africa with supplies to relieve the hard-pressed force of General von Lettow-Vorbeck. While the airship was en-route, erroneous reports arrived that von Lettow-Vorbeck had been defeated and it was not until the *Afrikaschiff* had overflown Khartoum that a recall message was received on board. She returned to base some four days after her departure, having flown a record breaking ninety-five hours and covering 4200 miles (6800 kilometres) in challenging and changing climatic conditions.

A mechanic crosses to the *Hindenburg*'s port forward engine gondola.

It was in the end a technological cul-de-sac, rigid airships were too slow and unwieldy to compete with fixed-wing aircraft, and, along with the flying-boat, are now icons of a time when air travel had glamour and style. They were not big enough to make their speed advantage over surface shipping

The *Graf Zeppelin* lands at Los Angeles, note the Goodyear blimp in the background.

commercially viable. The construction techniques and materials available at the time could not make craft (apart from a few notable exceptions) which were able to survive stormy weather. (It is of interest that Lord Rayleigh was of the opinion that there was nothing more difficult than calculating the stresses, particularly the torsional stresses of a rigid.)[9] The contemporary naval fixed-wing airman, Richard Bell Davies, had some interesting comments to make with regard to airships and safety:

> 'I have never been a great believer in the future of airships, but I think one of the reasons that they failed to do better than they did was due to the difficulty of giving long enough training to their captains. The master of a merchant ship has usually spent ten years or more in a subordinate position before he is given command. He has seen the ship berthed literally hundreds of times and has seen her handled in all sorts of weather. I suppose in the whole world there has only been one man who had experience with airships comparable to the ship experience of the average British Master Mariner. This was Dr Eckener when he commanded the *Graf Zeppelin*. She had no accidents and made trips all round the world.'[10]

There is much food for thought in this statement, as there also is in remarks made by Murray Sueter:

> 'The tide tables, laws of storms, etc, as applying to surface vessels, have been built up by years and years of patient labour by experts all over the world. Surely, then, it is not unreasonable to suppose that the same study of the conditions in the lower strata of the atmosphere in the England, Egypt, India, Australia, South Africa and Canadian air routes will have to be considered for the use of airmen navigating all types of aircraft, so that they can be guided in the same way as the seaman is in the normal conditions expected. The meteorological staff are not fools; they and the airship staff realize the importance of wind currents, both permanent and otherwise, and that is why they are analysing the lower strata of the atmosphere in the area of the England-Egypt-India route for every day of the year, in order to discover what are the normal conditions to be expected.'[11]

It remains a question, could a niche still be found for a rigid airship equipped with advanced avionics and engines, built from strong but light composite materials? Could it be used to deliver heavy plant and machinery to remote and inaccessible areas, or as an aerial cruise liner?

Non-Rigid Patrol Airships

In all, 147 Submarine-Scout type airships were constructed, twenty-nine with the BE2c fuselage, twenty-six Maurice Farman types, ten with an Armstrong-Whitworth car, six SS-Pushers (which had rubberized fabric petrol tanks, which were not a success and were soon replaced by aluminium ones) and seventy-six improved model SS Zeros. The SSZ was built to the design of three RNAS officers, Commander A.D. Cunningham, Lieutenant F.M. Rope and Warrant Officer Righton, at RNAS Capel, near Folkestone. Work started on building the prototype in June 1916. The car was specifically designed to be streamlined in shape and was constructed almost like a boat, with a keel and ribs of wood with curved longitudinal members. The whole frame was braced with piano wire and then floored from end to end. It was enclosed with eight-ply wood covered with aluminium. The crew of three consisted of the wireless telegraphist/observer/gunner in the front, with the pilot in the middle and the engineer in his own compartment to the rear. A machine gun could be mounted either to port or starboard, operated from the front seat, and two 110lb bombs could be carried. The car, as well as being boat-shaped, was watertight, so the airship could land on calm water. The engine was a great improvement. It is said that the engineering officer at Kingsnorth, Lieutenant T.R. Cave-Browne-Cave, had complained time and again about the adapted aero engines used in the SS Class, which because they were not designed for use in airships, were unsuitable for slow, sustained flight and were always giving trouble. His commanding officer, tiring of this, ordered him to go and do something about it. So, taking him at his word, Cave-Browne-Cave took the train to Derby and requested a meeting with Henry Royce. After only a few hours of discussion an engine specification was agreed. This became the 75 hp Rolls-Royce Hawk six-cylinder, vertical in-line, water-cooled engine driving a four-bladed pusher propeller; 200 of

An SSZ Class airship, looking over the pilot's head to the engineer's station at the rear of the car. (*via Tom Jamison*)

these were manufactured under licence by Brazil Straker of Bristol, which was the only company entrusted by Henry Royce to build complete engines. It was a superb creation and was test run for the first time at the end of 1915. The words of an airship pilot tell it all; 'The sweetest engine ever run – it only stops when switched off or out of petrol.'[12] It gave the airship a top speed of 53mph and a rate of climb of 1200 feet per minute. Slung on either side of the gasbag were two petrol tanks made from aluminium. The gasbag had a capacity of 70,000 cubic feet. It was of the same length as the SS Class gasbag, but was of a slightly greater diameter. The nose of the gasbag was reinforced by radially positioned canes to prevent it buckling at speed. As with the SS Class it was attached to the car with cables secured to the envelope by kidney-shaped *Eta* adhesive patches, which were also sown on, so spreading the load evenly. The SSZs, or Zeros as they were known, which first flew in September 1916, were more stable in flight than the SS Class and had much greater endurance. They were able to fly in weather conditions that would have prevented the earlier type from operating. Its unit cost was about £5000. It rapidly gained the approval of its pilots:

'The SSZs were dreams come true. I fell for them almost at once. At last we had a trouble-free engine and our engineers were able to get some sleep at nights.'[13]

The larger and longer range Coastal Class were the workhorses of the airship service, seeing more action than any other type; in all thirty-five of these were produced, flying from bases in Kent, Cornwall, Sussex, Norfolk, Wales and Scotland. The most famous of these was C9, which entered service at Mullion in Cornwall on 1 July 1915 and flew a record 2500 hours (averaging three hours six minutes per day flying time) and more than 68,000 miles (108,800 kilometres) before being retired from active service on 1 October 1918. She attacked several U-boats successfully. In 1917 the indefatigable Wing Captain Maitland made an experimental parachute jump from C17. It is believed that two, and possibly three, of this class were lost due to enemy action, two in duels with German seaplane fighters and one in an action with a U-boat, with the result that the order was given that their top gun, mounted on the envelope, should be manned at all times. It is thought that the two which were shot down by aircraft had strayed too close to enemy-occupied territory. They were the only airships destroyed by hostile fire.

The Coastal Class was followed by the improved C Star Class, ten of which were constructed. It was an interim type produced at short notice by the team at Kingsnorth because of problems with the development of the North Sea

Coastal Star Class airship C*7, note C*5 in the background. (*J.M. Bruce; G.S. Leslie Collection*)

Class. They were 207 feet in length (63 metres), 217 feet (66 metres) from C*4 onwards, with a maximum diameter of 47 feet (14 metres) and a capacity of 210,000 cubic feet (5943 cubic metres). The streamlined, tri-lobe envelope and the 220 hp (163kW) Renault engine aft, with a 110 hp (81kW) Berliet forward, allowed a faster top speed of 57mph (91kph). The car was clad in plywood rather than canvas, with portholes of Triplex glass to each side and in the floor. Provision was also made for static line parachutes for the crew in case of emergency. The longest flight made by a C* was one of thirty-four and a half hours, made by C*4 in May 1918.

A North Sea Class airship over East Fortune in 1917. (*Jack McCleery*)

North Sea Class airship NS4.

When the North Sea Class had recovered from its teething problems under the care of the Kingsnorth design team, it quickly proved to be the most efficient of the British blimps. The class was once more based on the Astra-Torres tri-lobe pattern, but was larger again, with a length of 260 feet (79 metres), maximum diameter of 57 feet (17 metres) and a capacity of 360,000 cubic feet (10,188 cubic metres). Power came from a pair of 250 hp (185kW) Rolls-Royce Eagle engines, with a design maximum speed of 55mph (88kph), though on occasions modified craft reached 70mph (112kph). Fifteen of this class were delivered before the Armistice, when production was cut short. The car, which contained control, navigation and wireless rooms, accommodation and sleeping space, was completely enclosed and was made from steel tubes clad in Duralumin and fabric. There was also a separate engine car connected by a walkway. The crew of ten were split into two watches, so patrols of several days in duration could be made. There were also cooking facilities on a hot-plate fitted to an engine exhaust. Up to five machine guns could be fitted and six 230lb (104kg) bombs could be carried. When the German High Seas Fleet surrendered and sailed into British waters in November 1918, NS-7 and NS-8, which were based at East Fortune on the Firth of Forth, escorted them in, positioned to starboard and in the centre of the fleet respectively. A world endurance record of 100 hours and 50 minutes was set by NS-11 in February 1919. In March, NS-11 and NS-12 made the first airship flights to Norway.

Three large non-rigids of the Parseval type were built by Vickers at Barrow and assembled at the airship station at Howden in Yorkshire, and also gave useful service, as did the thirteen SS Twin Class, of which 115 were planned and which were about half the envelope size and two thirds the length of the Coastal Class.

That their utility was valued throughout the war may be seen from two official documents, the first a memorandum from Captain F.B. Scarlett, DAD, and dated 26 March 1918:

'The following shows the number and types of different airships in commission:
'SS 9; SS Pusher 3; SS Zero 31; SS Twin 1; Coastal 9; Coastal Star 2; North Sea 3; Parseval 3 and Rigid 5.

Notes
'The SS Type was the first small airship commissioned, motive power supplied by one 75 hp engine. This type is now used for training.

'The SSP Type is a slight improvement on the former.

'The SSZ Type, which is in extensive use on most of the airship stations, is a decided improvement on the two foregoing types, and has proved extremely useful for anti-submarine patrol.

'The SST Type is similar to the SSZ, with the exception that it has two engines and is known as the SS Twin. The first unit of this type has just undergone its trials, which were extremely promising, the extra engine giving this ship a greater speed and making it much more reliable in case of engine failure.

'The C Type ship, known as the Coastal Patrol, will very probably be superseded by the SS Twin, although it has been extremely useful for patrol work.

'The C Star Type is an improvement on the C and has not been commissioned very long.

'The NS Type ship, known as the North Sea type, was designed for the purpose of doing extensive patrols in the North Sea, but up to the present has not given very good results.

'The P ship is the original German Parseval type.

'The R type ship is known as the Rigid and has been constructed on the lines of the German Zeppelins. These ships should still be considered as experimental.'[14]

The second is a planning paper written for the Board of the Admiralty, setting out airship requirements in the event that the war continued into 1919:

'In pursuance of Minute 354, the committee have reviewed the situation with regard to Rigid and Non-Rigid Airships, and they have agreed upon the following report and recommendations:

Non-rigid Airships

'In connection with the approved programme for completing 115 SS Twin-Type airships by June 1919, the committee found that the experiments with the Sunbeam Dyak engine, referred to in their previous report, have been successful, and that the Air Ministry are arranging to have this class of engine built for the Admiralty by the firm of Messrs Sunbeam. The delivery of this engine will commence in December, some months earlier than was anticipated, but on the other hand the dates for delivery of Rolls-Royce Hawk engines indicated in the previous report of the committee have been somewhat deferred.

'The approved programme of SST airships should therefore ensure the completion, by the end of June 1919, of 117 airships (including two experimental) which, with fifty-eight SSZ in commission and one in reserve, and thirteen SS and SSP airships (that is 189 in all), and allowing for a deletion of six for obsolescence, but making no allowance for casualties, would give us a stock of 183 airships from 1 July next.

Rigid Airships

'The committee found that the dates for the completion of rigid airships as indicated in their previous report had not been, and, cannot be realised, owing to difficulties in regard to construction and trials, shortage of labour, and in some cases alteration of design. By Board Minute 354, the number of rigid airships to be maintained in commission has been reduced to eleven, so that no further housing accommodation for rigid airships is required beyond that at present existing and in course of construction at Howden in Yorkshire and Killeagh in Co Cork, Ireland.

Generally

'The committee recommend that in future the situation with regard to rigid and non-rigid airships should be reviewed by them at intervals of three months, when account will be taken of any further orders rendered necessary by casualties which have occurred during the previous quarter.

Summary

'The report of the committee may be summarised as follows:

1. 'That the approved programme of SST airships should ensure the completion, by the end of June 1919, of 117 Airships (including two experimental) which, with fifty-eight SSZ in commission and one in reserve (obtainable by utilising large spares already in stock), and thirteen SS and SSP airships (that is, 189 in all), and allowing for a deletion of six for obsolescence, but making no allowance for casualties, would give us a stock of 183 Airships on 1 July 1919.

2. That no further housing accommodation will, prior to 1 October 1919, be required either for rigid or non-rigid airships beyond that already existing or approved.

Recommendations

1. 'That a further forty-eight SS Twin airships be now ordered for delivery in July, August and September 1919, in order to maintain continuity of production and to allow for casualties.

2. 'That no further large spare parts be ordered for SSZ Type, and that this type of vessel be allowed to die out as existing large spares are used up.

3. 'That the SS and SSP type be maintained as necessary by minor repairs only, and that they be allowed to die out when it becomes necessary to use large spares.

4. 'That non-rigid airships lost, prior to 1 October 1918, be made good from stock, but that subsequent to that date, ships completely lost be struck off the establishment, and ships partially destroyed, of which any material part remains, be replaced out of spares.

5. 'That the situation with regard to both rigid and non-rigid airships be reviewed by the committee at intervals of three months.'[15]

No other contemporary aircraft could have performed the jobs airships undertook. None could match the airships' endurance or slow speed capability. They could stay close to the convoys and their escorts for extended periods; either scouting ahead for submarines or mines, or standing off to windward, ready to swoop down rapidly to investigate a possible threat. Indeed, it could be said that the airships' potential was, even by the later stages of the war, not fully appreciated. Those operating with the Grand Fleet were sent ahead on scouting missions, but were forbidden by the C-in-C, Admiral Beatty, to go beyond visual range of the leading vessels, thus not breaking radio silence, but greatly limiting their range of vision over the horizon.

Another limitation imposed on the use of airships was described by Rear Admiral Murray Sueter, when he revealed in a book published after the war that he had proposed to the Admiralty in 1915 a scheme for the extensive aerial surveillance of shipping to be carried out by airship in the Mediterranean. This was turned down on the grounds of cost and in Sueter's opinion prevented the solution to what became a very costly destruction of shipping in that theatre.[16] He made this summary of the RN Airship Service's contribution in World War One, which had grown in size to 580 officers and 6534 men at eighteen airship stations:

	Hours	*Mins*	*Mileage*
1915	1496		41,675 (66,680km)
1916	8296		229,187 (366,699km)
1917	22309		579,188 (926,700km)
1918	56536	48	1,395,763 (2,233,220km)
Total	88717	48	2,245,810 (3,593,296km)[17]

On 1 November 1918 there were 103 airships in commission, five rigids, one Parseval, six North Sea, ten Coastal Star, four Coastal, twelve SST, fifty-three SSZ, three SSP and nine SS.[18] It should be noted that in the course of this valuable service only fifty-four airshipmen lost their lives from all causes. Sixteen airships in total were lost, mostly through accident or mishap. The most intense part of the campaign was from June 1917 to October 1918. During these sixteen months, on average, fifty-six airships were on duty every day and a total of 9059 patrols were carried out, the average duration of which was six hours and seventeen minutes. A total of 59,703 hours were flown, including 2210 escorts of shipping; 134 mines were sighted, of which seventy-three were destroyed; forty-nine U-boats were spotted, twenty-one of these were attacked with the help of surface craft and six by airships on their own. Their deterrence value was immense – during the entire war there was only one instance of a ship being escorted by an airship being sunk. This may be placed in context by considering the fact that of the 12,618,283 tons of merchant shipping lost in the First World War, 11,135,460 tons were sunk by U-boats – eighty-eight per cent of the total. During the final fifteen months of the war, SS type airships carried out over 10,000 patrols, flying nearly one and a half million miles in more than 50,000 hours. The submarines were kept below the waves, where they used up valuable battery power and were restricted to a speed of only eight or nine knots. A brief log entry from a captured U-boat speaks volumes; 'Sighted airship – submerged.' An analysis written in a respected, post-war, monthly magazine noted:

'The Germans stated that what they disliked most in the Irish Sea area were the airships that were always passing over them. They did not fear the bombs these craft carried, but they did dislike having their own position continually reported to the surface patrols, who, as a result, gave them little rest. There is no doubt that the morale of submarine personnel is much affected by continual nerve strain.'[19]

The Royal Navy's non-rigid airships did not win the battle against the U-boats on their own, but they made a highly important and unique contribution, without which the struggle would have been much more difficult. It was; 'An instrument of knowledge rather than power.'[20]

There is a remarkable consensus of opinion between contemporary commentators, politicians and airshipmen, as well as historians in later years. There is not a single dissenting voice, all agree on the utility, effectiveness and value for money of the naval non-rigid airships. Within a few months of the cessation of hostilities most of the non-rigids were withdrawn from service, as the RAF contracted hugely, and financial pressures bit into the budget. They were used extensively in mine-clearance operations, but by the summer of 1919 most had been deflated for the final time. The last non-rigid to serve with the RAF was NS-7, which was based at Howden in 1920, training the crew of R38. It flew for the last time on 25 October 1921.

It was to the airships' advantage that they operated in an environment without predators or effective countermeasures; there were no aircraft carriers to bring fighter aircraft within range and the U-boats were not equipped with anti-aircraft armament, nor did they really wish to remain on the surface and fight it out. Experimental use was made of SSZ1 in towing trials with the Lord Clive Class monitor, HMS *Sir John Moore,* off Dunkirk in 1916. The plan was to see if the airship could be used to spot for the monitor's 12 inch (304mm) guns as it bombarded German positions. It was quickly realised that the slow speed of the airship made her employment that close to the enemy coast impracticable. Another airship, SS-40, served briefly on the Western Front from Boubers-sur-Canche, near Arras, in the summer of 1916; she had a larger envelope, which was painted black. On a trial flight from Polegate it was noted by the War Office acceptance team; 'The ship became invisible as soon as she took off; seemed to go round in a circle and fade away. Never saw her again till she landed. Very good show!' However, in France, the results were disappointing as the *Black Ship,* or *Bertha the Black Blimp,* as she was known, could only operate safely at night, when there was little that could be seen, so the experiment was abandoned after

SS-40: The
Black Ship.

only two flights. Or was this merely a cover story? Interestingly, the memoirs of
one airship pilot, relating to his time at Kingsnorth, refer to SS-40:

'Disappearing from time to time, she was used for night work over France,
dropping men behind the lines.'[21]

This is corroborated to an extent in a memoir by Air Marshal Sir Victor Goddard
in preparation for a talk on the BBC in 1955, which was never broadcast:

'Many's the time that the *Black Ship* sailed over the lines at night through
that long summer and autumn of rumbling, bloody battle. But never once
with an agent to drop. Spies are brave men, but they didn't fancy our
airship as a mode of travel. Instead, Flight Sub-Lieutenant Billy Chambers
and Captain C.R. Robbins made night reconnaissance from which all too
little could be learned about the enemy's movements. Coming back from
a clandestine operation, the crew of the *Black Ship* would sing a bawdy
song as they approached their hangar at treetop height, with the engine
throttled back. The singing was to alert the ground crew and also to
discourage any Tommies below from taking pot shots at the almost silent
shape. Chambers was mentioned in dispatches in General Haig's report
on the Battle of the Somme.'[22]

Despite this hint of cloak and dagger work it can be said that the technology was
only able to survive in the context of the conditions pertaining between 1914
and 1918, or was it?

To war with the US Navy (Twice)

A small number of blimps were used for coastal patrol duties by the US Navy in 1917–18. An assortment of small non-rigids of various sizes was maintained by the US Army, and then exclusively the navy, between the wars. The major operator in the inter-war period was the Goodyear-Zeppelin Corporation of Akron, Ohio, which built the following small, helium-filled, non-rigid airships, including *Pony (1919–23)*, *Pilgrim (1925)*, and the extended fleet of the later 1920s and early 1930s: *Puritan*, *Volunteer*, *Mayflower*, *Vigilant*, *Defender*, *Reliance*, *Resolute*, *Rainbow*, *Enterprise*, *Ranger* and *Columbia*. A typical example would have been 140 feet (42.67 metres) in length, with a diameter of 40 feet (12.19 metres), a volume of 112,000 cubic feet (3169 cubic metres), driven by two 110 hp (81.4kW) engines, giving a speed of 60mph (96kph) and the ability to carry six passengers. By 1942 they had made 151,810 flights, 92,000 flying hours, with a total distance of more than 4,000,000 miles (6,437,000 kilometres)

A Goodyear blimp lands at the Century of Progress Exposition held in Chicago in 1933–34.

The Goodyear fleet at Akron.

in every state east of the Mississippi, but also to Texas, California, Cuba, Canada and Mexico, carrying 400,000 passengers in complete safety. Their versatility was immense: delivering mail and newspapers, taking aloft press reporters, newsreel cameramen and radio announcers to report on sports and other events, facilitating wildlife, civil engineering and traffic studies, disaster and emergency relief, rescues from the Everglades and at sea, and pleasure flights, to list just some of the roles for which they were used.[23] The pilots, crew and ground staff gained vast experience operating their craft in all weathers and became very confident with the ability of their ships to fly in all but the most adverse of conditions. Perhaps the worst hazards were the attentions of trigger-happy and thoughtless hunters, which at least proved that the blimps could sustain bullet damage and fly on. Many of the Goodyear pilots were commissioned as reserve officers in the USN, giving a nucleus of experience from which the naval airship service could expand. As for the Goodyear blimps, they had naval markings applied and were pressed into service for training duties.

USN blimp G-1.

USN blimp K-3.

In 1941 the US Navy had a handful of blimps. After the attack on Pearl Harbour in 1941, the Navy asked the US Congress for authorization to purchase many more. By June 1942 the construction of 200 helium-filled airships had been authorized. During the next three years Goodyear built a total of 168. At its production peak, the company was turning out eleven airships monthly. The United States was the only power to use airships during World War II, and the airships played valuable roles. The USN employed them for minesweeping, search and rescue, photographic reconnaissance, scouting, escorting convoys, and anti-submarine patrols.

In the bitter and crucial Battle of the Atlantic in 1942, nearly 500 merchant ships were sunk on the eastern seaboard of the USA alone. Remarkably, part of the answer was found to be the establishment of an eventual total of five Fleet Airship Wings, with a strength of more than 100 blimps in fifteen squadrons stationed not only on either side of the continental USA, but also in Jamaica, Brazil, Trinidad, French Morocco and Gibraltar; patrolling an area of over three million square miles (7.8 million square kilometres) over the Atlantic and Pacific Oceans, and the Mediterranean Sea between 1942 and 1945. They were very reliable, being available for duty eighty-seven per cent of the time; 35,600 operational flights were made in the Atlantic and 20,300 in the Pacific, for a total of 5,550,000 hours in the air escorting 89,000 ships loaded with troops, equipment and supplies. No ship escorted by a blimp was ever sunk and only one of the airships was lost to enemy action – K-74, which fought a duel with a U-boat.[24]

After 1945 the USN carried on with using blimps in anti-submarine warfare, search and rescue (SAR) and early warning roles. Some were equipped with huge airborne radar sets for early warning of bomber attacks against the USA. Two of the largest airships were the ZPG-2 at 324 feet (99 metres) in length and a capacity of 875,000 cubic feet (24,777 cubic metres), and the ZPG-3 at 403 feet (121 metres) long and a capacity of 1,516,000 cubic feet (43,000 cubic metres), the latter being the largest blimp ever built. An airship of this type could stay aloft without refuelling for more than 200 hours. On 31 August 1962, the navy ended its use of blimps. In the 1980s the USN examined once more the possibility of reviving airships, but Congress terminated funding for the project in 1989.

[Author's note: It is of interest to note that Betty Usborne's son, John Godley, later Lord Kilbracken, took part in successful anti-submarine operations, based in Ireland during the Second World War, which used what was regarded as outmoded technology. Maydown, in Co Londonderry, was the headquarters for MAC (Merchant Aircraft Carrier) ship operations. This type of aircraft carrier proved to be a highly effective countermeasure to the U-boat offensive from mid-1943 onwards. These were standard grain carriers or oil tankers fitted with an elementary flight deck from which a flight of three or four Swordfish biplanes was operated. Each flight of Swordfish flew from Maydown to join the carrier off the Irish coast, and returned to base after the journey across the Atlantic and back. It is a remarkable fact that, of the 217 convoys in which a MAC ship sailed, between May 1943 and the end of the war, only one was attacked successfully by a U-boat. Three parent units for the Swordfish were based at Maydown, 836 and 860 NAS, for operational deployment, and 744 NAS for training; 836 was the largest operational squadron in the FAA. Together, the Maydown squadrons provided over ninety Swordfish for some nineteen MAC ships. The last FAA squadron to relinquish the famous Swordfish was 836 at Maydown in July 1945. Northern Ireland remained a very important location for air anti-submarine activity for the next thirty years, with the Joint Air Submarine School (JASS) at Londonderry until 1969, the Air Anti-Submarine School at RNAS Eglinton (now City of Derry Airport) which closed in 1959 and RAF Coastal Command Shackletons flying from Aldergrove until 1959 and Ballykelly until 1971. The long tradition of maritime surveillance in Ireland is now maintained by the Irish Air Corps from its base at Baldonnel on the outskirts of Dublin.]

The British Army Considers an Airship

Remarkably, a plan conceived in the mid-1990s renewed the British Army's connection with lighter-than-air aviation after a gap of some eighty years – in the bulbous shape of ZH762, a Westinghouse Skyship 500 built by Airship Industries of Cardington. It was 170 feet (52 metres) long, 46 feet (14 metres) in diameter and had a capacity of 182,000 cubic feet (5150 cubic metres). The helium-filled envelope was laminated, lined with gas-retention film and sprayed externally with a polyurethane coating. The car was attached to the envelope and was made from reinforced plastic; it was powered by two Porsche 930 engines of 205 hp (151kW) each, and, as with previous blimps, they were fitted with swivelling propellers and its ballonets were fed from the slipstream. Skyships have been used for tourist flights, fishery patrols, aerial photography and a range of other activities. This airship was flown by Army Air Corps pilots in the course of an extensive trials programme, which included a visit to 5 Regiment AAC at RAF Aldergrove. It had the advantages of being able to lift a considerable quantity of mission-related equipment and of being able to remain in the air for protracted periods of time. Against these benefits had to be set the undeniable facts that it was slow, not being capable of more than 30–40 knots (34–45mph/55–74kph) cruising speed and that it was not well-suited to windy or icy weather conditions. Useful experience was gained, but the AAC decided in the end not to establish a new airship unit.

Westinghouse Skyship 500 ZH762 at RAF Aldergrove in 1995. (*5 Regiment AAC*)

The Airship Plane

The last scheme hatched by Neville Usborne was the one that would result in his tragic, early demise – the idea of an aeroplane carried aloft by an airship. Though further development of the AP-1 was terminated, aircraft were indeed to be borne aloft by airships. Trials were carried out by both the British and the Germans in 1918. On 26 January, an Albatros D.III single-seat fighter, serial number 3066, was fixed under the airship L35 (Zeppelin LZ 80) of the Imperial German Navy to test the idea of protecting airships by attaching a fighter which could fly off to defend the mother ship if it was attacked. The pilot was in the cockpit throughout and could not be transferred in flight. The trial was a success in that the Albatros, which had kept its engine running for the duration of the flight as there was no way of manually restarting it once the Zeppelin was airborne, was released from a height of some 5000 feet (1500 metres) and flew away safely. Then, on 6 November, Sopwith 2F.1 (or 'Ships Camel' as it was commonly known) N6814, flown by Lieutenant R.E. Keys, DFC, of No 212 Squadron RAF, was dropped from the British airship R23 and landed at Pulham in Norfolk. R33 was the next British rigid to be used for experiments of this nature, releasing a pilotless Sopwith Camel in 1920 and then from October 1925 not only releasing, but also recapturing aircraft in the air. A specially developed trapeze was attached to the envelope from which was suspended a DH53

R23 and Sopwith 2F.1 Ship's Camel N6622 in the shed at Pulham in 1918. It was also launched successfully and flown by Lieutenant Keys. Note C*9 in the background.

Hummingbird lightweight single-seater. When R33 had attained a height of 3800 feet (1150 metres), Squadron Leader Rollo Amyat de Haga Haig climbed down a ladder into the cockpit, the trapeze swung down and the Hummingbird, J7326, was released. He dived until the engine started, performed two loops and returned to the airship to hook on. As he came in to engage, the aircraft touched one of the trapeze stay wires and the propeller was smashed. The pilot then disengaged the suspension gear and dropped down to glide

R23 and Camel N6814.

to Pulham airfield below. On investigation it was decided that the approach of the pilot had been incorrect and the trapeze should have only been lowered when he was approaching from the stern, then there would have been a perfect

DH53 Hummingbird J-7326 suspended from R33 during trials in 1925.

approach with the nose gear slotting easily into place. The second attempt was also imperfect and once more the pilot landed on the ground. The third try, on 4 December, was completely successful, flying J7326. The following year the same experiment was made with a pair of Gloster Grebe II fighters, J7385 and J7400; both were dropped successfully in October and November, but no attempts were made to hook on again. The first successful launch was achieved on 21 October 1926. The pilot was Flying Officer R.L. Ragg (Later Air Marshal, CB, CBE, AFC) of the Royal Aircraft Establishment.

The most persistent and effective users of this idea were in the USA. The US Army Air Service experimented in 1923–1924 with a Sperry Messenger and Army Corps blimps TC-7 and TC-3, conducting numerous flights achieving successful launch and recovery. The US Navy devoted a great deal of time and resources to examining the possibility of using airship-borne aircraft as fleet scouts. Tests were conducted using the USS *Los Angeles*. A rigid 'trapeze' was installed on the airship and a programme of flights was undertaken from 1929 onwards, the first successful 'hook on' being made on 3 July 1929 by Lieutenant A.W. 'Jake' Gorton, flying a Vought UO-1.[25] In January 1928, the *Los Angeles* had also made a successful flight some 100 miles (161 kilometres) out to sea off the coast of Rhode Island, to land on the deck of the seaplane carrier, the USS *Saratoga*; she then followed up in March with a flight of 2265 miles (3624 kilometres) in forty hours from Lakehurst, New Jersey, to Panama, Cuba and back.[26]

The USS *Akron's* design included a hangar aft of the control car and crew's quarters. At the time of her early flights, however, no aircraft were carried. In

USS *Los Angeles* moored to USS *Patoka*.

February 1932 a trapeze was installed. Unlike the device on the *Los Angeles*, it included a winch which allowed the hooked-on airplane to be hoisted through a T-shaped door into the belly of the airship, where it was then transferred onto an overhead trolley system and rolled into one of the four spaces provided in the hangar. The hook-on operations began in May 1932. On 4 May 1932, a Consolidated N2Y-1 successfully hooked on to the *Akron's* trapeze and was hoisted inside the giant airship's hangar.

The USN then ordered a new design of aeroplane which many have believed was specifically for the role of airship operations, the Curtiss F9C-2 Sparrowhawk. It was in fact developed from a specification for a very small carrier-borne fighter.[27] It was a stubby little aeroplane and could fit inside the airship's hangar, and was first hooked-on to the *Los Angeles* in October 1931. The training carried out included night hook-ons for which the only illumination of the trapeze was by hand-held flashlights.[28] The Heavier-than-Air Unit of ZRS4 and ZRS5 began operating as scouts from the *Akron* the following year, but as mentioned above, the airship was destroyed in 1933. It had been discovered that the process of hooking-on required no extraordinary flying skills. The relative speed of the airship and the aeroplane were almost zero, the pilot approached the trapeze in an almost stalled attitude and slid his skyhook over the yoke of the trapeze. A spring-latch prevented him from drifting back off the yoke. If he stalled completely during his approach, he had at least 1000 feet (404 metres) of altitude in which to recover and then try again. Taking off was even easier, he simply pulled a lever in the cockpit to release the skyhook. The USS *Macon* also had provision for Sparrowhawks. They proved to be a success in scouting up to

On 7 July 1933 the first Sparrowhawks hooked on to the USS *Macon*.

A F9C-2 Sparrowhawk attached to the trapeze of the USS *Macon*.

200 miles (320 kilometres) ahead of the airship and their range was extended by removing their landing gear during over-water operations, replacing this with a belly fuel tank, which increased the aircraft's range by fifty per cent. On 19 July 1934, just how effective they could be was demonstrated. President Roosevelt was aboard the cruiser USS *Houston*, steaming west across the Pacific towards Hawaii. At noon, to the astonishment of the ship's crew, two tiny aircraft were spotted diving toward the ship, which they then circled – to the President's delight. As they were more than 1,500 miles (2400 kilometres) from land it seemed impossible that any aircraft could have the range required to operate so far from base. No aircraft carriers were operating anywhere nearby. Then *Macon* appeared overhead and orchestrated a series of demonstrations, during which the aircraft dropped mail and messages, which were recovered and winched into the airship's hangar. The President radioed the airship's commanding officer congratulating him; it had been a highly effective piece of publicity for the US Navy. Sadly, all such experiments came to an end when the *Macon* too was lost. Remarkably, the crash site was found in 2006 and the wreckage of several Sparrowhawks was discovered on the sea bed. A plan to construct the much larger ZRCV, which would have carried nine dive-bombers, was never taken beyond the concept stage.[29]

Finally, in the spring of 1937, General Ernst Udet, flying a Focke-Wulf FW-44 Stieglitz made either one or two in-flight hook-ons to a trapeze fitted to the German *Hindenburg*. The aim of this project was to develop an aerial delivery system for mail or passengers. The trials were not wholly successful as Udet experienced considerable difficulty attaching the light training biplane to the trapeze in the turbulent air underneath the airship.

Conclusions

It remains to evaluate and to guess where Neville Usborne's ability and desire for success could have taken him had he not met his untimely end. His ambition and technical ability took him to Barrow and HMA No 1, the ability he displayed there, despite the failure of the *Mayfly*, saw him posted to Farnborough, where he really learned to become an airshipman. Fortunately, the Royal Navy retained just enough of an interest in airships to allow Usborne to be in the right place at the right time, Kingsnorth, so that all that he had learned could be put into effect in the design of two highly successful classes of airship. Sadly his bravery and his questing intelligence, his desire to solve the pressing Zeppelin problem, resulted in his untimely and tragic death. He was admired by his peers, many of whom reached high rank in the RAF or the RN, or high positions in civil aviation. He was well-connected socially, ambitious, dynamic, commercially and mechanically minded, and also had the ear of a leading industrialist. In November 1915 Usborne drew up proposals for the formation of a post-war aeroplane company.[30] He envisaged a small number of skilled designers working for a company which would supply aircraft, flying schools, repair facilities, the design of aerodromes, and which would acquire the rights for mail services to developing markets in foreign countries (eg South America). His fertile mind also considered USA to Europe mail and passenger services. He had concluded that airships would not be viable as a commercial success except perhaps for very long overseas journeys. He was by no means alone in this supposition. For example, on 3 May 1919, a regular columnist for the Belfast daily morning newspaper, the *Northern Whig*, who wrote under the pseudonym 'An Old Fogey', wrote an article entitled 'Ulster's Great Aerodrome'. He was moved to quote Lord Tennyson, who foresaw, 'the nation's airy navies grappling in the central blue,' which had certainly been realised in the preceding four years, but he also looked forward to another of his lordship's predictions coming to pass, 'the heavens filled with commerce, argosies with magic sails, pilots of the purple twilight, dropping down with costly bales.' There then followed a speculative section entitled *Commercial Flying*; 'Now the Air Ministry have published a map showing several routes for the guidance of pilots, and have issued a set of rules of the road and a scale of the charges to be made for the accommodation of civil aviators and their machines at government aerodromes, including Aldergrove. Transatlantic commercial flying, in the opinion of experienced aviators, will come in the near future and the importance of Aldergrove may be still further enhanced by its becoming an important transatlantic air station. Then we may expect announcements in our Saturday morning newspaper such as the following – "Belfast and New York Air Service – Departures from Aldergrove next week as follows: Thursday, *Dalriada* 3000 hp: Saturday, *Ben Madigan* 4000 hp: both Belfast built airships. For passage apply etc."'

His letter of 7 January 1916 to Vickers, with his proposals for post-war aerial transport, received an encouraging reply from the chairman, Sir Trevor Dawson, who himself had been a gunnery officer in the Royal Navy in the 1880s and 1890. Success in the aviation business after the First World War was much on the minds of many of those who had gained vast flying experience during the conflict. Some tried breaking long-distance records, others joined the fledgling airlines and many more set up joy-riding companies. Few in the end made their fortunes. Two ex-military airmen were particularly successful; Sir Alan Cobham, who founded Flight Refuelling Limited after a decade of long distance flights and air displays all around the UK, and Ted Fresson, who was the pioneer of civil aviation in the far north of Scotland and the Isles. Perhaps Usborne could have joined this very short list, but it would have been a struggle. It was not until the 1930s that civil aircraft were designed in Britain that were sufficiently cost-effective to make running an airline in any way economically viable. Even then the biggest players were: the Government and Imperial Airways; the four big railway companies and Railway Air Services; and the investment house Whitehall Securities and British Airways. Industrially, Sopwith, Vickers, Handley Page, De Havilland, Avro and the rest survived on their wits, contracts for military aircraft, light sporting types from the late 1920s and civil airliners in penny packet numbers. If Usborne had gone into the administration of civil aviation, he might have prospered there, as did Sefton Brancker and Frederick Sykes. On the other hand many of his airship contemporaries rose to senior rank in the RAF or the Royal Navy; Masterman (1880–1957) and Maitland (1880–1921) were both Air Commodores, Elmhirst (1898–1982) became an Air Marshal, Sueter (1872–1960) a Rear Admiral, and both Bell Davies (1886–1966) and Usborne's own brother, Cecil, (1880–1951) reached the rank of Vice Admiral. It is safe to say, I believe, that he would have made a lasting mark and would not be such a forgotten figure.

Lighter-than-Air Flight Before the Advent of the Dirigible

In 1766 the English scientist, Henry Cavendish, announced his discovery of the density of inflammable air (or hydrogen as it was later named by Lavoisier) which was lower than that of any other element. By pouring sulphuric acid over iron filings, he was able to collect a sufficient quantity of the gas for his research. (Cavendish (1731–1810) was an English chemist, best known for his experiments on hydrogen, demonstrating its relative lightness compared to air. He announced the results of his research into the specific gravity of inflammable air (hydrogen) in 1766, which led the Professor of Chemistry at Glasgow University, Dr Joseph Black (1728–1799), to suggest the use of the gas for balloons.)

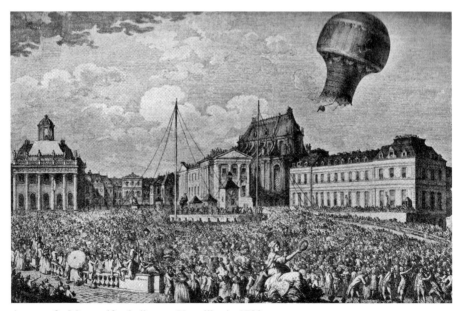

Ascent of a Montgolfier balloon at Versailles in 1783.

On 19 September 1783 a sheep, a cockerel and a duck became the first living creatures to make an ascent in a hot-air balloon constructed by Joseph and Étienne Montgolfier at Versailles, travelling 2 miles (3.2km).

This was followed, on 15 October 1783, by Jean-François Pilâtre de Rozier becoming the first man to ascend in a captive hot-air balloon, the outer envelope of which was made from light linen coated with alum, to a height of 82ft (25m) from the gardens owned by M Reveillon in the Faubourg St Antoine, Paris. Four days later his companion, Guillaume Grioud de Villette, remarked that a fairly inexpensive device of this nature would be very useful to an army intent on discovering, 'the enemy's position, manoeuvres, movement and supplies, and for reporting them by signals.'[1]

On 21 November 1783, de Rozier and François Laurent, Marquis de Arlandes, made the first flight in a free hot-air balloon of twenty-five minutes, ascending from the grounds of the Château de la Muette in the Bois de Boulogne.

It was thought at first that the hot-air balloon rose upwards because of 'Montgolfier's gas', which was created by the burning of wool and straw. It was not until a few years later that the physicist, de Saussure, correctly ascribed the ascensive power of the balloon to its true cause, the rarefaction of heated air.[2]

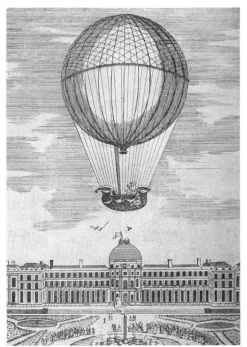

Ascent of Charles & Robert from the Tuileries in 1783.

On 1 December 1783, Professor Jacques Alexandre Cesar Charles and Marie-Noel Robert made the first flight in a hydrogen-filled balloon, with a rubberised silk envelope, of 27 miles (43km). This was something of an improvement on hot-air ballooning as they did not have to keep stoking the fire to stay aloft. The next day Charles flew alone to 9000 feet (2740 metres) and never flew again. It set the standard for all subsequent balloons – a net to surround the bag, wicker basket, safety valve and ballast.

The first manned balloon flight in Ireland, as recorded in *Faulkner's Dublin Journal*, was on 15 April 1784 from a field at Navan in Co

Meath by M Rosseau, accompanied by a small drummer boy. It would appear that they landed about an hour and a half later some miles away to the south, at Ratoath, in the same county.

On 25 April and 12 June 1784, Guyton de Morveau the Abbé Bertrand and M de Virly, at Dijon, carried out the first experiments in steering a balloon by means of oars, a rudder and 'a streamlined device' in front, which had the effect of turning the balloon a little. Over the next few years, sails, paddles and oars were all used by the early balloonists, but to little effect. The Archimedean concept of a screw propeller offered promise, but needed a practical power source. Dirigibility – altering the direction of the balloon in flight – would also be affected by changing the shape of the envelope from sphere to elongated shape, with the longer axis horizontal and in the direction of movement, so as to reduce air resistance.

The first manned flight in Great Britain was made by James Tytler (1745–1804), the editor of the *Encyclopaedia Britannica*, from Comely Gardens in Edinburgh on 27 August 1784. This was followed on 15 September by the first manned ascent in England by Vincento Lunardi (1759–1806) in London.

The first English aeronaut was James Sadler (1753–1828) at Oxford on 4 October 1784, in a home-made hot-air balloon.

The ascent of Vincento Lunardi in London.

On 16 October 1784, the first use of a rotating apparatus for propulsion, a hand-turned, six-bladed propeller fitted to the basket, was made by Jean-Pierre Blanchard in London. (Blanchard (1753–1809), who was born at Les Andelys in France, continued to make balloon ascents, making the first balloon flight in the USA on 9 January 1793. His last ascent, his sixtieth, was in February 1808. He was essentially a showman by nature and, though he became a skilled balloonist, helping to popularise the possibilities of flight, he added little to the science of the subject. He died in Paris on 7 March 1809.)

Two contemporary views may be cited, firstly from Dr Samuel Johnson:

'Happy you are that have ease and leisure to want intelligence of air-balloons. Their existence is, I believe, indubitable, but I know not that they can possibly be of any use. The vehicles, sir, can serve no use until we can guide them. I had rather now find a medicine that can cure an asthma.'[3]

Secondly, from Benjamin Franklin, who was serving as the US envoy to France:

'Since man may be supported in the air, nothing is wanting but some light and handy instrument to give and direct motion.'

In a letter of 16 January 1784 to Sir Joseph Banks, the President of the Royal Society, he wrote that he, 'believed that there was the possibility for the future that an army could use balloons for elevating an engineer to a view of an enemy's army, works, etc, conveying intelligence into or out of a besieged town, giving signals to distant places, or the like. Five thousand balloons, capable of raising two men each, could not cost more than five ships of the line; and where is the prince who can afford to cover his country with troops for its defense, as that "Ten Thousand Men descending from the Clouds" might not in many places do an infinite deal of mischief before a force could be brought together to repel them?'[4]

On 7 January 1785, Blanchard and Dr John Jeffries made the first international and cross-water flight from Dover to Foret de Felmores, Guines, taking two and a half hours in a hydrogen balloon. It cost Jeffries £800. A letter was carried from Ben Franklin's son to his father.

Irishman Richard Crosbie, who was a cousin of Arthur Wellesley, from Co Wicklow, ascended in a hydrogen balloon from Ranelagh Gardens in Dublin on 19 January 1785, watched by over 30,000 people and landing at Clontarf rather than attempt a crossing of the Irish Sea as planned. On 10 May, he was going to try again, but as the balloon would barely lift off he substituted a much lighter weight student from Trinity College by the name of Richard McGwire. The novice aeronaut had a fortunate escape, landing in the sea about nine miles (14 kilometres) out, but being rescued by a fishing boat. Crosbie tried again in July and made it halfway across before he too was forced to descend and be picked up by a barge.

The first British military personnel to make a balloon flight were Major John Money and George Blake of the Royal Navy, who ascended with the owner, Jonathan Lockwood, from Tottenham Court Road, London, on 3 June 1785. Money made several ascents in free balloons and narrowly escaped death in a balloon misadventure off the east coast, near Yarmouth, later that year.[5]

Blanchard and Jeffries cross the English Channel on 7 January 1785.

It was the 15 June 1785 that brought the first fatalities – de Rozier and Pierre Romain in a hybrid gas and hot-air balloon, which would seem to have been a rather dangerous idea.

On 2 April 1794, the world's first military aviation unit was established by the French Revolutionary Committee of Public Safety and, specifically, Jean Louis Guyton de Morveau. The first military use of a captive hydrogen balloon was *l'Entreprenant* of the Première Compagnie d'Aérostiers Militaires, which was sent up for observation at the Siege of Maubeuge on 2 June. Captain Jean-Marie-Joseph Coutelle was the aeronaut, accompanied by Brigade Adjutant General Étienne Radet. It was then used for observation and for dropping notes of orders from Major General Antoine Morlot at the Battle of Fleurus on 26 June, being airborne for some ten hours. The Austrians attempted in vain to shoot it down with cannon fire. Coutelle later said:

'I shan't say that the balloon won the Battle of Fleurus. What I can say is that, being trained to use my glasses, in spite of the oscillation and swaying due to the wind, I was able to distinguish infantry, cavalry and artillery, their movement and, in general, their numbers.'[6]

General Jean-Baptiste Jourdan was taken aloft on 5 July at the Battle of Sombreffe. The Aérostiers were given a uniform similar to that worn by the artillery. Further use of the balloons *Martial*, *Céleste*, *Intrépide* and *Hercule* was made at engagements and sieges in the German states and Italy. Napoleon Bonaparte intended to make use of balloons during his Egyptian campaign; unfortunately, most of the materials and equipment were lost when *Le Patriote* ran into rocks and sank off Alexandria on 4 July 1798. Further material may have been on board *L'Orient*, one of the French line-of-battle ships sunk by Nelson's fleet at the Battle of the Nile in Aboukir Bay on 1 August 1798. The balloon school at Meudon closed in 1802.

A contemporary illustration celebrating French military ballooning.

In 1803, Rear Admiral Charles Henry Knowles submitted a plan to the Admiralty for sending a balloon aloft from a ship to reconnoitre French invasion preparations at Brest, and in the same year, Major General John Money (1752–1817), the aeronaut of 1785, wrote a *Short Treatise on the use of balloons and Field Observators in Military Operations*, which concluded with the following accurate prediction as to the likely level of official interest and support:

'I would not consult old generals whether balloons of field observators could be of any use to the army, for I know what the answer would be, "that as we have hitherto done very well without them, then we may still do without them," and so we did without light artillery, riflemen and telegraphs, etc., and not till we had ocular demonstrations of their use were they adopted.'[7]

A short time later, in 1805–1806, one of the most skilled and inventive seamen of his generation, Captain Lord Cochrane, was the first British officer to use aerial devices in the furtherance of military objectives. He designed a kite to be flown from his ship, the thirty-eight gun frigate, HMS *Pallas*. Its first experimental use was as a means of giving the ship additional speed by sending a large spread of canvas soaring above the mastheads. It was not a success, as in Cochrane's own words:

'Possibly I might not have been sufficiently experienced in the mysteries of wings and tail, for though the kite pulled with a will, it made such occasional lurches as gave reason to fear for the too sudden expenditure of His Majesty's stores.'[8]

His next idea was to drop propaganda leaflets along the French coast by attaching them to small kites with yarn to which a length of slow burning match had been fixed. When it burnt through, the leaflets fell off inside enemy territory, 'much to the annoyance of the French Government.'[9]

Then in 1809, Captain T.H. Cooper, of the 56th Foot in *The Military Cabinet* – directed at the education of young officers – noted that balloons might be useful for exploration, reconnaissance and communication by signal. For the next fifty years there was little military interest in ballooning.[10]

Indeed, the traditional Anglo-French distrust and rivalry did not take long to surface in the new field of aviation, as exemplified in a doggerel rhyme of the period:

Les Anglais, nation trop fière,
S'arrogent l'empire des mers;
Les Français, nation légère,
S'emparent de celui des airs.[11]

On 3–4 October 1803, Jacques Garnerin (1770–1825) made the first long-distance balloon flight from Moscow to Polova of 200 miles (322km).

The first successful crossing of the Irish Sea by a balloon was made by Windham Sadler on 22 July 1817, flying from Portobello Barracks in Dublin at 1.20 pm and alighting near Holyhead at 6.45 pm. His father James (1751–1828) had failed in trying to accomplish the same feat on 1 October 1812, departing from the lawn of Belvedere House in Dublin and getting as far as the Isle of Man.

On 19 July 1821, Charles Green (1785–1870) of London made the first ascent in a balloon filled with coal-gas. It was heavier than hydrogen, but was comparatively economical to produce and more readily obtainable, having been in use for the street lighting of London since 1807. As his fame increased, the Gas-Light Company of London frequently provided supplies of the gas free of

James Sadler's ascent from Dublin on 1 October 1812.

charge. It is believed that the first aeronaut to accomplish 100 balloon flights was Green, who achieved this on 14 May 1832 in a flight from the Mermaid Tavern, Hackney. He also developed the idea of the guide rope suspended from the basket, which could trail along the ground at heights of up to 1000 feet (304 metres), relieving the balloon of a fraction of its load and causing it to adjust to a more or less constant altitude.[12]

A long-distance feat of note was achieved on 7–8 November 1836 when the hydrogen-filled *The Royal Vauxhall Balloon,* with a crew of three, Green, Robert Holland, MP, and Monck Mason, travelled from London to Weilberg in the Duchy of Nassau, some 486 miles (772 kilometres).

On 7 October 1849, M Farber made the first balloon flight over the Alps.

The most significant British aeronaut after Green was Henry Coxwell (1819–1900), whose ascents with James Glaisher (1908–1903) during 1862–1865 were undertaken for the purposes of scientific research, making meteorological and atmospheric observations, as well as experimenting with aerial photography.

Appendix II

Airship Terms

Airship designers needed to balance size, strength, engine power and lifting capacity against the weight of the structure, its payload and its drag – the greater the volume of gas, the greater the payload that could be carried – engines, fuel, passengers, freight and structural weight. The crew was carried in a cabin, box, or metal framework 'car' suspended from the envelope. For efficiency of movement an airship also had to be streamlined and firm in order to cut its way through the air.

Non-rigid – a gasbag or envelope with internal ballonets of air – limited in size of envelope due to the fact that the structure had no rigidity. This type is often known as a blimp.

Semi-rigid – the gasbag was the envelope of the non-rigid, but it also had a keel giving greater strength to the structure. Owing to the increased weight of structure, more lifting capacity had to be given over to lifting the weight of the airship rather than payload.

Rigid – had a strong but light metal (or wooden) framework with a doped fabric cover. Inside were suspended gasbags. This type could be built much larger, but with the penalty of a further increase in weight.

Envelopes were made of two thicknesses of rubberised fabric with rubber between and on the inside surface. They were doped (weatherproofed) on the outside. An old-fashioned Macintosh would be a reasonably near equivalent. Messrs Vickers formed a subsidiary company, the Ioco Rubber & Waterproofing Co, which cornered a large share of the market. Some early airships had envelopes made from goldbeater's skin: the outer membrane of part of the large intestine of the ox. Thousands of these were cleaned and dried then glued to a fine cloth backing and varnished. The result was light, gas-tight and flexible, but was also expensive and became brittle within three years. It had first been used by the Royal Engineers in the 1880s for balloon envelopes, the manufacturing process of which was a jealously guarded secret of the Weinling family of East London.[1]

Ballonets – bags smaller than the main gasbag and slung inside it. In flight air is pumped in or discharged as required, so maintaining the internal pressure and shape of the envelope as well as the trim of the airship.

Duralumin – the name given to a family of aluminium alloys containing small and varying amounts of copper, as well as iron, magnesium, manganese and silicon. It was found to be light, strong, very ductile, easily machined and pressed, with mechanical properties similar to those of mild steel. It has roughly the same tensile strength as mild steel, but with one third of its weight. Alfred Wilm patented the formula for the alloy in 1909, and granted an exclusive license for its manufacture to the company Dürener Metallwerke. The Duralumin name was derived from Dürener Metallwerke, and aluminium.

Hydrogen – the lightest gas known – colourless, odourless and tasteless. At major British airship stations it was produced in an on-site manufacturing plant, stored in gas-holders and piped underground to the airships' hangars. Gas cylinders were used for storage at out-stations. It was generally extracted using the Silicol Process which was by chemical reaction when powdered ferrosilicon was stirred with water and gradually admitted to a chamber containing a hot, strong solution of caustic soda. This resulted in 99.9% pure hydrogen within an hour. A large plant could produce 1,000,000 cubic feet (28,300 cubic metres) of hydrogen per day.

Eta patches – these were developed in 1913 for the final British Army airship, *Eta*. The rigging cables supporting the car beneath the envelope were subdivided into thirty-six attachment points, joined to the envelope by kidney-shaped adhesive patches which were also stitched in place. The load was by this means spread evenly without the need for the cumbersome netting and bridles used previously. The patches were essential to the development of the SS Class airship.

Steering is by means of control surfaces at the rear of the envelope – rudder for movement to left and right, and elevators to point the nose upwards or downwards – or by swivelling the engines or propellers.

Static Lift – by displacement of air as a balloon. If the total weight of the balloon or airship is slightly less than the weight of displaced air then it will rise. Hydrogen is the lightest of all gases, but has the disadvantages of being inflammable when pure and explosive when mixed with air. Helium is much rarer, is less buoyant than hydrogen, but does not burn. Air weighs about 75lbs (34kg) for 1000 cubic feet (28 cubic metres), while the same amount of hydrogen weighs only 5lbs (2kg), so giving 70lbs (32kg) of lift. The same volume of helium weighs 10lbs (4kg) and so gives 65lbs (30kg) of lift. Therefore for each 32,000lbs (907 cubic metres) of hydrogen contained in an airship's envelope there would be about one ton of gross lift. With a helium-filled envelope some 34,000lbs (977 cubic metres) would be needed for the same effect.

Dynamic Lift – from the reaction of airflow over the envelope and control surfaces when under way. This can be altered by trimming the control surfaces, eg nose down if light, or nose up if heavy.

Gross Lift – is the weight of the airship and all its contents.

Useful lift – is the weight that can be allocated to fuel, ballast, passengers and cargo.

Conditions of lift – these vary continually as gas (and the surrounding atmosphere) expands or contracts according to temperature and altitude. Moreover, the weather had a considerable effect, for example, rain falling on the envelope increased its weight, so making the airship loose height. The strength and direction of the wind also had a considerable effect on the airship's speed and progress through the air.

Control of lift – in flight this is controlled by regulating the lift, releasing gas to descend and discharging ballast (normally water) to ascend.

Size – as an airship becomes larger in size its surface area increases as the square of its linear dimensions. If a large airship is three times longer than a small one, it has nine times as much surface area, but twenty-seven times as much volume and lift.

Mooring – an airship would come in to land nose to wind. The pilot then threw down a rope for the mooring party to grab hold of. It was prudent to let the rope earth itself to the ground first, as too eager a lunge for it would result in an electric shock. When it drew closer to the ground party they could reach up for the guy-ropes attached to the bows and the stern. When it was close enough to the ground, they moved forward tugging on the ropes to 'walk' the airship into the shed. Handling on the ground could be a tricky business as an airship presented a sizeable bulk to the wind and was naturally buoyant in this element. When safely in the shed maintenance could be carried out by the riggers and mechanics, with their patches, rubber solution and dope.

Take-off – the airship would be made positively buoyant so that it could be 'walked' out of the shed. Trim would be checked, the engine started, the order to, 'Let go' would be given and the craft would rise gently into the wind.

Good Qualities – airships are economical, quiet and capacious. They can fly long distances without refuelling and are, despite the popular misconception, safe in which to fly. Most of the notorious accidents were due to design faults, the use of hydrogen, or poor weather forecasting. The only paying passengers ever to die in an airship accident were the thirteen souls who were lost in the *Hindenburg*.

Bad Points – they are very slow, of very light construction and thereby prone to being flimsy. Large airships of the Zeppelin type are very expensive to construct. They are difficult to handle on the ground and need large hangars in order to protect them from the elements.

Blimp – there are a number of theories regarding the origin of this word, but it would appear that it is onomatopoeic and can be traced specifically to 5 December 1915, when Lieutenant A.D. Cunningham, RNAS, playfully flicked a finger against the envelope of SS-12 at the Capel air station in Kent and then mimicked aloud the sound it had made. A young midshipman, Victor Goddard, repeated the tale to his fellow officers in the mess hall before lunch the same day. It is believed that by this route the word came into common usage.

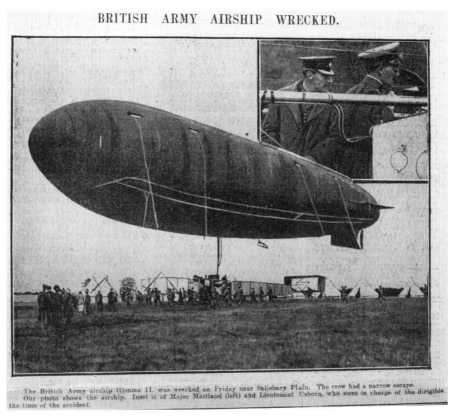

BRITISH ARMY AIRSHIP WRECKED.

The British Army airship Gamma II. was wrecked on Friday near Salisbury Plain. The crew had a narrow escape. Our photo shows the airship. Inset is of Major Maitland (left) and Lieutenant Usborn, who were in charge of the dirigible the time of the accident.

Gamma's mishap of September 1912 is described on page 149. This contemporary press report captioning the photograph is something of an exaggeration.

Appendix III

'Air Battles of the Future'

The following article appeared in the *Daily Mail* in October 1907 and was copied to other newspapers around the world:

AIR BATTLES OF THE FUTURE.
TERRIBLE POSSIBILITIES OF AERIAL WARFARE.
By Dr Rudolf Martial, a Councillor of the German Government.

The battle-airships possessed by Great Britain, France and Germany: Great Britain – *Nulli Secundus*, constructed at Aldershot; travelled on Saturday fifty miles, crossed London, was in the air 3–4 hours, and the highest speed attained in light air was at the rate of forty miles an hour. France – *La Patrie*; has manoeuvred over Paris, travelled through the air for 6 hours and 15 minutes, and covered forty miles. Her speed against wind was at the rate of eighteen miles an hour, Germany – The Gross and the Parseval, both constructed by German Army officers; each has manoeuvred over Berlin. The Gross is said to carry six men, searchlights, and wireless telegraphy instruments; she remained in the air 3 hours 50 minutes, and went against the wind at a speed equal to 12 miles an hour. Count Zeppelin's large aluminium airship, which is also reported to have been bought by Germany, can carry thirty persons, and is said to be capable of travelling 528 miles. In the aerial war of the near future man will be staggered, not by the spectacle, but by the slaughter. For the spectator there will be little to see beyond a number of faint grey linear objects, like whetstones silhouetted against the sky. But each of these drab-coloured objects is an airship which can easily carry from ten to fifty torpedoes, weighing from 110lb to 165lb. The havoc wrought by a small fleet of Zeppelin airships would be frightful. It could pursue the fastest battleship and send it to the bottom. The battleship is at a terrible disadvantage: it is easily damaged from above; it has a speed of twenty-five knots, against a speed of nearly thirty knots possessed by its adversary.

Pursue the comparison to questions of cost and of crew. *La Patrie*, costing £12,000, with a crew of three, and Count Zeppelin's giant airship, costing £25,000, with a crew of six, are each capable of annihilating a battleship, value £2,000,000, with a crew of nearly 1000 men.

Small flexible motor-airships, of so little bulk that they can be stowed away in a couple of carts, can easily be carried on a battleship and inflated on board with compressed gas from steel bottles. Thus the battle-airship will take its place with the heavy guns and the torpedoes as part of the equipment of a battleship. To a motor-airship, the North Sea or the Mediterranean is no more than a large pond. Count Zeppelin's aluminium airship can travel 850 kilometres without taking in any benzine. The action of radius of Lebaudy's *Patrie*, or of the Parseval motor-airship, both of which have a considerably smaller gas capacity, may be 'estimated' at from 225 kilometres to 250 kilometres. At its narrowest point the English Channel only measures 31 kilometres across and the distance from Nordholz to England is about 400 kilometres. With airfleets constructed upon Count Zeppelin's system it would be possible to drive away from the North Sea all squadrons of the fleet which are not protected by battle-airships. An aerial fleet which, during the day, has helped to decide the issue of a battle near Sedan, can, the same evening or during the night, annihilate a battle-fleet in the English Channel, which is only 200 kilometres distant. The air-fleet which has been beaten in battle on land will be driven to sea by the enemy's air-fleet. It will be put out of action by being prevented from taking in a fresh supply of benzine. A fleet so pursued would probably be fired upon by the victor, at the same time, from the land and from the sea. The most important principle of strategy and tactics will be – the attacking airship must be directly above its opponent, as, of course, it can only hit the enemy by letting fall torpedoes. According to an accomplished German authority on aeronautics it will never be possible – owing to the danger of an explosion – to use guns from the cars. This question brings us to a consideration of the fight between airship and airship, surely the most thrilling contest in which man could engage. The opposing airships will strive to rip up each other's envelopes. This coup, bringing instant destruction upon the airship and its occupants, can be effected, of course, by piercing the thin gas-bladder with a sharp missile. There is another weapon. A missile charged with phosphorus solution or carbonic bisulphide would explode the gas-envelope and so destroy the airship. In an aerial battle the Zeppelin airship, with its aluminium envelope, will be a formidable foe. Not only would it be much easier to rip up the gas-bladder of the *Patrie*, or any other Lebaudy airship, with a sharp object, than it is the aluminium envelope of the Zeppelin airship, but in the event of a collision between the two types, the semi-flexible, or flexible one, would sink on account of the damage done to its air-bladder. An especially important mission of the motor-airship will be the laying of mines near the enemy's harbours by night, along the enemy's coast, or directly in the midst of the enemy's fleet. The Zeppelin motor-airship is even able to descend upon the surface of the water. On account of its large tonnage it is especially adapted for the laying of mines. With a dozen such enormous airships it would be possible to lay mines in a few hours time, and so completely block up the mouth of the Thames or the Elbe.

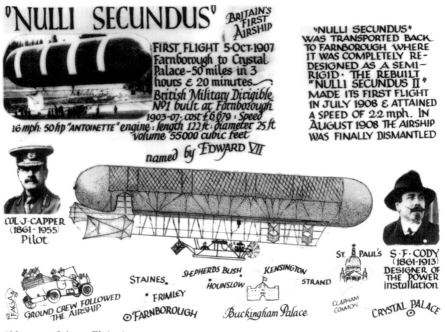

'NULLI SECUNDUS' BRITAIN'S FIRST AIRSHIP

FIRST FLIGHT 5·Oct·1907 Farnborough to Crystal Palace - 50 miles in 3 hours & 20 minutes.
British Military Dirigible Nº1 built at Farnborough 1903-07· cost £6,679 : Speed 16 mph: 50 hp "ANTOINETTE" engine: length 122 ft: diameter 25 ft volume 55000 cubic feet

named by EDWARD VII

"NULLI SECUNDUS" WAS TRANSPORTED BACK TO FARNBOROUGH WHERE IT WAS COMPLETELY RE-DESIGNED AS A SEMI-RIGID· THE REBUILT "NULLI SECUNDUS II" MADE ITS FIRST FLIGHT IN JULY 1908 & ATTAINED A SPEED OF 22 mph. IN AUGUST 1908 THE AIRSHIP WAS FINALLY DISMANTLED

COL·J·CAPPER (1861-1955) Pilot

ST. PAUL'S   S·F·CODY (1861-1913) DESIGNER OF THE POWER installation

GROUND CREW FOLLOWED THE AIRSHIP

STAINES·   SHEPHERDS BUSH   KENSINGTON
· FRIMLEY   HOUNSLOW   STRAND
⊙FARNBOROUGH   Buckingham Palace   CLAPHAM COMMON   CRYSTAL PALACE⊙

(Museum of Army Flying.)

The *Clément-Bayard* Airship

The War Office Tests:

1. The balloon to carry a crew of six, together with wireless telegraph apparatus up to 300lb, and petrol and ballast together making up a total weight of not less than one-fourth of the full total lift.
2. The balloon to have two similar engines, of equal horsepower, all parts of which are interchangeable. Either engine independently or both together to be used at will in working propellers.
3. The ballonet capacity to be one-fourth of the total capacity of the balloon.
4. The balloon to be of the non-rigid or semi-rigid type.
5. The balloon to be portable – ie, to be capable of being taken to pieces easily when deflated and packed on wagons for land transport.
6. The balloon to have anchor ropes and guiding ropes, and to be capable of being taken in or out of its shed by not more than thirty men.
7. The balloon to be capable of anchoring in the open for twenty-four hours, in moderate winds, up to 20 miles an hour.
8. The stability and steering capability of the balloon must be satisfactory.
9. The balloon not to lose, by leakage, more than one-hundredth part of its capacity for every day of twenty-four hours.
10. The balloon must be capable of rising 6,000ft. with its full crew and wireless apparatus, and must then have in hand fuel sufficient for three hours' run at full speed, together with one-fifth of the original complement of ballast.
11. The balloon must complete a triangular course of 100 miles each side, or 300 miles, in not more than fourteen hours, travelling fully equipped. For four hours of this journey the height above sea level not to be less than 3,000ft. Any suitable day may be chosen.
12. The speed of the balloon on a measured course of five miles with and against the wind (due allowance being made for the velocity of the wind) shall not be less than thirty-two statute miles an hour.[1]

Appendix V

The Lebaudy Airship of 1910

MORNING POST NATIONAL FUND AIRSHIP:

Although it is hoped that the airship will not be out of commission more than a month, it was exceedingly unfortunate that disaster should have fallen upon the *Morning Post* dirigible after making such a splendid journey from France. We were just able to record in our last issue, very briefly, particulars of this voyage, and we now give them in fuller detail. Carrying eight persons on board, including M Julliot, who was responsible for the design, M Capazza, the chief pilot, M Leon Berthe, second pilot, MM De Brabant, Boutteville and Lucas, engineers, Major Sir Alexander Bannerman, and the representative of the *Morning Post*, Mr H. Warner Allen, the airship rose from her shed at Moisson at 10 o'clock on Wednesday of last week, and, during the first stage of the journey, followed the course of the Seine to Rouen, where the river was left, and the course continued straight on to St. Valery en Caux on the French coast. This point was passed at 12 o'clock exactly, and with the two 120 hp Panhard engines working steadily, the English coast was soon sighted and the captive balloon at Brighton guided the dirigible on her way. The cross-Channel trip actually occupied two hours eighteen minutes, and an hour and ten minutes later, at 3.28 pm, the airship was over Aldershot. The full journey of 197 miles, from Moisson to Aldershot, having occupied five hours twenty-eight minutes, the speed working out to about 36 miles an hour, which, considering the adverse wind conditions met with during part of the journey, was very satisfactory. When the airship arrived at Aldershot she was at a height of 1,600 feet, and the landing operations were rendered somewhat difficult by a 25 miles per hour wind which was blowing, and she had therefore to tack several times before she was finally got into position. However, this was eventually accomplished and then the work of getting her into the shed was started. Three-quarters of the envelope had already disappeared inside when the stern of the ship was seen to be rising, and, before steps could be taken to rectify matters, a projecting beam caught the fabric and tore a large hole in it. This allowed the gas to escape very rapidly and the fabric fell like a great yellow pall over the car. Several of the men who were handling the dirigible were covered by the fabric, but fortunately no one was injured. It is stated the rent will take about a month to repair. The car was a little strained through falling over on its side when the envelope collapsed and the propeller also was damaged, but this is not a very serious matter. During the journey 528lbs of ballast were used, sometimes in the form of water, sometimes in the form of petrol. During the journey 400 litres of petrol were used by the engines, and on landing there were about 200 litres in the tanks and 990lbs of petrol was still held in reserve as ballast, with 880lbs of water. The highest altitude reached during the trip was 2,120 feet, but during the cross-Channel trip the altitude was 200 feet.[1]

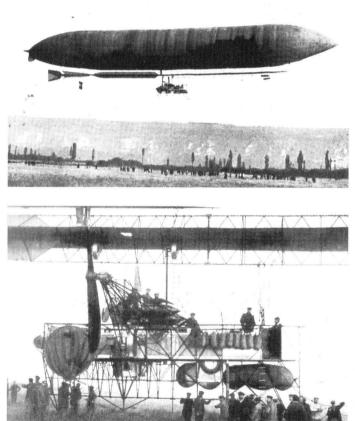

The *Morning Post* Lebaudy departs on 26 October 1910.

Appendix VI

The British Army – Early
Heavier-than-Air Craft

On 16 October 1908, British Army Aeroplane No 1, piloted by Samuel Cody, made its first short flight from Farnborough. This was the first officially recognised aeroplane flight in Great Britain. The aircraft was a single engine biplane of fragile aspect. Two pusher propellers were linked to the 50 hp Antoinette power unit by drive chains. The pilot sat with his back to the engine in a triangular canvas pram, manipulating a control wheel of the type normally associated with a tram.

Despite opposition from some in high quarters, army fixed-wing aviation slowly but steadily began to make its mark, another significant step taking place almost two years later. Two Bristol Boxkites were provided by the British & Colonial Aeroplane Company for use during the army annual manoeuvres on Salisbury Plain. On 21 September 1910, Captain Bertram Dickson, who had recently left the Royal Field Artillery, demonstrated the flying and reconnaissance capabilities of his Bristol Boxkite, No 9. Later the same day he was joined by Lancelot Gibbs, flying his own 'clipped-wing racing Farman'. Five days later a wireless transmission was made from the air to a portable station on the ground at Larkhill using the other Boxkite, No 8, flown by Robert Loraine.

Volunteer pilots for the Air Battalion had to learn to fly at their own expense and, if successful, were reimbursed £75 by the government. One officer, Lieutenant R.A. Cammell, RE, even brought his own aircraft, a Blériot XXI monoplane, which was also used in early wireless experiments in June 1911 and was acquired for the Air Battalion in August, being given the serial number B2. Not only officers became pilots, as on 4 June 1912, Corporal Frank Ridd became the first NCO to gain a Royal Aero Club 'ticket', as the flying certificate was commonly known.

Appendix VII

The Origins of Fixed-wing
Aviation in the Royal Navy

The first official mention of aviation in the Royal Navy goes as far back as July 1908, when it was proposed that the new post of Naval Air Assistant should be established at the Admiralty. This was despite a very brusque dismissal given to the Wright brothers the previous year; 'Their Lordships are of the opinion that aeroplanes would not be of any practical use to the Naval Service.' A number of young and ambitious naval officers seized the opportunity to become involved with this new branch. Many served with distinction in the First World War and achieved high rank in the Royal Navy or the Royal Air Force.

The story of HMA No 1 is told in the main text; meanwhile, heavier-than-air aircraft were making progress. The first Royal Naval officer to learn to fly was Lieutenant G.C. Colmore, who did so at his own expense, gaining his Royal Aero Club Aviator's Certificate (No 15) at Eastchurch on 21 June 1910, flying a Short biplane. He was followed early in 1911 by the first four naval officers to be selected for flying instruction. The Admiralty had been made a very generous offer by F.K. McClean (who himself qualified for his Royal Aero Club 'ticket' No 21 in September 1910) that he would pay for the training at Eastchurch and lend two of his aircraft for the purpose. The instructor, G.B. Cockburn, who held Certificate No 5, also provided his services free of charge. The only fees paid by the Admiralty were £20 per officer paid to Short Brothers for six months' technical instruction. The four officers were Lieutenants Samson, Longmore, Gregory, (all RN) and Gerrard (RMLI). They were awarded Certificates 71 and 72 (on 25 April), 75 and 76 (on 2 May).

The *Mayfly's* misfortune was soon to be offset by two very important events in the story of British naval aviation; the first (relatively) successful ascent from water by a British seaplane on 18 November 1911 by Commander Oliver Schwann flying an Avro Type D biplane at Barrow-in-Furness. The expenses for this effort were funded by a syndicate comprised of Schwann, Captain Sueter, Commander Masterman, Flight Lieutenant Boothby, Engineer Lieutenant

Randall and Mrs Sueter. The second was on 12 January 1912; the first take-off from the deck of a British warship. This was accomplished by Lieutenant Charles Rumney Samson in a Short S.38. He flew from an improvised platform on the foredeck of HMS *Africa*, and then anchored in the Medway off Sheerness, landing safely at Eastchurch. A few months later, on 2 May, came the first take-off from a ship under way, again by Samson with a Short S.38. The ship was HMS *Hibernia* and the location Weymouth Bay. Both *Africa* and *Hibernia* were King Edward Class battleships.

Further organisational progress was made on 13 May 1912 with the formation of the Royal Flying Corps, which consisted of separate Naval and Military Wings. The Naval Wing was commanded by Samson. In the words of the Military Wing's CO, Lieutenant Colonel Frederick Sykes; 'Very early, a rift appeared between the Naval and Military wing, which gradually widened until two rival bodies emerged, competing against each other for men and material.' In September 1912, the Admiralty set up an Air Department to administer the Naval Wing; by the end of that year it comprised sixteen aircraft, of which three were 'hydro-aeroplanes'. The term seaplane was not introduced until the following year. Progress was swift; by 1913 experiments in bomb dropping, spotting submarines, night flying and wireless telegraphy took place; an aircraft with wings which could be folded for easier stowage on board ship was developed (the Short Folder); naval air stations were established at the Isle of Grain, Calshot, Cromarty, Felixstowe and Great Yarmouth; naval aircraft took part in fleet manoeuvres; on 28 July 1913 the Caudron G.II biplane amphibian, serial No 55, was flown off the temporarily converted cruiser, HMS *Hermes*, by Flight Lieutenant F.W. Bowhill, the first naval aeroplane to fly from a ship specifically equipped to operate them.

At the beginning of 1914 there were over 100 trained naval pilots. Further technical innovations were made. Only a few days later, on 28 July, Lieutenant Arthur Longmore made the first successful torpedo drop from the air flying a Short seaplane at Calshot. Moreover, firing trials were carried out by Lieutenant Clark Hall with a 1½ pounder gun mounted in the nose of a Short Gun-Carrier.

At the outbreak of war in August 1914, the RNAS consisted of 130 officers, and some 700 petty officers and ratings. Its aircraft strength was a total of seventy-eight, of which forty were landplanes, thirty-one seaplanes and seven were airships – not all of which were fit for any type of operational duties. The foundations had been laid and it would perform heroically over the next four years in a great variety of roles including; air defence, aerial dog-fighting, long-range and strategic bombing, torpedo attack on shipping from the air, anti-submarine and anti-Zeppelin patrols, convoy protection and reconnaissance;

with landplanes, seaplanes, flying-boats and airships; in and around the British Isles, on the Western Front, in Salonika, Gallipoli, Mesopotamia and East Africa; with great names including Samson, Marix, Warneford, Culley, Collishaw, Little and Dallas. When the RNAS was merged with the RFC to create the RAF on 1 April 1918, it had a strength of 2900 aircraft, as well as 55,000 officers and men.

Samson lifting the Short off *Hibernia* in Weymouth Bay on 2 May 1912, in the first take-off of an aeroplane from a moving vessel. (*Bombardier, Belfast*)

Notes

Chapter 1

1. *Before the Aircraft Carrier,* p 13.
2. *Aviation The Pioneer Years,* p 64–65.
3. For a brief history of ballooning from 1783 to the mid-19th century see Appendix 1.
4. *Irish Times,* 29 June 1859.
5. In July 2012, Lowe's great-great-great nephew, Terry Lowe, took to the air in a near-exact replica of the *Intrepid* over Buffalo, New York.
6. *The Illustrated History of the Army Air Corps,* p 13.
7. *Before the Aircraft Carrier,* p 115.
8. *Irish Times,* 16 June 1862.
9. *Before the Aircraft Carrier,* p 115.
10. Ibid, p 14.
11. *The Air Weapon,* p 56.
12. Ibid, p 41.
13. *The History of Aeronautics in Great Britain,* p 272.
14. *Dr Eckener's Dream Machine,* p 27.
15. Ibid, p 29.
16. *The Father of British Airships,* p 47.
17. Grover attained the rank of colonel and died in 1893.
18. *On the Uses of Balloons in Military Operations,* p 71.
19. Ibid, p 84.
20. Beaumont also attained the rank of colonel and died in 1899.
21. *On Balloon Reconnaissances,* p 101.
22. Later Sir Frederick Abel, Bart, KCB, 1827–1902.
23. *The Air Weapon,* p 54.
24. *The Times,* 24 August 1878.
25. *The Eye in the Air,* p 18.
26. Elsdale was one of the pioneers of balloon photography. In 1883, when in Halifax, Nova Scotia, he carried out successful experiments with small balloons, and he used an automatic camera. *The Use of Balloons in War 1784–1902,* p 74.
27. *The Complete book of Aviation,* p 550.
28. *British Aviation: the Pioneer Years,* p 26.
29. *Early Aviation at Farnborough, Balloons, Kites and Airships,* p 44.
30. *The Times,* 13 December 1881.
31. *The Times,* 1 February 1952.
32. Usborne papers.

33. Allen Crosbie in e-mail to author.
34. *Isambard Kingdom Brunel*, p 218–20, 223.
35. *Ships of the Victorian Navy*, p 38.
36. *Aviation: The Pioneer Years*, p 95.
37. *Irish Times*, 30 September 1884.
38. *Aviation: The Pioneer Years*, p 96.
39. Ibid, p 97.
40. *Irish Times*, 6 September 1884.
41. *Expectation and Reality the Great War in the Air*, p 1.
42. *The History of Early British Military Aeronautics*, p 2.
43. *The Eye in the Air*, p 19.
44. *The Air Weapon*, p 67.
45. Ibid, p 67.
46. *Military Ballooning in the British Army*, p 48.
47. *Suakin 1885*, p 135.
48. *Irish Times*, 26 March 1885.
49. *Military Ballooning in the British Army*, p 48.
50. *The History of Early British Military Aeronautics*, p 8.
51. Ibid, p 8.
52. *The Army in the Air*, p 9.
53. *Military Ballooning in the British Army*, p 51.
54. Ibid, p 52.
55. *The Eye in the Air*, p 19.

Chapter 2

1. *Britannia at Dartmouth*, p 120.
2. *A Sailor's Odyssey*, p 16.
3. Ibid, p 16
4. *Britannia at Dartmouth*, p 112.
5. *A Sailor's Odyssey*, p 16.
6. *The Story of the 'Britannia'*, p 161.
7. *Admirals*, p 338.
8. *A Sailor's Odyssey*, p 15–16.
9. *Britannia at Dartmouth*, p 109.
10. Ibid, p 117.
11. Ibid, p 120.
12. *Leadership: Followership*, p 31.
13. *Sailor in the Air*, p 2.
14. *The Story of the 'Britannia'*, p 160.
15. *My Naval Life 1886 – 1941*, p 7.
16. *The Story of the 'Britannia'*, p 113–14.
17. Ibid, p 120.
18. Ibid, p 127.
19. *The Northern Whig*, 24 July 1899.
20. Ibid.
21. Ibid.

22. Neville Usborne's logbook.
23. *My Naval Life 1886 – 1941*, p 20–21.
24. According to a contemporary of Usborne's the subjects covered under this heading included mathematics, statics, hydrostatics, physics, magnetism, electricity, marine surveying, the steam engine and French. *A Sailor's Odyssey*, p 35.
25. Ibid, p 36.
26. ADM/196/47
27. *The History of Early British Aeronautics*, p 10.
28. *Military Ballooning in the British Army*, p 53.
29. Ibid, p 54.
30. *Strand* Magazine, July 1895.
31. *The Times*, 13 October 1897.
32. *From Balloon to Boxkite*, p 38.
33. *Early Aviation at Farnborough: Balloons, Kites and Airships*, p 34.
34. *Early Aviation at Farnborough: Balloons, Kites and Airships*, p 35–36.
35. *From Balloon to Boxkite*, p 50.
36. *The Last Place on Earth*, p 151.
37. *Military Ballooning in the British Army*, p 58.
38. *Early Aviation at Farnborough: Balloons, Kites and Airships*, p 172.
39. *Military Ballooning in the British Army*, p 59.
40. *The History of Early British Aeronautics*, p 21.
41. *From Balloon to Boxkite*, p 54.
42. *Dr Eckener's Dream Machine*, p 39.
43. Ibid, p 39.
44. *Expectation and Reality: The Great War in the Air*, p 1.
45. *Lighter-than-air-Craft*, p 43.
46. *Early Aviation at Farnborough: Balloons, Kites and Airships*, p 54.
47. *The British Rigid Airship 1908 – 1931*, p 84.
48. *Early Aviation at Farnborough: Balloons, Kites and Airships*, p 76.
49. *My Fifty Years in Flying*, p 69.
50. *British Aviation: the Pioneer Years*, p 29.
51. *Early Aviation at Farnborough: Balloons, Kites and Airships*, p 183.
52. *From Many Angles*, p 47.
53. Ibid, p 47.
54. Ibid, p 48.
55. Ibid, p 48.
56. Ibid, p 49.
57. Ibid, p 49.
58. *British Aviation: the Pioneer Years*, p 28.
59. *Early Aviation at Farnborough: Balloons, Kites and Airships*, p 79.
60. *From Balloon to Boxkite*, p 57–59.
61. *British Aviation: the Pioneer Years*, p 22.
62. *The History of Early British Aeronautics*, p 27–28.
63. Quoted in *From Balloon to Boxkite*, p 104.
64. *The History of Early British Aeronautics*, p 27–28.
65. *The Good Soldier*, p 143.

66. Usborne papers.
67. ADM/196/47.
68. *Early Aviation at Farnborough: Balloons, Kites and Airships*, p 144.
69. *The History of the Fleet Air Arm from Kites to Carriers*, p 7–8.
70. ADM/196/47
71. ADM/196/47
72. Usborne papers.
73. ADM/196/47
74. Usborne papers.
75. ADM/196/47
76. Usborne papers.
77. ADM/196/47
78. ADM/196/47
79. *Early Aviation at Farnborough Volume II*, p 157.
80. *My Fifty Years in Flying*, p 73.
81. Air 1/669/17/122/792
82. *Early Aviation at Farnborough Volume II*, p 158.

Chapter 3

1. ADM/196/47
2. Reginald Bacon (1863–1947) retired from the Royal Navy in 1909 to join the Coventry Ordnance Works as Managing Director. He returned to naval service during the war, and when he retired again it was as a full Admiral and Knight of the Realm.
3. John Arbuthnot Fisher (1841–1920) was one of the greatest and most controversial naval officers of his time.
4. *The Air Weapon*, p 104.
5. *The Impact of Air Power on the British People and Their Government 1909–14*, p 98.
6. *Zeppelins over England*, p 29.
7. Reginald Balliol Brett (1852–1930) succeeded as 2nd Viscount Esher in 1899.
8. *Dr Eckener's Dream Machine*, p 51.
9. Ibid, p 52.
10. *Irish Times*, 2 April 1909.
11. Ibid, 5 April 1909.
12. *The Air Weapon*, p 197.
13. For details of Samuel Cody's heavier-than-air flight in 1908 see Appendix 6.
14. *My Fifty Years in Flying*, p 75.
15. *The Air Weapon*, p 194.
16. *Irish Times*, 11 September 1907.
17. *My Fifty Years in Flying*, p 77–78.
18. *Irish Times*, 4 October 1907.
19. *Clive Maitland Waterlow*, p 219.
20. *Early Aviation at Farnborough Volume 2*, p 177.
21. *Irish Times*, 9 October 1907.
22. Ibid, 7 October 1907.
23. *Belfast Telegraph*, 3 December 1907.

24. *Early Aviation at Farnborough Volume 2*, p 217.
25. *Early Aviation at Farnborough Volume 2*, p 85.
26. *Battlebags*, p 4 and also *The Father of British Airships*, p 22.
27. Quoted in the *Irish Times*, 4 August 1908.
28. Ibid, 28 July 1908.
29. *Airship Navigator*, p 20.
30. Quoted in *Tumult in the Clouds*, p 1.
31. *Expectation and Reality: the Great War in the Air*, p 1.
32. For a longer contemporary assessment of the changes it was thought that airships could impose on conventional methods of warfare, see Appendix 3.
33. *The Army in the Air*, p 13–14 and Cab.38/15/3.
34. *The Impact of Air Power on the British People and Their Government 1909–14*, p 17.
35. Ibid, p 10.
36. Ibid, p 3.
37. *Irish Times*, 21 April 1909.
38. *The Impact of Air Power on the British People and Their Government 1909–14*, p 6–7.
39. Ibid, p 126.
40. *The Times*, 22 February 1909.
41. Ibid, 22 March 1909.
42. *The Impact of Air Power on the British People and Their Government 1909–14*, p 49.
43. Ibid, p 89, quoting C.H. Gibbs-Smith's *Aviation 1970*.
44. *Morning Post*, 26 August 1909.
45. *The Impact of Air Power on the British People and Their Government 1909–14*, p 99–101.
46. *The History of Early British Military Aeronautics*, p 36.
47. *The History of Royal Air Force Cranwell*, p 2.
48. *Documents Relating to the Naval Air Service Volume I*, p 57.
49. *The Impact of Air Power on the British People and Their Government 1909–14*, p 11.
50. Ibid, p 45.
51. *The War in the Air*, p 158–160.
52. *British Aviation: the Pioneer Years*, p 97.
53. *The Impact of Air Power on the British People and Their Government 1909–14*, p 107.
54. *Flight*, 15 January 1910.
55. *Irish Times*, 3 August 1903.
56. *Irish Times*, 13 March 1909.
57. CID 106B, Cab. 38/15/3
58. *British Aviation: the Pioneer Years*, p 146.
59. *Airmen or Noahs*, p 49.
60. Quoted by Jack Bruce Short 184, p 3.
61. *Band of Brigands*, p 37.
62. *Flight* Magazine, 30 July 1910.
63. Air 3/1
64. Usborne papers.
65. *Flight* Magazine, 25 March 1911.

66. *The Airship No 3*, p 47.
67. Ibid, p 47.
68. *Flight* Magazine, 26 June 1909.
69. *British Aviation: the Pioneer Years*, p 102.
70. *Irish Times*, 4 May 1910.
71. *The British Rigid Airship 1908–1931*, p 16.
72. ADM/196/47
73. *The Air Weapon*, p 180.
74. *Flight* Magazine, 24 September 1910.
75. *The British Rigid Airship 1908–1931*, p 18.
76. *British Aviation: the Pioneer Years*, p 125.
77. *The Impact of Air Power on the British People and Their Government 1909–14*, p 105.
78. Ibid, p 153.
79. Ibid, p 153.
80. *The Irish Times*, 5 May 1911.
81. *The Impact of Air Power on the British People and Their Government 1909–14*, p 66.
82. *Flight* Magazine, 12 November 1910.
83. *The Father of British Airships*, p 66.
84. *The Air Weapon*, p 120.
85. *Irish Times*, 14 February 1910.
86. *Irish Times*, 16 March 1910.
87. Ibid, 11 June 1910.
88. *My Fifty Years in Flying*, p 82.
89. *My Fifty Years in Flying*, p 83.
90. *Irish Times*, 16 March 1910.
91. *Flight* Magazine, 25 June 1910.
92. Ibid, 16 July 1910.
93. *Irish Times*, 13 July 1910.
94. Ibid, 14 July 1910.
95. See Appendix 6.
96. *From Many Angles*, p 90.
97. *Irish Times*, 26 September 1910, *Flight* Magazine, 1 October 1910.
98. *Battlebags*, p 9.
99. *The AERO*, 28 September 1910, p257.
100. *From Many Angles*, p 91.
101. *The Observer*, 12 February 1911.
102. *A Brief History of the Royal Flying Corps in World War One*, p 12.
103. *The History of Early British Military Aeronautics*, p 39–40.
104. *Irish Times*, 5 October 1910.
105. *Flight* Magazine, 21 January 1911.
106. *From Balloon to Boxkite*, p 63.
107. *Flight* Magazine, 4 February 1911.
108. *The Air Weapon*, p 145.
109. Air 3/1.
110. *Airmen or Noahs*, p 113.

111. Air 3/1.
112. Ibid.
113. *Flight* Magazine, 27 May 1911.
114. Air 3/1.
115. Ibid.
116. *Airmen or Noahs*, p 114–115.
117. *From Dreadnought to Scapa Flow*, p 332–3.
118. *Airmen or Noahs*, p 114.
119. Ibid, p 149.
120. *Air Power and the Royal Navy*, p 112.
121. Air 3/1.
122. *Airmen or Noahs*, p 116.
123. Air 1/2626.
124. *Flight* Magazine, 16 September 1911.
125. Ibid, 30 September 1911.
126. *The Air Weapon*, p 155.
127. ADM/196/47.
128. Ibid
129. *Airmen or Noahs*, p 115–17.
130. *The British Rigid Airship 1908–1931*, p 57.
131. *Flight* Magazine, 18 March 1911.
132. *The War in the Air*, p 160–61.
133. *From Many Angles*, p 91.
134. *The Air Weapon*, p 126.
135. Ibid, p 127.
136. *The Impact of Air Power on the British People and Their Government 1909–14*, p 164.
137. *Flight* Magazine, 27 May 1911.
138. Ibid, 1 July 1911.
139. Ibid.
140. Ibid.
141. Ibid.
142. Ibid, 5 August 1911.
143. Ibid, 12 August 1911.
144. Ibid, 16 September 1911.
145. Ibid, 23 September 1911.
146. Ibid.
147. Ibid, 30 September 1911.
148. *Irish Times*, 18 October 1911.
149. *Flight* Magazine, 7 November 1911.
150. *The Birth of Military Aviation*, p 176.
151. *The Air Weapon*, p 157.
152. For details of Samson's remarkable and daring aviation firsts see Appendix 7.
153. *The Impact of Air Power on the British People and Their Government 1909–14*, p 198, quoting a letter in the Henderson papers from the official historian H.A. Jones to Lady Henderson.
154. *The Impact of Air Power on the British People and Their Government 1909–14*, p 215.

155. Ibid, p 216.
156. CID 172B Cab. 38/23/11.
157. *Air Power and the Royal Navy*, p 111.
158. *The Impact of Air Power on the British People and Their Government 1909–14*, p 216.
159. *The Impact of Air Power on the British People and Their Government 1909–14*, p 189.
160. Cab. 38/22/32.
161. *Flight* Magazine, 9 March 1912.
162. *The War in the Air Volume II*, p 393.
163. Cab 38/22/32.
164. Ibid.
165. *Flight* Magazine, 24 August 1912.
166. *The Times*, 12 August 1912.
167. ADM/196/47.
168. *Flight* Magazine, 1 June 1912.
169. *Flight* Magazine, 27 April 1912.
170. *From Many Angles*, p 95.
171. *From Balloon to Boxkite*, p 225–26.
172. *Flight* Magazine, 8 June 1912.
173. AIR 1/796/204/4/924.
174. *The Father of British Airships*, p 85 and *Battlebags*, p 5.
175. *The Airship No 3*, p 48.
176. *Airmen or Noahs*, p 133.
177. *The Impact of Air Power on the British People and Their Government 1909–14*, p 217–18.
178. *The Air Weapon*, p 182.
179. *The Impact of Air Power on the British People and Their Government 1909–14*, p 218.
180. *The Good Soldier*, p 166.
181. *From Many Angles*, p 103–104.
182. *From Many Angles*, p 105.
183. *The Good Soldier*, p 144.
184. *Expectation and Reality: the Great War in the Air*, p 1.
185. *Airmen or Noahs*, p 23.
186. *The War in the Air Volume I*, p 226–27.
187. *Flight* Magazine, 28 August 1913.
188. *From Many Angles*, p 105.
189. *Flight* Magazine, 12 October 1912.
190. Ibid, 19 October 1912.
191. *The Father of British Airships*, p 88.
192. *Flight* Magazine, 23 November 1912.
193. Ibid, 14 December 1912.
194. *History of British Aviation 1908–14*, p 149–50.
195. *The Impact of Air Power on the British People and Their Government 1909–14*, p 222.
196. Ibid, p 233.
197. *Flight* Magazine, 7 December 1912.
198. *Flight* Magazine, 25 January 1913.
199. Ibid, 1 February 1913.

200. Ibid, 8 February 1913.
201. *The Air Weapon*, p 205.
202. *The Impact of Air Power on the British People and Their Government 1909–14*, p 236.
203. *The Achievement of the Airship*, p 88.
204. *British Aviation the Pioneer Years*, p 230.
205. Ibid, p 238.
206. Cab 38/23/9.
207. *Flight* Magazine, 5 April 1913.
208. Ibid.
209. *Flight* Magazine, 25 January 1913.
210. Ibid, 8 March 1913.
211. Ibid, 29 March 1913.
212. Ibid.
213. Ibid
214. Ibid, 30 August 1913.
215. Ibid, 29 March 1913.
216. *Flight* Magazine, 5 July 1913.
217. *Airmen or Noahs*, p 119.
218. *Flight* Magazine, 26 July 1913.
219. *Irish Times*, 24 July 1913.
220. Usborne papers.
221. CID 179B Cab 38/24/21 dated 7.6.13
222. Usborne papers.
223. *The Airship No 3*, p 48.
224. *Irish Times*, 27 May 1913.
225. *Flight* Magazine, 17 May 1913.
226. Ibid
227. Ibid, 6 June 1913.
228. *The Airship No 3*, p 48.
229. *Irish Times*, 13 June 1913.
230. Ibid, 18 June 1913.
231. Ibid, 27 June 1913.
232. *The Air Weapon*, p 224.
233. Air 1/627/17/100, dated 14 September 1913.
234. *New York Times*, 21 August 1913.
235. AIR 1/627/17/100.
236. *The Father of British Airships*, p 114.
237. AIR 1/627/17/100.
238. *Flight* Magazine, 30 August 1913.
239. *From Many Angles*, p 110.
240. *The War in the Air*, p 229.
241. *The Times*, 4 October 1913.
242. *Airmen or Noahs*, p 126.
243. *The Air Weapon*, p 225.
244. *Flight* Magazine, 11 October 1913.
245. Usborne papers.

246. *The Times*, 13 September 1913.
247. Ibid, 27 September 1913.
248. *Clive Maitland Waterlow*, p 231.
249. *Flight* Magazine, 1 November 1913.
250. *Daily Chronicle*, 20 October 1913.
251. *Airmen or Noahs*, p 119.
252. *A Brief History of the Royal Flying Corps in World War One*, p 10.
253. *Edward M. Maitland*, p 36.
254. Ibid.
255. *The Impact of Air Power on the British People and Their Government 1909–14*, p 219–220.
256. Usborne papers.
257. *The Airship No 3*, p 48.
258. *Airship Navigator*, p 12.
259. *Flight* Magazine, 13 December 1913.
260. Ibid.
261. Ibid.
262. Ibid.
263. Ibid.
264. Ibid.
265. ADM 1/8378 (1.7.14)
266. *The Airship No 3*, p 48.
267. *Flight* Magazine, 10 January 1914.
268. *The Times*, 24 February 1913.
269. Cab 37/119/47
270. CID 190B Cab 38/27/22
271. Adm 1/8621 (7.6.14)
272. *The Airship No 3*, p 48.
273. Usborne papers.
274. *Kingsnorth Airship Station*, p 19.
275. Ibid, p 20.

Chapter 4
1. *Kingsnorth Airship Station*, p82.
2. *The War in the Air*, p 361–64.
3. *Airmen or Noahs*, p 121.
4. DAD No 12055 August 1914.
5. Usborne papers.
6. Ibid.
7. Ibid.
8. AIR 1/240/15/226/69
9. *Tumult in the Clouds*, p 165.
10. *Flight* Magazine, 25 September 1914.
11. Cab 37/121/125 (16.10.14)
12. *Airmen or Noahs*, p 166.
13. Cab 37/121/125 (16.10.14)

14. Usborne papers.
15. Ibid.
16. *Kingsnorth Airship Station*, p 35.
17. Airship Experimental Report 1915.
18. *Flight* Magazine, 25 December 1914.
19. Cab 37/123 (1.1.15).
20. Usborne papers.
21. *Airship Pilot No 28*, p 36.
22. *Flight* Magazine, 30 April 1915.
23. *Airships over the North Channel*, p 13.
24. Handbook of SS Type Airships.
25. Usborne papers.
26. *The Times*, 18 July 1925.
27. *The Airship No 3*, p 48.
28. *The War in the Air*, p 463.
29. *Airship Navigator*, p 20.
30. *The British Airship at War 1914–18*, p 45.
31. *Airmen or Noahs*, p 122.
32. *The World Crisis*, p 1623–1624.
33. Ibid, p 285.
34. Elmhirst papers.
35. *Airship Pilot No 28*, p 67.
36. Usborne papers.
37. *Airship Pilot no 28*, p 47.
38. Ibid.
39. *Airmen or Noahs*, p 124.
40. Elmhirst papers.
41. *The World Crisis*, p 284.
42. *Dr Eckener's Dream Machine*, p 59.
43. Appendix 3 to CID 137B Cab 38/19/60
44. *Great Britain and Sea Power 1815–1853*, p 202.
45. *Flight: 100 Years of Aviation*, p 94.
46. *Expectation and Reality – the Great War in the Air*, p 1.
47. *The World Crisis*, p 284–85.
48. *Tumult in the Clouds*, p 144.
49. *Zeppelins over England*, p 49.
50. *Dr Eckener's Dream Machine*, p 71.
51. Ibid.
52. *Sailor in the Air*, p 145.
53. Air 1/2633 dated 18 October 1915.
54. Usborne papers.
55. *Airmen or Noahs*, p 16.
56. Usborne papers.
57. Air 1/2633 dated 18 October 1915.
58. Air 1/2639 dated 19 February 1916.
59. *Irish Aviators of World War 1*, p xxv.

60. Air 1/2639 undated.
61. *The Airship No 3*, p 46.
62. Usborne papers.
63. *Airship Navigator*, p 20.
64. *The War in the Air Volume II*, p 386.
65. Usborne papers.
66. *The Times*, 10 October 1931.
67. *Dr Eckener's Dream Machine*, p 98.
68. Ibid, p 94.
69. *Airmen or Noahs*, p 22.
70. Ibid, p 130, quoting from *The Grand Fleet* by Lord Jellicoe, p 489.
71. *The Times*, 31 August 1921.
72. Usborne papers.

Chapter 5
1. *Airmen or Noahs*, p 125.
2. Ibid, p 3
3. *Battlebags*, p 136.
4. *The British Airship at War 1914–18*, p 48.
5. *Battlebags*, p 143.
6. *Vickers Aircraft since 1908*, p 27.
7. *Zeppelins: German Airships 1900–40*, p 33–34.
8. *Zeppelins: German Airships 1900–40*, p 46.
9. *Airmen or Noahs*, p 128.
10. *Sailor in the Air*, p 206.
11. *Airmen or Noahs*, p 137.
12. *Battlebags*, p 80.
13. *Airship Pilot No 28*, p 64–65.
14. Air 1/275 (26.3.1918)
15. Adm. 167/55 (26.10.1918)
16. *Airmen or Noahs*, p 35–36.
17. Usborne papers.
18. *The RNAS Airship Service*, p 88.
19. *Airmen or Noahs*, p 26, quoting *Blackwood's Magazine*, April 1919, page 561, Vol MCCXLII
20. *The War in the Air*, p 464.
21. *Airship Pilot no 28*, p 36.
22. *The Black Ship*, p 157.
23. *The Story of the Airship (Non-Rigid)*, p 48.
24. *The Forgotten Blimps of World War Two*, p 3.
25. *Trapeze Artists*, p 382.
26. *Airmen or Noahs*, p 148.
27. *Trapeze Artists*, p 383.
28. Ibid, p 383.
29. Ibid, p 385.
30. Usborne papers.

Appendix 1

1. *First Military Aviator*, by Jon Guttman, in *Aviation History*, November 2012.
2. *Lighter-than-air-Craft*, p 15.
3. *The Air Weapon*, p 26.
4. *Army Wings*, p 7 and *Balloons in War 1784–1902*, p 69.
5. *Balloons in War 1784–1902*, p 73.
6. *The Eye in the Air*, p 14.
7. *The Air Weapon*, p 33.
8. *Cochrane – the Life and Exploits of a Fighting Captain*, p 72.
9. Ibid, p 76.
10. *The Eye in the Air*, p 16.
11. *The Air Weapon*, p 27.
12. *Lighter-than-air-Craft*, p 22.

Appendix 2

1. *The History of Early British Military Aeronautics*, p 5–6.

Appendix 4

1. *The Times*, 19 October 1910.

Appendix 5

1. *Flight* Magazine, 5 November 1910.

References

Primary Sources
Private papers of Wing Commander Neville F. Usborne (Kilbracken Family Archive).
Files in the AIR, ADM, Cab and CID series held at the National Archive Kew.
ADM/196/47
ADM 1/8621 (7.6.14)
ADM 1/8378 (1.7.14)
ADM 167/55 (26.10.1918)
AIR 1/275 (26.3.1918)
AIR 1/796/204/4/924
AIR 1/627/17/100
AIR 1/669/17/122/792
AIR 1/168/15/226/5
AIR 1/240/15/226/69
AIR 1/2564
AIR 1/2626
AIR 1/2633
AIR 1/2639
AIR 3/1
AIR 3/3
AIR 3/6
AIR 3/7
Cab 38/22/32 (30.7.12)
Cab 38/22/42 (6.12.12)
Cab 38/23/9 (6.2.13)
Cab 38/15/3 (23.10.08)
Cab 37/119/47 (20.3.14)
Cab 37/121/125 (16.10.14)
Cab 37/123 (1.1.15)
CID 179B Cab.38/24/21 (7.6.13)
CID 190B Cab.38/27/22 (9.5.14)
CID 172B Cab. 38/23/11 (Feb 1912)
CID 106B (28.1.09)
Appendix 3 to CID 137B Cab 38/19/60 (11 July 1911)

Files held at the RAF Museum Hendon, particularly Airship Experimental Report 1915, the Royal Aero Club Collection and, Price, Gilbert Holland, *The Innocent Erk – RNAS and RAF Memoirs –* unpublished manuscript held in the RAF Museum archives.

Official Publications
RNAS Pilot's Flying Logbook – Lieutenant A.H. Crump, RAF
RNAS Pilot's Flying Logbook – Flight Sub-Lieutenant B.W. Hemsley, RN
Airship Logbook SS20
Handbook of SS Type Airships. Compiled by the Instructional Staff at the Airship
    Deport, Wormwood Scrubs, 1917

Journals and Newspapers
Arden-Close, Colonel Sir Charles, *The Use of Balloons in War 1784–1902* (The Royal
    Engineers Journal, March 1942)
Beaumont, Captain F., *On Balloon Reconnaissances – as practised by the American Army*
    (Professional Papers of the Corps of Royal Engineers Vol xii, New Series, 1862)
Bruce, J.M., *The Birth of Military Aviation Part 1, the RFC before World War 1* (Air
    Pictorial, May 1987)
Chilton, Edward, *Rear Admiral Sir Murray Sueter, CB* (Cross & Cockade Vol 15, No 2,
    1984)
Cross, Captain J.R., *British Military Ballooning* (The Army Air Corps Journal, 1980)
Dunn, Michael J., *James Templer and the Birth of British Military Aviation* (RAFHS
    Journal 55, 2013)
Edge, Brian, *HMA No 1* (Dirigible No 52, Autumn 2007)
Elmhirst, Air Marshal Sir Thomas, *First Across the Irish Sea* (Aerostat Vol.8, No.1, 1977)
Fletcher, Lieutenant J.N., Detailed report on a trip from Larkhill to Farnborough
    12.8.12. (via Nigel Caley)
Geoghegan, John J. III, *Watery Grave of the Sparrowhawks: An inside look at the Navy's
    first parasitic fighter* (Flight Journal, August 2008)
Goddard, Air Marshal Sir Victor, *The Black Ship* (Cross & Cockade Vol 12, No 4, 1981)
Goodall, M., *The RNAS Order of Battle, August 2, 1914* (Cross & Cockade Vol 3, No 4,
    1972)
Grossnick, Roy A., *Kite Balloons to Airships: the Navy's Lighter-than-Air Experience*
    (Washington, DC, no date)
Grover, Lieutenant G.E., *On the Uses of Balloons in Military Operations* (Professional
    Papers of the Corps of Royal Engineers Vol xii, New Series, 1862)
Grover, Lieutenant G.E., *On Reconnoitring Balloons* (Professional Papers of the Corps
    of Royal Engineers Vol xii, New Series, 1862)
Guttman, John, *First Military Aviator* (Aviation History, November 2012)
Jackson, Robert, *Airships in the war against the U-boats* (The Rolls-Royce Magazine,
    September 1992)
Jarrctt, Philip, *At the drop of a Camel* (Cross & Cockadc Vol 7, No 3, 1977)
Jarrett, Philip, *Camel Droppings* (*Aeroplane*, May 2011)
Keillor, Lynn, *Hitch Hikers Ten Aircraft that owed it all to their motherships* (Air & Space
    Smithsonian, July 2012)
Knight, Charles, *War Ballooning* (Strand Magazine 1895)
Layman, R.D., *Dirigibles, Airships, Zeppelins and Blimps* (Relevance – The Quarterly
    Journal of The Great War Society, Winter 1996)
Masterman, Air Commodore, E.A.D., *Airship Pioneers* (The Airship No 3, 1934)
Montgomery, Bob, *Flight Lines* (Flying in Ireland, June 2009)

Morrow, John H. jr, *Expectation and Reality: The Great War in the Air* (Airpower Journal, Winter 1996)

Mottram, Graham, *The Early Days of the RNAS* (Cross & Cockade Vol 10, No 3, 1979)

Mottram, Graham, *The Royal Naval Air Service* (Cross & Cockade Vol 31, No 3, 2000)

Mowthorpe, Ces (greatly assisted by Cooke, D.), *Howden Airship Station 1916–1930* (Cross & Cockade Vol 10, No 4, 1979)

Nugent, Edward E., *The Forgotten Blimps of World War II* (The Naval Aviation Museum Foundation Magazine, Spring 1995)

O'Grady, Kent, *Britain's Rigid Airships* (Aerostation Vol 27, No 1, Spring 2004)

Rumerman, Judy, *Lighter-than-air Airships in WWII* (US Government Centennial of Flight Essay, 2003)

Sanger, Ray, *Clive Maitland Waterlow* (Cross & Cockade Vol 34, No 4, 2003)

Sharples, Wing Commander Simeon, *Leadership: Followership* (Spirit of the Air, Vol 3, Nos 5 & 6, 2008)

Skelton, Marvin L., *Edward M. Maitland* (Cross & Cockade Vol 10, No 1, 1979)

Slocombe, K., *Blimps – Notes on the British Non-rigid Airships* (Cross & Cockade Vol 4, No 1, 1973)

Smith, Richard K., *Trapeze Artists: The US Navy's ZRS4 & 5 HTA Unit* (Air Pictorial, December 1963)

Thetford, Owen, *50 Years of British Naval Aviation* (Flight Deck, Autumn 1958)

Turpin, Brian J., *Coastal Patrol Airships 1915–18* (Cross & Cockade Vol 10, No 3, 1979)

Watson, Colonel C.M., *Military Ballooning in the British Army* (Royal Engineers Institute, Occasional Papers, Vol XXVIII, 1902)

Wright, Peter, *The RNAS Airship Service and the Air Construction Corps Parts I, II & III* (Cross & Cockade Vol 32, No 4, 2001; Vol 33, No 1, 2002; Vol 33, No 2, 2002)

Belfast Evening Telegraph: 22 July 1899, 12 August 1899, 2 December 1907, 3 December 1907

Cork Examiner: 9 July 1925

Daily Chronicle: 20 October 1913

Flight Magazine: 26 June 1909, 15 January 1910, 25 June 1910, 16 July 1910, 30 July 1910, 17 September 1910, 24 September 1910, 1 October 1910, 22 October 1910, 5 November 1910, 12 November 1910, 21 January 1911, 28 January 1911, 4 February 1911, 18 March 1911, 25 March 1911, 13 May 1911, 27 May 1911, 1 July 1911, 5 August 1911, 12 August 1911, 16 September 1911, 23 September 1911, 30 September 1911, 7 November 1911, 25 November 1911, 3 February 1912, 9 March 1912, 27 April 1912, 1 June 1912, 8 June 1912, 25 June 1912, 12 August 1912, 24 August 1912, 12 October 1912, 19 October 1912, 23 November 1912, 7 December 1912, 14 December 1912, 25 January 1913, 1 February 1913, 8 February 1913, 1 March 1913, 8 March 1913, 15 March 1913, 29 March 1913, 5 April 1913, 17 May 1913, 6 June 1913, 5 July 1913, 26 July 1913, 23 August 1913, 30 August 1913, 13 September 1913, 20 September 1913, 27 September 1913, 11 October 1913, 1 November 1913, 13 December 1913, 28 February 1914, 11 April 1914, 24 July 1914, 25 September 1914, 25 December 1914, 30 April 1915, 24 February 1916, 15 September 1921, 22 July 1920, 14 December 1956.

Irish Times: 29 June 1859, 5 July 1859, 7 August 1861, 7 December 1861, 16 June 1862, 1
    October 1870, 6 October 1870, 17 December 1881, 6 September 1884, 16 September
    1884, 20 September 1884, 30 September 1884, 20 November 1884, 12 March 1885,
    26 March 1885, 4 April 1885, 11 September 1907, 4 October 1907, 7 October 1907,
    9 October 1907, 28 July 1908, 4 August 1908, 13 March 1909, 2 April 1909, 5 April
    1909, 21 April 1909, 22 July 1909, 3 August 1909, 14 February 1910, 16 March 1910,
    4 May 1910, 11 June 1910, 13 July 1910, 14 July 1910, 26 September 1910, 5 October
    1910, 5 May 1911, 18 October 1911, 27 May 1913, 13 June 1913, 18 June 1913, 27
    June 1913, 24 July 1913, 9 July 1925, 18 July 1925, 23 April 1928.
Larne Times: 5 September 1986.
The Lifeboat: May 1920.
Morning Post: 26 August 1909.
New York Times: 21 August 1913.
Northern Whig: 21 July 1899, 24 July 1899, 26 July 1899, 3 May 1919.
The Observer: 12 February 1911.
The Times: 24 August 1878, 1 November 1880, 13 December 1881, 13 October 1897, 26
    December 1908, 22 February 1909, 22 March 1909, 7 April 1910, 19 October 1910,
    27 February 1913, 20 August 1913, 4 October 1913, 9 October 1913, 10 October
    1913, 24 October 1913, 31 December 1913, 10 January 1914, 24 February 1914, 23
    February 1916, 5 November 1920, 31 August 1921, 8 July 1925, 6 March 1928, 20
    May 1931, 10 October 1931, 1 February 1951, 28 August 1957, 17 March 1958.
Wigtown Free Press: articles by Donnie Nelson: 26 June 1986, 18 September 1986, 25
    January 1996.

Books
Abbott, Patrick, *Airships* (Princes Risborough 1991)
Abbott, Patrick, *The British Airship at War 1914–1918* (Lavenham 1989)
Abbott, Patrick and Walmsley, Nick, *British Airships in Pictures* (Trowbridge 1998)
Allen, Hugh, *The Story of the Airship (Non-Rigid)* (Chicago 1942)
Andrews, C.F. and Morgan, E.B., *Vickers Aircraft since 1908* (London 1988)
Barker, Ralph, *A Brief History of the Royal Flying Corps in World War One* (London
    2002)
Barry, Michael, *Great Aviation Stories Vol 1* (Fermoy 1993)
Bartlett, C.J., *Great Britain and Sea Power 1815–1853* (Oxford 1963)
Beauchamp, K.G., *History of Telegraphy* (London 2001)
Bell Davies, Vice Admiral Richard, VC, *Sailor in the Air* (Barnsley 2008)
Bilbé, Tina, *Kingsnorth Airship Station* (Stroud 2013)
Blundell, W.D.G., *Royal Navy Battleships 1895–1946* (New Malden 1973)
Botting, Douglas, *Dr Eckener's Dream Machine* (London 2002)
Brett, Dallas, R., *History of British Aviation 1908–14* (London 1933)
Broke-Smith, Brigadier P.W.L., *The History of Early British Military Aeronautics*
    (London 1952)
Bruce, J.M., *Britain's First Warplanes* (Poole 1987)
Bruce, J.M., *Short 184* (Berkhamsted 2001)
Burge, Squadron Leader C.G., *The Complete Book of Aviation* (London 1935)
Campbell, Christy, *Band of Brigands* (London 2008)

Campbell, Christopher, *Aces and Aircraft of World War One* (Blandford 1981)

Castle, Ian, *British Airships 1905–30* (Oxford 2009)

Castle, Ian, *London 1914–17: The Zeppelin Menace* (Oxford 2008)

Churchill, Winston S., *The Great War* (London 1933)

Connon, Peter, *An Aeronautical History of the Cumbria, Dumfries and Galloway Region (Part II)* (Penrith 1984)

Connon, Peter, *In the Shadow of the Eagle's Wings – Aviation in Cumbria 1825–1914* (Penrith, 1982)

Cooper, Peter J., *Farnborough: 100 Years of British Aviation* (Hinckley 2006)

Cork & Orrery, Admiral of the Fleet The Earl of, *My Naval Life 1886–1941* (London 1942)

Cunningham of Hyndhope, Admiral of the Fleet Viscount, *A Sailor's Odyssey* (London 1951)

Davy, M.J.B., *Lighter-Than-Air-Craft* (London 1934)

Dennehy, Rev. Henry Edward, *The History of Great Island* (Cork 1990)

De Syon, Guillaume, *Zeppelin! Germany and the Airship, 1900–1939* (Baltimore 2002)

Dixon, Conrad, *Ships of the Victorian Navy* (Southampton 1987)

Elmhirst, Air Marshal Sir Thomas, *Recollections of,* (London 1991)

Farrar-Hockley, General Sir Anthony, *The Army in the Air* (Stroud 1994)

Finnis, Bill, *The History of the Fleet Air Arm From Kites to Carriers* (Shrewsbury 2000)

Gambier Parry, Major E., *Suakin 1885: Being a Sketch of the Campaign of this year* (London 1886)

Gibson, Mary, *Warneford VC* (Yeovilton 1979)

Gleeson, Joe, *Irish Aviators of World War 1: Volume 1* (North Charleston 2012)

Gollin, Alfred, *The Impact of Air Power on the British People and Their Government, 1909–14* (Stanford 1989)

Grant, R.G., *Flight: 100 Years of Aviation* (London 2004)

Gray, Edwin, *A Damned Un-English Weapon* (London 1973)

Green, Rod, *The Illustrated History of the Army Air Corps* (Middle Wallop 2008)

Grey, C.G., *Sea-Flyers* (London 1942)

Hall, Malcolm, *From Balloon to Boxkite* (Stroud 2010)

Hampshire, Cecil, A., *A Short History of the Royal Navy* (London 1971)

Harper, Harry, *My Fifty Years in Flying* (London 1956)

Hartcup, Gary, *The Achievement of the Airship* (Newton Abbot 1974)

Harvey, Robert, *Cochrane: the Life and Exploits of a Fighting Captain* (London 2002)

Haslam, E.B., *The History of Royal Air Force Cranwell* (London 1982)

Hayes, K.E., *A History of the RAF and USNAS in Ireland 1913–1923* (Dublin 1988)

Hayward, Roger, *The Fleet Air Arm in Camera 1912–1996* (Stroud 1998)

Herrmann, David G., *The Arming of Europe and the Making of the First World War* (Princeton 1997)

Higham, R., *The British Rigid Airship 1908–1931* (London 1961)

Hildebrandt, A., *Airships Past & Present* (London 1908)

Hodgson, J.E., *The History of Aeronautics in Great Britain* (Oxford 1924)

Huntford, Roland, *Shackleton* (London 1996)

Huntford, Roland, *The Last Place on Earth* (London 1985)

Jackson, A.J., *De Havilland Aircraft since 1909* (London 1987)

Jackson, Robert, *Army Wings: A History of Army Air Observation Flying 1914–1960* (Barnsley 2006)

Jefford, Wing Commander C.G., *RAF Squadrons* (Shrewsbury 1994)

Johnston, E.A., *Airship Navigator* (Stroud 1994)

Kent, Barrie H., *Signal! A History of Signalling in the Royal Navy* (London 2004)

Kilbracken, John, *Bring back my Stringbag* (Barnsley 1996)

Killen, John, *A History of Marine Aviation* (London 1969)

Lambert, Andrew, *Admirals* (London 2008)

Layman, R.D., *Before the Aircraft Carrier* (London 1989)

Leland, Mary, *That Endless Adventure: A History of the Cork Harbour Commissioners* (Cork 2001)

Longmore, Air Chief Marshal Sir Arthur, *From Sea to Sky* (London 1946)

Mackworth-Praed, Ben, *Aviation: the Pioneer Years* (London 1990)

Macmillan, Norman, *Sefton Brancker* (London 1925)

Magnello, Eileen, *A Century of Measurement* (Bath 2000)

Marder, A.J., *From Dreadnought to Scapa Flow, Volume 1* (Oxford 1961)

Mason, Francis K., *The British Fighter since 1912* (London 1992)

Massie, Robert K., *Dreadnought* (London 2004)

McKinty, Alec, *The Father of British Airships: A Biography of E.T. Willows* (London 1972)

Mead, Gary, *The Good Soldier: The Biography of Douglas Haig* (London 2008)

Mead, Peter, *The Eye in the Air* (London 1983)

Mowthorpe, Ces, *Battlebags: British Airships of the First World War* (Stroud 1998)

O'Riordan, Patrick, *Portraiture of Cork Harbour Commissioners (Profiles of Cork Harbour Commissioners 1814-1997)* (Cork 2014)

Oughton, Frederick, *The Aces* (London 1961)

Pack, Captain S.W.C., *Britannia at Dartmouth* (London 1966)

Palmer, A.W., *A Dictionary of Modern History* (Harmondsworth 1971)

Palmer, Alan, *The Penguin Dictionary of Twentieth Century History 1900–1978* (Harmondsworth 1979)

Penrose, Harald, *British Aviation: the Pioneer Years* (London 1967)

Poolman, Kenneth, *Zeppelins over England* (London 1960)

Probert, Air Commodore Henry, *High Commanders of the Royal Air Force* (London 1991)

Raleigh, W. and Jones, A.H., *The War in the Air* (London 1922)

Reynolds, Quentin, *They Fought for the Sky* (London 1960)

Robertson, Bruce, *Aviation Enthusiast's Data Book* (Cambridge 1982)

Robertson, Bruce, *The Army and Aviation* (London 1981)

Rolt, L.T.C., *Isambard Kingdom Brunel* (London 1957)

Roskill, Captain S.W., *Documents Relating to the Naval Air Service Volume I 1908–1918* (London 1969)

Saunders, Hilary St George, *Per Ardua: The Rise of British Air Power 1911–1939* (London 1944)

Snowden Gamble, C.F., *The Air Weapon Volume I* (Oxford 1931)

Statham, Commander E.P., *The Story of the 'Britannia'* (London 1904)

Steel, Nigel and Hart, Peter, *Tumult in the Clouds* (London 1997)

Stephenson, Charles, *Zeppelins: German Airships 1900–40* (Oxford 2004)
Sturtivant, Ray and Page, Gordon, *Royal Navy Aircraft Serials and Units 1911–1919* (Tonbridge 1992)
Sueter, Rear Admiral Murray F., *Airmen Or Noahs* (London 1928)
Swanborough, Gordon and Bowers, Peter M., *United States Navy Aircraft Since 1911* (Annapolis 1976)
Sykes, Major General Sir Frederick, *From Many Angles* (London 1942)
Taylor, M.J.H. and Mondey, D., *Milestones of Flight* (London 1983)
Thetford, Owen, *British Naval Aircraft since 1912* (London 1971)
Till, Geoffrey, *Air Power and the Royal Navy* (London 1979)
Trotter, Wilfrid Pym, *The Royal Navy in Old Photographs* (London 1975)
Turner, Major Charles Cyril, *The Old Flying Days* (London 1927)
Usborne, Vice Admiral C.V., *Blast and Counterblast* (London 1935)
Walker, Percy B., *Early Aviation at Farnborough: Balloons, Kites and Airships* (London 1971)
Walker, Percy B., *Early Aviation at Farnborough Volume 2: The First Aeroplanes* (London 1974)
Warner, Guy, *Airships over the North Channel* (Belfast 2005)
Warner, Guy, with Boyd, Alex, *Army Aviation in Ulster* (Newtownards 2004)
Williams, T.B., *Airship Pilot No.28* (London 1974)

Websites
www.airshipsonline.com (Airship Heritage Trust)
www.geocities.com (U-boat war 1914–18)
www.gwpda.org/naval (German Admiralty Declaration 4 February 1915 and following events)
www.rafweb.org (Air of Authority: a History of RAF Organisation)

Index

People

Abel, Professor Frederick, 11
Agg-Gardner, James, 13–14
Alcock, Captain Sir John, 226
Allen, Captain C.R.W., 137
Allen, Mr H.Warner, 274
Arlandes, François Laurent, Marquis de, 259
Ashton, Lieutenant C.J., 82
Asquith, H.H. (later Earl), 89–90, 131, 155

Bacon, Captain R.H.S. (later Admiral Sir Reginald), 74, 83, 89, 92, 100
Baden-Powell, Major B.F.S., 44–5, 84, 177
Balfour, Arthur (later Earl), 90, 117, 206
Banks, Sir Joseph, 261
Bannerman, Major Sir Alexander, 101–102, 110, 112, 126, 134, 274
Battenberg, Vice Admiral Prince Louis of (later Admiral of the Fleet), 117, 131
Baumann, M, 156
Beatty, Admiral Sir David (later Admiral of the Fleet Earl), 242
Beaulieu, Lord Montagu of, 84, 155
Beauman, Flight Sub-Lieutenant Eric (later Major), 213
Beaumont, Captain Frederick (later Colonel), 9–11
Beedle, Captain William, 67
Berthe, M Leon, 275
Bertrand, Abbé, 260
Blake, George, 262
Blakeney, Major R.D.B., 53
Blanchard, Jean-Pierre, 261
Bland, Lilian, 77
Blériot, Louis, 86
Bonaparte, Napoleon (later Emperor), 263
Booth, Squadron Leader R., 230
Boothby, Lieutenant F.L.M. (later Commander), 136, 157, 161, 179, 277
Boutteville, M, 274
Bowhill, Flight Lieutenant F.W. (later Air Chief Marshal Sir Frederick), 278
Boyle, Flight Commander J., 184
Brancker, Major Sefton (later Air Vice Marshal Sir), 173, 229, 257
Breguet, Louis, 104
Broke-Smith, Lieutenant P.W.L. (later Brigadier), 64–5, 108, 111–113, 128, 130, 134

Brown, Lieutenant Sir Arthur Whitten (later Lieutenant Colonel), 226
Brunel, Isambard Kingdom, 17

Cahill, Engine Room Artificer, 161
Cammell, Lieutenant R.A., 108, 112–113, 276
Capazza, M, 274
Capper, J.E. (later Major General Sir John), 13, 57, 62–3, 67–8, 76–82, 84, 87, 90–2, 99, 101–102, 104–105, 107, 109, 111, 113, 122
Capper, Mrs Edith Mary, 77
Carden, Captain A.D., 104, 107
Carfrey, Lieutenant C.T., 137
Caulfield, Lieutenant W.T.M., 76
Cave-Browne-Cave, Engineer Lieutenant T.R. (later Wing Commander), 172, 202, 236
Cavendish, Henry, 258
Cayley, Sir George, 3–4
Chalmers, Sir R., 131
Chambers, Flight Sub-Lieutenant Billy, 245
Charles, Professor Jacques Alexandre Cesar, 259
Churchill, Winston (later Sir), 117, 122, 131–2, 151–3, 172–3, 198, 205, 212, 219
Clark Hall, Lieutenant R.H., 278
Clement, M, 97–8, 104
Cobham, Sir Alan, 257
Cochrane, Captain Lord, 263–4
Cockburn, G.B., 277
Cody, Samuel Franklin, 44, 65, 70, 72–3, 77, 79, 81, 102, 112, 276
Collins, Sergeant, 141
Colmore, Flight Lieutenant G.C. (later Squadron Commander), 222, 277
Cook, Petty Officer H.G. (later 2nd Lieutenant), 190
Cooper, Captain T.H., 264
Corbett Wilson, Denys, 167
Cork & Orrery, 12th Earl of, 35
Coutelle, Captain Jean-Marie-Joseph (later Colonel), 262
Coxwell, Henry, 7–8, 10, 12, 265
Cradock, Commander Christopher (later Rear Admiral), 31
Cronje, General Piet, 54
Crosbie, Richard, 261–2
Cunningham, Flight Lieutenant A.D. (later Wing Commander), 184, 190, 222, 236, 269

Cunningham, Cadet A.B. (later Admiral of the
    Fleet Viscount), 33
Curzon-Howe, Captain the Hon A.G., 31, 34
Curzon-Howe, Mrs, 31

Daimler, Gottlieb, 21, 29
Dalgleish, Flight Lieutenant J.W.O. (later Wing
    Commander), 196, 222
Davies, Vice Admiral Richard Bell, 35, 179, 235,
    257
Dawson, Sir Trevor, 257
de Brabant, M, 274
de Fouville, M, 22
de Havilland, Geoffrey (later Sir), 102
de Morveau, Jean Louis Guyton, 260, 262
de Saussure, Horace-Bénédict, 259
de Virly, M, 260
Deutsch de la Meurthe, M, 59
Dickson, Captain Bertram, 276
Driant, Emile, 82
Du Cros, Arthur, 97–8
du Maurier, Guy, 83

Eckener, Dr Hugo, 59, 211, 232, 235
Edwards, Colonel, 24
Ellis, Herbert, 98
Elmhirst, Midshipman Thomas (later Air
    Marshal Sir), 205–206, 210, 227, 257
Elsdale, Captain Henry (later Major), 12–13, 22,
    26, 55
Esher, 2nd Viscount, 75, 83, 131
Ewart, Major General J.S., 83

Fanshawe, Admiral Sir Arthur, 73
Farber, M, 265
Ferber, Captain F., 8
Ferguson, Harry, 77
Fisher, Admiral Sir John (later Admiral of the
    Fleet Lord), 74, 92, 117, 123, 199–200, 202,
    205, 216, 227
Fitzmaurice, Commandant James, 226
Fletcher, Lieutenant J.N. (later Wing
    Commander), 141–2, 147, 184, 190, 222
Foch, Généralissimo Ferdinand (Maréchal de
    France), 148
Fossett, Steve, 177
Fox, Lieutenant A.G., 129
Franklin, Benjamin, 261
French, Lieutenant General Sir John (later Field
    Marshal Viscount), 68, 110, 147
Fresson, Ted, 257
Fullerton, Colonel J.D., 88
Fulton, Captain J.D.B., 126
Fyfe, Hamilton, 101

Gambetta, Léon, 7
Garnerin, Jacques, 264
Gaudron, Professor Auguste, 190

Gerrard, Lieutenant E.L. (later Air
    Commodore), 277
Gibbs, Lancelot, 276
Giffard, Henri, 2, 4, 19
Gilbert, Sir W.S., 17
Glaisher, James, 265
Grioud de Villette, Guillaume, 259
Glazebrook, Dr R.T., 89, 123
Godard, Eugène, 4
Goddard, Air Marshal Sir Victor, 249, 265
Godley, Hugh (2nd Lord Kilbracken), 220
Godley, John (3rd Lord Kilbracken), 220, 249
Gooden, Frank, 102–103
Gordon, Major General Charles, 21, 23
Gorton, Lieutenant A.W. 'Jake', 253
Green, Charles, 264–5
Green, F.M., 92, 104, 108, 177, 202
Green, Gustavus, 88, 104, 107
Greener, Sergeant-Major, 46, 49, 52
Gregory, Lieutenant R., 277
Grey, Sir Edward (later Viscount), 192
Grierson, Lieutenant General J.M., 146–7,
    149
Grover, Lieutenant George (later Colonel), 8,
    10–11, 24
Gunner, W.H., 182

Hadden, Major General Sir Charles, 83, 89,
    131
Haig, Lieutenant General Sir Douglas (later
    Field Marshal Earl), 145, 147–8, 169, 245
Haig, Squadron Leader Rollo Amyat de Haga,
    252
Haldane, R.B. (later Viscount), 69, 83–4, 88,
    90–2, 99, 102, 111, 122, 124, 131–2, 138, 148,
    153
Hamilton, General Sir Ian, 172, 179
Hamilton, Vereker, 179, 220
Handley Page, Frederick (later Sir), 133
Harper, Harry, 62, 73, 75, 77, 79, 105–106
Harris, Lieutenant Arthur (later Air Chief
    Marshal Sir), 191
Hartford, Flight Sub-Lieutenant I.H.B. (later
    Squadron Commander), 190, 222
Heath, Major G.M., 52–3
Heathcote, Rear Admiral Edmund, 2
Heckstall-Smith, S., 167
Henderson, Brigadier General David (later
    Lieutenant General Sir), 131
Hicks, Flight Lieutenant W.C. (later Group
    Captain), 157, 172, 184, 190, 196, 217, 222
Holland, Robert, 265
Holt Thomas, George, 200–202
Hugon, M, 171
Hume, Lieutenant A.H.B., 47, 55
Hunefeld, Baron von, 226
Husband, Lieutenant, 157
Hyde-Thomson, Lieutenant, 95

Ireland, Squadron Commander Wyndor
    Plunkett de Courcy, 217, 219
Irving, Mr, 137
Ivy, Sergeant William, 29

Jackson, Admiral Sir Henry (later Admiral of the
    Fleet), 206
Jeffries, Dr John, 261
Jellicoe, Commander John (later Admiral of the
    Fleet Earl), 34, 117, 124, 153, 221, 224
Johnson, Dr Samuel, 261
Jolly, Warrant Officer, 68
Jourdan, General Jean-Baptiste, 263
Julliot, Henri, 60, 101, 274

Kaiser Wilhelm II, 75, 86, 214, 221
Keys, Lieutenant R.E., 251
King Edward VII, 55, 76, 83
King George V, 89, 108, 138, 163, 192
King, Captain W.A., 79
Kitchener, Field Marshal Lord, 211
Knabe, Herr, 29
Knowles, Rear Admiral Charles Henry, 263
Kohl, Captain Hermann, 226
Krebs, Captain Arthur, 19–21
Kruger, President Paul, 55

La Mountain, John, 6
Lambton, Rear Admiral H., 58
Lavoisier, Antoine, 258
Lebaudy, Paul, 60, 101
Lebaudy, Pierre, 60, 101
Lee, Captain R.P. (later Major), 12, 22
L'Estrange Malone, Lieutenant Cecil (later
    Lieutenant Colonel), 95, 156, 172, 179
Lefroy, Captain H.P.T. (later Major), 112–3, 137,
    170
Lloyd George, David (later Earl), 83, 86
Locke, Flight Lieutenant K.J., 192
Lockwood, Jonathan, 262
Lockwood Marsh, Lieutenant Colonel W., 221
Lodge, Reverend N.B., 31
Longmore, 'Commandant' (later Air Chief
    Marshal Sir Arthur), 148, 277–8
Loraine, Robert (later Lieutenant Colonel), 276
Lowe, Thaddeus, 6
Lucas, Mr, 274
Lunardi, Vincento, 260
Lynch, Colonel Arthur, 54–5

McClean, F.K. (later Lieutenant Colonel Sir
    Francis), 277
McClellan, Major General George B., 6
McGrane, Sergeant, 141
McGwire, Richard, 262
McKechnie, J., 117
McKenna, Reginald, 83, 92, 117

Mackenzie, Lieutenant R.J.H.L., 24
McQuade, Mr, 104
Mackworth, Flight Commander J.D. (later
    Colonel), 184
Mahdi, The, 24
Maitland, Lieutenant E.M. (later Air
    Commodore), 82, 113, 126, 128, 130, 137,
    139, 147, 149, 157, 165, 167, 170–1, 173, 178,
    184, 189–90, 192, 196, 221, 228, 237, 257
Marchant, Engine Room Artificer, 161
Markham, Rear Admiral Sir Albert Hastings
    (later Admiral), 35
Martial, Dr Rudolf, 270
Martin, Rudolf, 82
Martin-Leake, Lieutenant T.E., 76
Mason, Monck, 265
Masterman, Commander E.A.D. (later Air
    Commodore), 96, 136, 154–5, 157, 161,
    163–4, 167, 171–2, 174, 177–8, 182–3,
    189–90, 200, 202, 219, 223, 257, 277
Mathy, Kapitän-Leutnant Heinrich, 213
Maxim, Hiram, 45, 84
Methuen, Lieutenant General Lord, 58
Metzing, Korvettenkapitän, 212
Meusnier, Lieutenant Jean-Baptiste Marie,
    3–4
Moltke, Field Marshal Helmuth von, 212
Money, Major John (later Major General),
    262–3
Montgolfier, Étienne, 259
Montgolfier, Joseph, 259
Montsiou, 27
Moore, Captain A.W., 35
Morlot, Major General Antoine, 262
Mowthorpe, Ces, 202, 216

Nelson, Vice Admiral Lord, 32, 263
Niblett, Captain H.S.F., 41
Nicholson, General Sir W.G., 83–4, 92, 110
Norway, N.S. (Neville Shute), 230

O'Gorman, Mervyn, 89, 91–2, 99, 124–5, 128,
    130–2, 143, 177
Otto, Nikolaus, 21
Paget, Major General A.H., 58
Pilâtre de Rozier, Jean-François, 259
Powell, Walter, 13–14
Pratt, H.B., 93
Prince Albert, 1
Prince Fushimi, 76
Prince of Wales (later Duke of Windsor), 165
Princess Maria Theresa, 76
Princess Mary, 163
Princess Victoria, 163

Queen Mary, 108, 163, 192
Queen Victoria, 1, 32–3

Radet, Brigade Adjutant General Étienne, 262
Ragg, Flying Officer R.L. (later Air Marshal), 253
Ramsey, Sergeant, 108
Randall, Engineer-Lieutenant C.R.J., 93, 278
Rawlinson, Major General Henry (later General Lord), 169
Rawson, Vice Admiral Sir Harry Holdsworth (later Admiral), 40
Rayleigh, Lord, 89, 91, 99, 235
Renard, Captain Charles (later Colonel), 8, 19–21, 57, 62
Reveillon, M, 259
Reynolds, Lieutenant H.R.P., 108
Ridd, Corporal Frank (later Sergeant), 276
Ridge, Lieutenant T.J., 105, 108, 128
Righton, Warrant Officer, 236
Robbins, Captain C.R., 245
Robert, Marie-Noel, 259
Roberts, Field Marshal Lord, 54
Robertson, Charles G., 93
Robida, Albert, 22
Rolls, Charles, 84
Romain, Pierre, 262
Roosevelt, President Franklin Delano, 255
Roosevelt, President Theodore, 55
Rope, Lieutenant F.M., 236
Rousell, M, 164, 171
Rosseau, M, 260
Royce, Henry (later Sir), 236–7
Ryan, Mr, 161

Sadler, James, 260
Sadler, Windham, 264
St Aldwyn, Viscount, 132
Salisbury, Marquess of, 27, 132
Samson, Lieutenant C.R. (later Air Commodore), 131, 148, 171, 173, 184, 200, 277–9
Santos-Dumont, Alberto, 57, 59, 77
Sayyīd Muhammad `Abd Allāh al-Hasan, 179
Scarlett, Wing Commander F.R. (later Air Vice Marshal), 183, 240
Schaak, Herr, 161
Schwann, Commander Oliver (later Air Vice Marshal), 93, 171, 183, 192, 277
Schwarz, David, 29, 58
Schweiger, Kapitänleutnant Walther, 198
Scott, Major G.H., 229
Scott, James William, 1
Scott, Captain Robert Falcon, 56
Scott, Philip, 1
Scovell, Corporal, 137
Seely, Colonel J.E.B. (later Major General), 128, 131–2, 138, 158–9, 173–4
Shackleton, Lieutenant Ernest (later Sir), 56
Sharpe, Chief Artificer Engineer A., 93

Shaw, Dr W.N., 89
Shone, Major General W.T., 62
Short, Horace, 133
Smith, Major General William Farrar "Baldy", 6
Smith-Dorrien, Lieutenant General Sir Horace (later General), 109
Spaight, 2nd Lieutenant T.H.L., 55
Sparling, Flight Lieutenant E.H., 190, 222
Spencer, C.G., 193
Spencer, Stanley, 60
Sperling, Major, 76
Spooner, Stanley, 194
Standford, William J., 196
Stelling, Lieutenant, 160
Stephan, Heinrich von, 7
Strasser, Korvettenkapitän Peter (later Fregattenkapitän), 212–3
Stroehle, Hans-Paul, 177
Sturdee, Vice Admiral Sir Doveton (later Admiral of the Fleet), 122
Sueter, Captain Murray (later Rear Admiral), 62, 89, 93, 95–6, 116–7, 119, 123, 132–3, 143, 161, 168, 170–3, 183, 187, 189, 192, 200–202, 208, 215, 219, 221, 223, 235, 243, 257, 277
Sueter, Mrs, 278
Sullivan, Sir Arthur, 17
Sykes, Lieutenant F.M. (later Major General Sir Frederick), 62–5, 147, 257, 278

Talbot, Lieutenant C.P., 93, 123
Templer, Lieutenant J.L.B. (later Colonel), 12–14, 23, 25–6, 43, 45–6, 52, 55–6, 62, 67–8, 77, 80–81, 88, 122
Thomson, Lord, 229
Tissandier, Albert, 18–19
Tissandier, Gaston, 18–19
Tournachon, Felix (Nadar), 4
Trench, Colonel Frederick, 87
Trenchard, Marshal of the RAF Lord, 131, 180
Trollope, Lieutenant Francis (later Major), 22, 55
Tryon, Vice Admiral Sir George, 34–5
Tupper, Captain Reginald (later Admiral), 14, 73
Turner, Major Charles C., 190
Tytler, James, 260

Udet, General Ernst, 255
Usborne, Ann, 195, 220
Usborne, Betty (nee Hamilton), 179, 195, 219–20, 249
Usborne, Cecil Vivian, 16, 72–3, 257
Usborne, Captain George, 1–2, 14–15
Usborne, Josephine (nee Scott), 1
Usborne, Neville Florian, 1, 16–18, 28, 30–43, 69–74, 93, 95–7, 100, 113, 119, 123, 133–4, 136–41, 150–1, 153–4, 156–7, 161–8, 171–4, 177–9, 182–93, 195–6, 200–202, 207–208, 210–11, 214–23, 228, 251, 255–7

Usborne, Philip Osbert Gordon, 16
Usborne, Vivian Mary, 17

Vaughan-Lee, Rear Admiral Charles, 217
Verne, Jules, 21

Wake Walker, Captain Sir Baldwin (later Vice
    Admiral), 41
Wallis, Barnes (later Sir), 228–30
Ward, Lieutenant Bernard (later Captain), 27, 52
Warneford, Flight Sub-Lieutenant Rex, 215, 279
Warren, Major General Sir Charles (later
    General), 22
Waterlow, Lieutenant Clive (later Lieutenant
    Colonel), 79, 105, 107, 112–3, 126–9, 133–4,
    137, 139, 147, 167, 169, 171, 173, 175, 177,
    184, 194
Watson, Lieutenant Charles (later Colonel), 11,
    57
Watson, Captain Sir Hugh D., 124
Weinling, family, 266
Wellesley, Arthur (later Duke of Wellington), 261
Wells, Lieutenant G.F., 66
Wells, H.G., 82–3
Wildman-Lushington, Captain G.V., 171
Williams, Captain T.B., 206
Willows, Ernest, 67, 102–104, 113, 133, 140,
    151, 177
Wilm, Alfred, 267
Wilson, Flight Lieutenant A.C., 161, 222
Wilson, Admiral of the Fleet Sir Arthur, 117,
    123, 132
Wilson, Dr Edward, 56
Wilson, Colonel H.H. (later Field Marshal Sir
    Henry), 58
Wöelfert, Dr Karl, 28–9
Wood, Lieutenant General Sir Evelyn (later
    Field Marshal), 27
Woodcock, Lieutenant H.L. (later Wing
    Commander), 136, 157, 167, 170, 184, 190,
    220
Wright, Orville, 68–9, 75, 77, 87, 277
Wright, Wilbur, 45, 68–9, 77, 87, 277

Zeppelin, Count Ferdinand von, 6, 8, 58–9,
    75–7, 84, 270–1

Places
Abbotsbury, 76
Akron, Ohio, 246
Aldershot, 10, 13, 27, 43, 45, 49, 52, 56–7, 62,
    68, 82, 84, 99, 108–110, 113, 128, 153, 156,
    163, 167, 170, 270, 274
Andover, 109, 113, 130
Anglesey, Isle of, 207–208
Antwerp, 213
Ashdown Copse, 141

Aspern, 143
Australia, 16, 41, 55, 235
Auteuil, 18
Aylesbury, 169

Bagshot, 79
Baldonnel, 226, 249
Ballyliffin, 207–208
Bangor, Co Down, 40
Barrow-in-Furness, 74, 93, 95–6, 99–100, 117,
    120, 123, 203, 223, 240, 256, 277
Basingstoke, 130
Basingstoke Canal, 151
Battersea, London, 105
Bay of Whales, Antarctica, 56
Beaminster, 13
Beauvais, 229
Bechuanaland, 22, 55
Belfast, Co Antrim, 256
Belfast Lough, 40, 80
Bentra, Co Antrim, 207–208
Berbera, 180
Berlin, 2, 7, 28, 55, 82, 87, 89, 124, 270
Berlin-Schöneberg, 21
Berlin-Templehof, 29
Bexhill, 103
Bois de Bologne, 19
Boubers-sur-Canche, 244
Bournemouth, 108–109, 171
Bracknell, 164
Brentford, 79
Brest, 263
Bridport, 13, 76
Brighton, 12, 274
Brooklands, 105, 160
Bulford, 63
Bull Run, Battle of, 5

Calais, 187
Calshot, 184, 278
Capel, 207, 236, 269
Cardiff, 67, 150
Cardington, 227–8, 250
Cavendish Dock, 93, 114
Chalais-Meudon, 19, 21, 58, 62, 78
Chancellorsville, Battle of, 5
Chatham, 13, 25–7, 43, 55, 84, 102, 172–4, 181,
    185
Clifden, 226
Clontarf, 262
Cobh, Co Cork, (see Queenstown)
Cologne, 87
Copenhagen, 211
Corbehem, 103
Cork, 1, 17
Cove, Co Cork, (see Queenstown)
Cove Common, 81, 113, 140, 151, 173

Cowes, 161
Crewkerne, 13
Cromarty, 278
Crystal Palace, London, 49, 60, 79, 82, 190

Daventry, 169
Dayton, Ohio, 68
Devizes, 149
Dijon, 260
Donegall Quay, Belfast, 40
Douai, 103
Dover, 12, 84, 185, 187, 207, 261
Dublin, 16, 91, 249, 261, 264
Dunchurch, 169–70
Dunkirk, 190, 196, 204, 244
Düsseldorf, 214

East Fortune, 226, 239
Eastbourne, 207
Eastchurch, 171, 173, 183–4, 277–8
Edinburgh, 260
Elancourt, 4
Enniscorthy, Co Wexford, 167
Epinel, 193
Epsom, 226

Fair Oaks, Battle of, 5
Farnborough, 44, 62–3, 66, 76–7, 79–81, 84, 87,
    90–1, 98, 101–102, 104–105, 107–109, 111–
    13, 125–129, 130, 136–9, 141, 147, 149–51,
    154, 157, 160–4, 166–7, 169–173, 177–8, 184,
    189, 191, 195–6, 202–203, 210, 256, 276
Faversham, 171, 185
Felixstowe, 184, 278
Finsbury, London, 22
Fischamend, 143
Fishguard, 167
Fleurus, Battle of, 262
Folkestone, 2, 16, 236
Foret de Felmores, Guines, 261
Fredericksburg, Battle of, 5
Friedrichshafen, 58, 74, 76, 87, 214
Frimley, 79

Geneva, 75
Ghent, 215
Gibraltar, 41, 66, 248
Glasgow, 137, 226
Grain, Isle of, 172–3, 184, 278
Great Yarmouth, 184, 214, 217, 262, 278
Greenly Island, Labrador, 226
Guildford, 78, 108, 128, 144

Hamburg, 143, 211
Hampton Roads, 6
Hasheen, Battle of, 25
Haywards Heath, 138

Heligoland, 211
Hendon, 156–7, 213
Holywood, Co Down, 80
Hoo, 174, 183, 196
Hounslow, 79, 105
Howden, 210, 223, 225, 229, 240–1, 244
Hull, 214
Hurlingham, 105

Isle of Man, 264
Issy-les-Moulineaux, 104

James River, 6
Jarrow, 214
Johnstown Castle, 207
Jutland, Battle of, 221, 224

Khartoum, 21, 23, 234
Kiel, 143
Killeagh, Co Cork, 241
Kimberley, Siege of, 53
King's Lynn, 214
Kingsnorth, 174, 181–3, 185, 187, 190–1, 193–6,
    202–204, 209–210, 217–8, 220, 222, 236–7,
    239, 245, 256
Kinsale, 199

La Brayelle, 104
Ladysmith, Siege of, 53, 58
Lake Constance, 58, 75, 78
Lakehurst, New Jersey, 233, 253
Langley Field, Virginia, 230
Larkhill, 126, 130, 141, 276
Leatherhead, 113
Lidsing, 26
Lisbon, 70
London, 22, 28, 32, 42, 55, 70, 79, 83–5, 87, 91,
    97–8, 100, 103, 105, 108, 128, 137, 144,
    147–8, 154, 157–8, 160, 171, 176–7, 183,
    191–2, 194, 211, 213–5, 224, 260–2, 264–6,
    270
Long Island, 226,
Longparish, 141
Lough Swilly, 40
Lubeck, 143–4
Luce Bay, 207–208
Lucerne, 75
Lydd, 26, 52

Mafeking, 22, 53
Magersfontein, Battle of, 53
Malahide Castle, 208
Manassas, Battle of, 5
Mateki Derevni, 190
Marolles-en-Brie, 19
Maubeuge, Siege of, 262
Milford, 10

Moisson, 60, 274
Mława, 213
Moscow, 264
Moville, Co Donegal, 2
Muette, Château de la, 259
Mullion, 207, 237
Munich, 21, 76

Navan, Co Meath, 259
New Jersey, 230, 233, 253
Nile, Battle of the, 263
North Foreland, 170
Northampton, 61
Northolt, 191

Odiham, 165–6
Ohio, 230, 246
Oakhampton, 52
Ostend, 190, 196
Oxford, 108, 260

Paardeberg, Battle of, 53
Palma, Majorca, 70
Panama, Cuba, 253
Paris, 4, 8, 19, 22, 54, 55, 57, 60, 97, 100, 103,
    112, 176–7, 193, 259, 261, 270
Paris, Siege of, 6–7
Peking, 55
Pembroke, 70, 207–208
Petersfield, 82
Point Sur, California, 230
Polegate, 207, 244
Polova, 264
Portsmouth, 42, 69, 70, 72–3, 82, 84, 96, 105,
    113, 144, 147, 153–4, 163, 169, 171, 173, 184
Potomac River, 6
Pretoria, 53–4
Pulham, 224, 226, 251–2

Queenstown (now Cobh), 1–2, 14, 16–17, 136,
    199

RAF Aldergrove, 249–50, 256
Ratoath, Co Meath, 260
Rawalpindi, 55
Redhill, 196
Reims, 86
Richmond, Battle of, 6
River Medway, 217, 278
Rochester, 183, 196
Roehampton, 191
Rouen, 7, 274
Rugby, 61, 169

Saint-Cloud, 59
St John's, Newfoundland, 226
St Louis, 68

St Paul, Minnesota, 6
St Paul's Cathedral, London, 79, 105, 137–8,
    160, 171, 192
St Pol sur Mer, 148
St Valery en Caux, 274
Salisbury Cathedral, 111
Salisbury Plain, 98, 109, 130, 276
San Juan Hill, Cuba, 29
Savannah, Georgia, 6
Seven Pines, Battle of, 5
Sheerness, 71, 84, 150, 154–5, 171, 173–4, 181,
    183, 278
Sheppey, Isle of, 171
Soissons, 101
Solferino, Battle of, 4
Somaliland, 179
Sombreffe, Battle of, 263
Suakin, 24–5
Southend, 214
Staines, 79, 105
Strood, 218
Stuttgart, 74–5
Sudan, 23–4, 55
Sunningdale, 79
Sunninghill, 105
Symonsbury, 13
Teddington, 87–8, 99
Thames Ditton, 105
Thetford, 147
Tidworth, 109
Tripoli, 34, 136, 180

Upavon, 138

Venice, 2
Versailles, 232, 259
Vienna, 21
Villacoublay, 21

Weilberg, 265
Weybridge, 105
Weymouth Bay, 278
Wolverhampton, 115
Woodstock, 170
Woolwich, 10–12, 44, 192
Wormwood Scrubs, London, 98, 100, 103,
    191–2, 205

Balloons
Alice, 205
Atlantic, 4
Bristol, 53
Céleste, 263
Constitution, 5
Crusader, 12
Duchess of Connaught, 53
Eagle, 5

Enterprise (19th Century), 5–6,
Evening Star, 10
Excelsior, 5
Feo, 22
Fly, 13, 23, 25
Hazel, 205
Hercule, 263
Heron, 13, 22
Intrepid, 5
Intrépide, 263
Joan, 205
l'Entreprenant, 262
Mammoth, 190
Martial, 263
May, 205
Neptune, 7
Pegasus, 82
Pioneer, 12
Sapper, 13, 23
Saratoga, 5
Scout, 23–5
Spy, 13, 22
Teviot, 55
The Royal Vauxhall Balloon, 265
Thrasher, 76
Tugela, 55
Thrasher
Union, 5
United States, 5
Washington, 5

Aeroplanes
35 hp Caudron, 156–7
80 hp Gnome-Caudron, 156
Albatros D.III, 251
Avro 510, 209
Avro Type D, 277
BE2, 164, 200–202, 205, 213, 216–7, 221, 236
Blériot XI, 164, 167
Blériot XXI, 276
Bristol Boxkite No 8, 276
Bristol Boxkite No 9, 276
British Army Aeroplane No 1, 276
Caudron G.II, 278
Consolidated N2Y-1, 254
Curtiss F9C-2 Sparrowhawk, 254
DH53 Hummingbird, 251–2
Focke-Wulf FW-44 Stieglitz, 255
Gloster Grebe II, 253
Henri Farman F.20, 164
Junkers W33, 226
Maurice Farman S.7, 164, 236
Morane Parasol, 215
Short Biplane No 3, 173
Short Folder, 278
Short Gun-Carrier, 278
Short S.27, 171

Short S.38, 278
Sopwith 2F.1 Ships Camel, 251–2
Sperry M-1 Messenger, 253
Vickers Vimy, 226
Vought UO-1, 253

Airships
23r, 224
24r, 224
25r, 224
Airship Plane AP-1, 216–8
Airship Plane AP-2, 218
Albatross, 177
Astra-Torres XIV HMA No 3, 164–5, 171, 176,
      183–5, 190–3, 196
Baby, 87–8, 99, 104
Beta HMA No 17, 99, 104–13, 122, 125–6,
      134–5, 137–9, 145–7, 149–50, 153, 161,
      163–5, 169, 172–3, 175, 191–2, 196
Clément-Bayard, 98, 110
Clément-Bayard II, 97, 99–102, 120, 153, 273
Colonel Renard, 110
Coastal Class: 208–209, 223, 230, 237, 240
      C1, 210
      C9, 237
      C17, 237
      C19, 210
Coastal Star Class: 237–8, 240
      C*4, 238
Columbia, 246
Defender, 246
Delta HMA No 19, 138, 145, 147, 150, 158, 161,
      163, 165, 169–73, 175, 184, 193, 196
Deutschland, 28–9
Epsilon, 161
Enterprise, 246
Eta HMA No 20, 161, 167–70, 172–3, 175, 180,
      196, 237, 267
Gamma HMA No 18, 99, 107–108, 111, 122,
      125–6, 128–31, 136–9, 141, 147, 149–50, 154,
      156–7, 161, 163–4, 173, 175, 184, 196
Giffard, 2, 4, 19
HMA No 5, 190
HMA No 6, 190
HMA No 7, 190
HMA No 8, 192–3, 196
HMA No 9r, 223–4
HMA No 10, 192, 209
K-74, 249
La France, 19–20, 58
La Patrie, 78, 80, 270–1
Lebaudy, 60
Liberté, 110
L33, 226
L35 (LZ 80), 251
LZ1, 58–9, 74
LZ2, 74

LZ3 (SMS Z-I), 74, 76
LZ4, 75
LZ5 (SMS Z-II), 76
LZ6, 211
LZ7 *Deutschland*, 211
LZ8 *Deutschland II*, 211
LZ10 *Schwaben*, 124, 211
LZ11 *Viktoria Luise*, 211
LZ13 *Hansa*, 211
LZ14 (L1), 212
LZ17 *Sachsen*, 211
LZ37, 215
LZ104, 234
LZ120 *Bodensee*, 232
LZ121 *Nordstern*, 232
LZ126/ZR-3 USS *Los Angeles*, 232, 253–4
LZ127 *Graf Zeppelin*, 233–5
LZ129 *Hindenburg*, 177, 233, 255, 268
LZ130 *Graf Zeppelin II*, 177, 233
Mayflower, 246
Metallballon, 29
Morning Post Lebaudy, 99, 101–102, 120, 153, 274–5
Naval Airship No 1 *Mayfly*, 92–6, 113–123, 133, 277
North Sea Class: 237–40
    NS-7, 239, 244
    NS-8, 239
    NS-11, 239
    NS-12, 239
Nulli Secundus I, 76–9, 270
Nulli Secundus II, 80–1
P1, 136
P3, 136
Parseval (P Type): 76, 143, 240
PL.18 HMA No 4, 136, 152, 160, 183–5, 187, 189–90
Pilgrim, 246
Pony, 246
Puritan, 246
R23, 251–2
R26, 224
R27, 225
R29, 225
R31, 225
R.32, 225
R33, 226, 230, 251–2
R34, 226, 232
R36, 227
R38 (ZR-2), 227–8, 244
R80, 228, 230
R100, 229–30
R101, 228–30
Rainbow, 246
Ranger, 246
Reliance, 246
Resolute, 246

Roma, 230
Santos-Dumont No 6, 59
Schütte-Lanz Type, 213, 221, 225
Spencer No 1, 60
SS Class: 196–202, 204–208, 216, 223, 227, 230, 237, 240–3
    SS-1, 201–202
    SS-2, 201–202
    SS-3, 201–202
    SS-12, 269
    SS-40, 244–5
SS-Pusher Class, 236, 240–3
SS Twin Class, 240, 242–3
SSZ Class: 236–7, 240–3
    SSZ1, 244
    SSZ11, 223
    SSZ20, 223
TC-3, 253
TC-7, 253
Tissandier, 18–19
USS *Akron* ZRS-4, 230, 253–4
USS *Macon* ZRS-5, 177, 230, 254–5
USS *Shenandoah* ZR-1, 230
Vigilant, 246
Volunteer, 246
Westinghouse Skyship 500, 250
Willows No 1, 67
Willows No 1A, 81
Willows No 3, 102–104, 139
Willows No 4 HMA No 2, 136, 139–40, 150–1, 161, 165–7, 175, 195, 201–202
Zeppelin NT, 177
Zeta, 101
Zodiac, 110
ZPG-2, 249
ZPG-3, 249

Kites
Kite Balloon, 58, 143, 152, 171, 193, 210, 215
Man-lifting, 44–5, 61, 65–6, 70, 72, 78, 93, 125–6, 138, 177, 183
Naval, 263–4

Ships and Shore Establishments
Britannia Royal Naval College, Dartmouth, 30
Devonport, 42
Fanny, 6
George Washington Parke Custis, 6
HMS *Actaeon*, 71
HMS *Africa*, 278
HMS *Agamemnon*, 17
HMS *Ariadne*, 71
HMS *Berwick*, 71–2
HMS *Britannia*, 30–7
HMS *Camperdown*, 34–5
HMS *Canopus*, 37, 41
HMS *Cruiser*, 38

HMS *Defiance*, 70
HMS *Devastation*, 18
HMS *Doris*, 69–70
HMS *Dreadnought*, 73
HMS *Empress*, 2
HMS *Enchantress*, 173
HMS *Excellent*, Whale Island, 42, 72–3, 163
HMS *Fervent*, 73
HMS *Firequeen*, 70
HMS *Grafton*, 73
HMS *Havock*, 27
HMS *Hermes*, 163, 278
HMS *Hermione*, 95–6, 113, 123
HMS *Hibernia*, 278
HMS *Hindustan*, 31
HMS *Indomitable*, 205
HMS *Inflexible*, 18
HMS *King Edward VII*, 82
HMS *Lightning*, 18
HMS *Malaya*, 16
HMS *Pallas*, 263–4
HMS *Prince George*, 37, 40–1
HMS *Racer*, 32–3
HMS *Recruit*, 73
HMS *Resolution*, 16
HMS *Revenge*, 2
HMS *Revenge*, 70, 73
HMS *Royal Sovereign*, 17
HMS *Sans Pareil*, 17
HMS *Sir John Moore*, 244
HMS *Thames*, 69
HMS *Tyne*, 38
HMS *Vernon*, 43, 70, 74, 147
HMS *Victoria*, 34
HMS *Victory*, 134
HMS *Warrior*, 17, 70
HMS *Zealous*, 2
HMY *Victoria and Albert*, 33
Hydrographic Department, Whitehall, 42
Le Patriote, 263
L'Orient, 263
RMS *Lusitania*, 198–9
RMS *Titanic*, 136
Royal Naval College Greenwich, 2, 41–2, 70
Royal Naval College, Portsmouth, 42
RRS *Discovery*, 56
Schouwen Bank lightship, 190
SMS *Scharnhorst*, 72
SS *Manx Queen*, 40
SS *Oroya*, 41
SS *Princess Victoria*, 193
Teaser, 6
U-1, 73
U-20, 198
UB-115, 225
USS *Houston*, 255
USS *Saratoga*, 253

Vulcano, 2
Woolwich Dockyard, 11
Wye, 33

Units, Organisations
Academie de Aérostation, 22
Advisory Committee on Aeronautics, 88, 120
Aerial League of the British Empire, 84
Aéro-Club de France, 59
Air Ministry, 225, 241, 256
Airship Industries, 250
American Army Balloon Corps, 4
Astra Airship Company, 112, 152
Austria-Hungary, Balloon Corps, 21

Barr and Stroud, 137
Barrow Steam Navigation Company, 40
Bavarian Army, School of Ballooning, 21
Bengal Sappers, 13
Brazil Straker, 237
British Army: 8, 9, 22, 55, 76, 134, 158, 167, 250,
     267, 276
   2nd Middlesex Militia, 12
   5 Regiment Army Air Corps, 250
   7th Battalion King's Royal Rifle Corps, 12
   56th Foot, 264
   Berkshire Regiment, 25
   British Expeditionary Force, 109, 185, 211
   Essex Regiment, 126, 178
   General Staff, 126, 131, 146, 174
   Grenadier Guards, 22
   Irish Guards, 164
   Scots Guards, 44
   Oxford University Territorials, 108
   Royal Arsenal, Woolwich, 10
   Royal Engineers: 8, 11–12, 22, 52, 62, 81, 126,
        178, 266
     Air Battalion, 125–9, 134, 138, 178, 276
     Balloon Factory, 27, 52, 54–5, 57, 61, 66–7,
          76–7, 89–92, 105, 108, 112–13, 124–5, 138
     Balloon School, 25–6, 45, 52, 60, 67, 74,
          78–9, 82, 91–2, 99, 102, 111, 122, 125,
          178, 190
     Balloon Section, 22–3, 43–55, 60, 62–66
     London Balloon Company RE
          (Territorials), 108, 128
     Wireless Company, 81–2
   Royal Field Artillery, 276
   Royal Flying Corps: 63, 135–6, 138, 146, 148,
        152, 155, 157, 161, 164, 174, 178–80, 211,
        221, 229, 278–9
     Central Flying School, 138
     Military Wing, 63, 135, 138, 148, 161, 174,
          177, 278
     Naval Airship Section, RFC Airship Wing,
          136, 179
     Naval Wing, 135, 138, 161, 278

British & Colonial Aeroplane Company, 276

Camel Constabulary, 179
C.G. Spencer & Sons Ltd, 193
Civil Service Commission, 28
Committee of Imperial Defence: 83, 92–3,
    131–3, 138, 144, 153, 155
    Aerial Navigation Sub-committee, 83, 131–2,
    138
    Technical Sub-Committee, 133
Committee of Public Safety, 262
Cork Harbour Board, 14–15
Cork Lifeboat, Queenstown Station, 14

Deutsche Luftschiffahrt Aktien Gessellschaft
    (DELAG), 211
Dürener Metallwerke, 267

Ewen School of Flying, 157

Flight Refuelling Limited, 257
French Army Balloon Corps, 19
French Army Balloon School, 263

Gas-Light Company of London, 264
Goodyear-Zeppelin Corporation, 246

Imperial German Admiralty: 197
    High Seas Fleet, 213, 221, 239
    Imperial German Navy Airship Division, 212
Imperial German Air Service, 126
Ioco Rubber & Waterproofing Co, 266
Irish Air Corps, 226, 249
Italian Army, 136

James Scott and Company, 1

Knowles Oxygen Co, 115

Lebaudy-Frères, 101
L'Établissement Central de Aérostation
    Militaire, 8

Meteorological Office, 89

National Physical Laboratory, 87–91, 99, 123,
    125, 225

Ordnance Board, 136
Orient Line, 41

Parliamentary Aerial Defence Committee, 97
Première Compagnie d'Aérostiers Militaires,
    262
Preussische Luftschiffer-Abteilung, 21

Prussian Army, Luftschiffer detachments, 7
Physikalisch Technichse Reichsanstalt, 89

Queenstown Coastguard, 14

Royal Aero Club, 113, 134, 156, 171, 276–7
Royal Aeronautical Society, 221–2
Royal Air Force: 178, 180, 221, 225, 229, 244,
    249, 251, 256–7, 277, 279
    No 212 Squadron, 251
Royal Aircraft Factory, 138, 155, 167, 202
Royal Airship Works, 227
Royal Navy: 2, 16–18, 28, 30, 34, 36–7, 70, 73–4,
    83–4, 92, 95, 117, 123, 132, 144, 152, 159–60,
    171, 180, 182, 184, 199, 221, 225, 230, 256–7,
    262, 277–9
    Admiralty, 17, 40, 42, 70–1, 73–4, 83, 89, 92,
    117, 119, 122–4, 131, 137, 139, 143, 151–4,
    161, 163, 167, 173–4, 177, 179–81, 183,
    185, 189, 191–4, 197–200, 202–203, 205,
    210–12, 215, 218–9, 223, 225, 240–1, 243,
    263, 277–8
    Air Department, 89, 143, 179, 183, 189, 192,
    194, 223–4, 278
    Airship Branch, 135, 182, 202–203
    Central Air Office, 183
    Royal Marine Light Infantry, 277
    Royal Naval Air Service, 178, 180, 183, 185,
    189–90, 204, 210, 213–14, 221, 230, 236,
    278–9
    Royal Naval Flying School, 183
Royal Observer Corps, 219

Short Brothers, 94, 115, 201, 277

Union Army, 9
United Services Institution, 70
US Army Air Service, 253
US Navy: 176, 227, 233, 246, 248, 253, 255
    Fleet Airship Wings, 248
US Signal Corps Balloon Section, 29

Vickers, Son & Maxim, 74, 93–4, 96, 115–6, 119,
    121, 161, 190, 201, 203, 215, 223, 228, 240,
    257, 266

War Office, 8, 11, 26, 44, 52, 57, 62, 68, 74, 77–9,
    84, 87, 98–9, 101–102, 110–111, 126, 131,
    133, 138, 144, 149, 152, 174, 211, 244, 273
William Beardmore, 226
Women's Aerial League, 111
World Postal Union, 7

Zeppelin Company, 58–9, 74–6, 84, 211, 232